Whispers In A Dark Closet

Regina Wachtel

Like spider webs, lives
Are spun with fragile threads that
great strain tears apart.
                    - rw

TAPROOT PRESS
Publishing Company

Illustrations by Tikvah Feinstein

Whispers In A Dark Closet is Regina Wachtel's first novel. She began writing at an early age. *LifeLines,* a collection of poetry by Wachtel, has been a remarkable success. She is a divorced mother of five grown children, and is retired from a career with a national retail chain. She is a former editor/writer of a newsletter. Wachtel is currently working on a sequel to *Whispers In A Dark Closet.*

WHISPERS IN A DARK CLOSET, first printing 1998
previous title: Web of Deception
Published in the United States of America
Through TAPROOT PRESS Publishing Company

Printed in Canada by Hignell Book Printing.

This book is entirely the property of the author. The author assumes all rights, royalties and accountability for the story, characters, content, its production and distribution. This is a work of fiction.

© 1998 by Regina Wachtel, all rights reserved

All rights reserved under copyright laws. No part of this book may be reproduced or transmitted in any form or by any means, electronic or mechanical including photocopying, recording, or by any informational storage and retrieval system without the author's written consent, except by a reviewer or writer who may quote a short section or part to be printed in a magazine or newspaper.

Library of Congress United States Copyright Office
registration number TXu 750-260
1 2 3 4 5 6 7 8 9 10
FIRST EDITION

Library of Congress Catalog Card Number: 98-60901

ISBN 1-890269-03-4 $16.95

In memory of fellow-writer, Paul Alexander, my first critic.

To Tikvah Feinstein, my esteemed mentor, editor, and friend. It was through her encouragement and support that this work came to fruition.

To Nola,
Thank you
Regina Wachtel

Whispers In A Dark Closet

To Jena and victims of abuse, that they may find courage to declare the perpetrator of the crime to be the guilty one.

If Jena's story helps one person find release from guilt and fear, and reclaim for herself or himself the emotionally healthy, functional life that God intended, this book will have served its purpose.

The Rape and Incest National Hotline number is 1-800-656-Hope (4673).

The 24-hour hotline is available for victims of sexual assault providing support and information. A free call allows the caller to speak confidentially to a trained volunteer.

Whispers In A Dark Closet

FOREWORD

Jena was a vibrant, mischievous, happy girl as a child. We were kindred spirits who shared similar backgrounds and avid interests in poetry and music. At age ten we separated when she suddenly withdrew from friends and classmates.

Years later we were reunited during a critical period in her life. It was then I learned the reason for her strange childhood behavior. She revealed to me that she was sexually molested when she was ten. Shock and guilt caused her withdrawal into self-isolation. For years she was tortured by anger and shame. Through professional help she was able to legitimately place the blame on the perpetrator of that heinous crime.

To free herself from bondage to the past, Jena expressed to me a desire to make known her life of agony and fear. Her story is one of faith and courage as she makes a bittersweet journey through joy and sorrow. It shows the transformation she experienced following that traumatic event. She wants others who experienced similar tragedies to realize, when they confront the gruesome past, it is possible for contentment and joy to enter their lives.

This book is a work of fiction based on a true story. The names of President Franklin D. Roosevelt, General Dwight D. Eisenhower and other world leaders have been mentioned in passing to fix time and locale of the story, but are not characters in the story. Any resemblance of other characters to actual persons living or dead is purely coincidental.

PROLOGUE

In the darkness of night, streaks of lightning rip through the sky. They light up the bedroom where Sarah lies alone. A sharp, brilliant flash clearly illuminates the woman's face. She jumps from the bed and runs to the steps, then hurries up them. Loud bursts of thunder roar through the night air. Upstairs, she rushes from room to room, lowering blinds in every bedroom. Another loud burst of thunder wakens ten-year-old Jena from a peaceful sleep. The young girl lies motionless. She listens to her mother gasp, "Lord help us! Lord save us!"

This is Dad's first bank conference. Just when he's out of town, we get a bad storm. I wish Mother was not so scared. Maybe if she's not alone in bed she won't be so afraid, she thinks.

The woman does not hear her daughter get out of bed. Jena creeps down the stairs and crawls into her parents' empty bed. Sarah's brown eyes dart about in her terror. Her face turns ashen.

She dashes down the steps.

The distraught woman rushes to lower the living room, dining room and kitchen blinds. She runs slender, delicate fingers through her short, black wavy hair. Sarah shuts out the storm believing the act will protect her family from nature's fury.

Jena quietly waits in the large bed. She prays that her presence will comfort her mother. As Sarah draws the blinds, she is overcome by memories of long past terrors.

The year is 1907. Sarah is an excited six-year-old the morning she arrives at the pier with her parents. Her mother wears a long beige dress, a wool shawl wrapped around her shoulders and a head scarf. Her father, a tall thin man, wears a long black coat. His thick, dark beard covers the bottom-half of his face. Sarah is happy in the new white dress under her navy-blue coat. She is anxious as she walks up the gangway beside her parents onto a huge ship. The trio gazes in amazement as they walk along the deck of the enormous liner. As the boat sails out to sea, the curious young voyager looks over the rail. She watches foam thrash against the side of the ship.

"Why are we here, Mama?" Sarah inquires.

The young woman smiles. Her hazel eyes twinkle with expectations of a bright and prosperous future.

"Papa can not get a job in Germany. We go now to a country where there is work for a carpenter. This long journey is the start of a great life for us. Our future is in America."

Sarah leans on the rail looking at the ocean. She watches a flock of birds follow the vessel out to sea. "Mama, why do these big white birds fly all around the ship?"

"The gulls eat food scraps thrown overboard."

Papa leads Mama and Sarah inside the liner. Their small cabin is located on the bottom deck. It has a single lower bed and a narrow upper berth. A bath area is shared with other passengers. They walk a long distance to the diner. Small delicate flowers are painted on china bowls and plates that sit at ends of long tables. Silver knives and spoons rest in square wicker baskets beside the dishes. A cook wears a tall white hat and carries a huge kettle to the table. He serves a long line of people politely and rapidly.

The curious girl stares into her bowl. She stirs the hot soup. She frowns as she asks, "Where are they, Mama? I can't find them."

"The cooks don't make special food for us, Sarah. They serve bread to eat with their beef soup. We will have chicken soup with matzo balls when I cook our meals in America. Now eat this food. It will keep you strong and healthy."

Sarah delights in each new discovery. Then one gray afternoon she observes the sea change from calm friend to furious foe. The sky turns black. Gusty winds toss the giant vessel against violent waves.

The storm forces the ship's passengers to remain in their quarters. Sarah and her parents suffer seasickness. When a dreadful plague spreads through the vessel, Sarah watches her mother and father grow feverish and weak. She is helpless as they cough, constantly at first, then less and less. They become too weak almost to talk. Her parents are among several hundred persons who die aboard ship. The tiny girl is counted among those who escape the epidemic that ran rampant throughout the vessel.

Weeks later, a petite, frail, terrified waif descends the gangway. She clutches the hand of a traveler she met the first day of her journey. Tears stream down her pale cheeks. She arrives alone and desolate in a foreign country, surrounded by strangers. She begins a new life owning a suitcase stuffed with clothing and a broken heart filled with shattered dreams.

For eight years, the devastated and lonely child endures life in an orphanage. Under the supervision of nuns she is taught to keep rooms neat and clean. Sarah learns a new language and practices an alien faith. A Catholic benefactress takes Sarah into her home. There, *the teen-aged girl cares for two small children. The doctrines introduced to her in the institution continue to control her life.*

Sharp bursts of thunder snap Sarah to the present. She paces back and forth between the living room and dining room. Crystal rosary beads slip through her trembling fingers. She bows her head and repeats over and over, "Lord help us! Lord save us!"

Sarah walks into the master bedroom. Jena hears her mother heave a deep sigh. Her mother's hand quivers as she reaches to lower the blind. A flash of lightning brightens the room. Sarah sees her youngest daughter snuggled in the big bed.

"Mother," Jena begs, "let me stay here until the storm stops. You won't have to be afraid with me beside you. I'll go upstairs to my bed when Dad comes home."

"Your father phoned me earlier. He won't be here tonight. There's a storm where he is, too. He must wait it out. Then he'll start for home."

Jena cuddles beside her mother and falls asleep. The woman lies awake, immobilized by her fears and memories, unaware her husband is on his way home.

From the bus window, Al sees tree limbs and debris scattered along the roadway. Headlights dance across rain-drenched streets. He sits alone in the bus. The solitude gives him time to gloat over praise heaped on him by his former boss. He was ecstatic at the meeting when John Grason announced, *"Al Bordeau is the new manager of Sage Bank."* After years of struggle and sacrifice, he achieves success.

Al stares at the attractive blond seated under a dim light four rows in front of him. She wears a stylish rose-colored dress. He glances at his valise on the seat beside him. His hands tighten into fists. *I'll bet that woman would not be apathetic if her man got a great promotion.* He scowls. He thinks about Sarah's indifference when he told her the good news. *Damn it. She wasn't even pleased with my offer that we go out for dinner and dancing to celebrate. What the hell's the use working so hard to succeed? The only thing my promotion means to her is more money for household expenses. Some day she'll regret not buying herself pretty clothes. She always dressed nice when I courted her and after we first were married. She'll learn too late how her attitude changes my feelings toward her. I'll be damned if the only praise and appreciation I get will come from my colleagues,* he groans.

The summer storm subsides but Al's fury rages on. He leans his head on the back of the seat and closes his eyes. In the darkness he recalls bygone years.

Al envisions being reared in the farmhouse located near the abbey. His parents were farmers from France. They arrived in America following priests who came to start a new religious community. His early life was dominated by strict parents. Nine children are verification of the parents' submission to rigid church laws. Al and the other children worked as farm hands and obeyed their father's commands: "You will attend Mass every Sunday and all Holy days. Friday meals are meatless. No food or liquids will be taken after midnight Saturday when you are to receive Holy Communion on Sunday. The path to heaven is narrow. Only the guiltless will enter its door."

The boy became an adolescent believing that to touch or kiss a girl would cast him into the fiery pits of hell. He was drafted shortly before World War I ended. This provided liberation from a tyrannical father.

His basic training was in Georgia, far from home. This environment gave him freedom to enter the world of wine, women and good times. His youthful desire to explore primal urges was sampled. The soldier returned home and met Sarah, an innocent, naive, beautiful black-haired young girl. Together they went to dances, picnics and long walks.

One evening Al's strong kisses and fondling overwhelm Sarah. New sensations, and the sense of feeling accepted, lead the nineteen-year-old to her first sexual encounter. The young couple never discusses intimacy. Several impulsive unions result in an unplanned pregnancy. A church wedding follows for her and twenty-four-year-old Al.

In the solitude of the quiet bus, Al dwells on Sarah's aversion to sex. His need for satisfaction makes their bed a battlefield, not a blissful sanctuary.

"Oh, how I wish you would be a less dedicated mother and perfect housekeeper, and a more loving and devoted wife," he hears himself whisper, thankful for vacant seats around him.

Al arrives home at dawn. He is not surprised to find Sarah in the laundry. A load of clothes swishes in the washer.

"You're up early, Sarah. Looks like you had a bad night here, too. The town's a mess."

There are no words of welcome. Affectionate greetings ceased ages ago. They communicate with polite conversation.

"Jena slipped into our bed last night to comfort me. She fell asleep as I lay awake, terrified of the storm."

"That sounds like something she'd do. This afternoon she can work with me outside. She'll want to help rake the twigs. They're scattered every where. I'm going to take a shower. After a few hours sleep I'll tackle that job."

"Have Jena come down here to help with the laundry."

Al turns and heads for the basement steps.

Outside, dew drops linger on thin blades of grass. A crest of orange sun peeks through the clouds. A radiant sunbeam shines through sheer white curtains and brightens the room. Robins chirp from branches of tall fruit trees. The scent of apple blossoms drifts through an open window.

Jena does not waken as her father enters the bedroom. He's weary from hours cramped on a bus. A tired heap of pent-up frustration, he slides into bed beside his sleeping daughter. Al is surprised by his response to Jena's warm body.

Overcome by strong desire, he explores the newly developed form. Jena wakens as strong hands caress and glide over her soft body. Strange, sensuous feelings stir within her. Losing all self-control, Al abruptly draws the child close to him. He succumbs to temptation.

"Get out. Get out of this bed," he growls. "Don't ever do that again. Never again!"

Jena is bewildered by her father's mysterious actions. She is unaware of the danger or sinfulness of this sordid exploitation. She does not understand.

"Why not?" she asks in a low, innocent voice.

His face turns red as he fumes. "Because it's bad."

"Why is it bad?" she pleads. She sees wrath in his

deep blue eyes. His anger confuses her.

He makes no attempt to explain. He clutches her arm and roars once more, "It's bad. Don't ever do that again."

Al is relieved to hear Sarah call from the basement, "Jena get up. I want you to help with the laundry."

The young girl jumps from the bed. Upstairs in her room, a light-blue cotton dress replaces a pink batiste night gown. She brushes her bangs and short brown hair. She goes to the kitchen and sits at the table. A bowl of cold cereal with milk satisfies her hunger.

Sarah carries a basket of wet clothes to the back yard. Jena dismisses the perplexing moments with her father and concentrates on the laundry she hangs on lines stretched from pole to pole.

The happy girl continues to go about her random chores in her usual way. Sexual feelings surface for brief moments. Occasionally she reflects on the curious event she experienced with her father early this morning. The child believes it to be a natural gesture of his affections for her. *Dad loves me,* she reasons. The smile on her face portrays a picture of innocence.

Al is unable to sleep. For five hours he lies tormented with notions that demons must have caused him to commit such an act.

How will I face my wife and daughter? What will happen to our lives? Sarah's neglect of my needs and Jena's submission to my desires have kindled the fire of this transgression. We are all equal in guilt. I will not assume all the blame. Thoughts of his sinful act overpower him. They hold his mind hostage.

Al tosses and turns. He conjures up specters of the

past. *Sarah survived her grim childhood. I weathered my severe youth. Now there is more pain for both of us.* Visions of tranquil, happy times emerge. Times when he and Jena enjoyed wonderful moments together rise up to haunt him. He is tortured by memories of an innocent, free-spirited child, far from harm's way. From this day forward, the sight of his youngest daughter will forever remind him of his sin.

"Oh God, free me from this agony." Al cries.

CHAPTER 1
1933 - LIFE ON THE HILL

    Al and Sarah Bordeau live quiet lives in Sage, population 5,500. During their thirteen years of marriage they have lived in a rented house in the center of town. Five small rooms no longer accommodate the growing family of six. With three daughters and one son, ages three through twelve, another bedroom is needed. Al is a teller at Sage Bank, where he obtains a mortgage to build a two-story house. It is a spacious building with four bedrooms upstairs and a large parlor and kitchen on the first floor. The frame house stands alone, surrounded by dense woodland, one mile up a steep hill, far from the heart of town. A water pump is near the back of the house. A privy stands at the edge of the yard.
    Their only neighbors, Otto and Nita Kale and son Barry, eleven, live one-half mile down the hill from them. A dirt road passes the Kale house and ends at the Bordeau place.
    The move requires major adjustments for the family. With no municipal water lines constructed along the hillside, water must be carried into the house for cooking and laundry. A large metal tub, in a secluded coroner of the kitchen, is used for Saturday baths. A four-burner, wood-burning stove stands in the center of the kitchen.
    Jena is four years old by the time the house is built. The family moves from town to the hill on a cold winter

day. The tiny girl's short bangs peek beneath her red bonnet. Her dark brown eyes grow wide with curiosity as she stands and stares at the huge house.

"Why are there so many steps, Mama?" she asks, as she watches her father and brother help two men carry furniture from the large green moving-van up to the house.

"They go up to the front porch," Sarah answers. "There are many big rooms in this house. Your father and I have one bedroom. Phil and Rita each have a room of their own. You and Laura will share a room together."

Satisfied for the moment, Jena pulls her dark blue mittens tight over her hands. She ponders her mother's words as she climbs bravely up the ten steep steps. She counts each one and gently brushes delicate snowflakes from them. She ascends slowly until she reaches the porch. Her twinkling eyes open wide, sparkling like the glistening snow as she stands proudly by the front door. Her chubby cheeks are cherry-red like the coat and bonnet she wears. Frost flows from her tiny mouth as she calls out, "Mama, I can see Dad and Phil lift my bed from the truck. Come up here and watch them," she exclaims breathlessly and shakes snow from her coat and mittens.

The thin woman struggles up the steps. Her arms are wrapped around a large cardboard box filled with bed linens. Jena scurries through the house as the movers help her father and brother place heavy furniture in the rooms. By bedtime the house is in good order.

"This really is a big house," Jena whispers to Laura as the girls lay in their double bed. "I'm going to like living here," she sighs as the girls drift off into peaceful slumber.

Four months later, on a balmy spring day, Sarah and Al return from town. The handle on a tan wicker basket hangs over the woman's arm. When she sets it on the ground near the steps, Laura, six, calls to her younger sister, "Jena come here. Look what Mother brought home."

Sarah takes a tiny shepherd-collie pup from the basket. Jena runs to see the rusty-brown ball of fur. His front paws stretch upward as he struggles onto the bottom step.

The little girl swoops the puppy into her arms. He licks her face. Her cheerful giggles ring through the warm breeze.

"His fur tickles my face. Look Mama, he likes me."

"Keep the puppy away from your mouth," Sarah cautions her.

"Is he mine, Mama?" her daughter asks. "Is he mine?"

"He belongs to the family, Jena. He's all of ours. What do you think we should name him?"

Phil, eleven, looks at the puppy. He speaks up. "Let's call him Rusty. It's the color of his fur."

"That's a good name," Sarah agrees. "It does suit him."

The months Rusty lives inside the house he and Jena become inseparable. By summer's end, Rusty has grown to be very large.

"I'm tired of this dog always being in our way," Al often complains.

One bright Saturday morning Al and Phil carry a hammer, saw and heavy lumber to the back yard. They work together as they build a large dog house in the corner of the yard.

"This will keep the dog out of the house," Al tells his son.

"I'll make a strong rubber flap for a door," Phil says, as he measures the opening. "When it gets cold outside, I'll get him an old blanket to lay on. That should keep him warm in the wintertime."

"You can handle that. I've done enough for this dog."

Al turns away and walks to the house.

Every morning, Jena comes out to see her special friend. "Good morning, Rusty. How are you today?" she greets him. The dog jumps up and down and wags his tail when he sees the small girl, anxious for his customary daily hug.

Day after day Sarah watches Jena and the dog from the kitchen window. Often the two friends play together for hours.

It is a brisk fall day. The girl and dog escape from the yard to enjoy a romp in the woods. It is cool and the pair has been gone a long time. Sarah puts her hands in her apron pockets as she walks outside. She searches for her daughter. There is neither sight nor sound of girl or dog. She does not hear Jena's impish laughter.

"Laura," she calls to her daughter inside the house, "is Jena in there with you?"

"No. She and Rusty are in the woods."

The sky is growing dark. Heavy rain clouds hover above. Sarah paces frantically in the yard. "Jena! Rusty!" she calls. "Come back to the house Jena," she shouts.

Several minutes pass before the distraught woman sees a red coat and hat appear from among the trees. The tiny girl's flushed cheeks are as colorful as her clothes. She runs from the woods across the yard with Rusty close by her side. There is a mischievous grin on her face as she reaches the porch.

"Jena," Sarah scolds, "you mustn't go alone in the woods. I wouldn't be able to help you if you got hurt in there."

"Oh Mother, nothing will happen to me." Her brown eyes glisten as she laughs. "Don't worry. Rusty takes care of me."

A flash of lightning streaks through the sky, followed by a loud burst of thunder and a torrent of rain. Sarah runs inside the house. She hopes to find refuge from a fear she can't control.

Jena stands on the porch. The wind blows a heavy spray of rain. It sprinkles water on her and Rusty. They watch the storm from outside. Sarah goes through the house and pulls down all the blinds. The woman paces back and forth in the parlor, praying for the storm to end. "God help us!" she sighs over and over as she clutches crystal rosary beads in her hands.

Sarah relates the incident to Al when he comes home from work. "This morning Jena went into the woods with that dog. They were there for over an hour. I had to call her to come home," she says, with a quiver in her voice. "She reached the back porch just as the rain began to pour down. One of these days something dreadful will happen to her. I wish you'd tell that girl to stay in the yard where I can keep an eye on her."

"You worry too much, Sarah. Nothing will bother Jena. Not while that dog is with her. She won't be a child forever. Let the kid enjoy the woods."

"I know she loves the woods and being with Rusty. But I worry so much about her." Sarah pauses. "I guess you're right, though. I'm powerless to keep that pair away from their beloved sanctuary. It's just," she hesitates again, "I'm sure she'll be safe in the yard."

Sarah goes to the kitchen. She takes two pumpkin pies from the oven. She sets them on the high window sill to cool. Rusty sniffs the spicy aroma. Unable to reach the after-dinner treats, he lies patiently on the porch.

After dinner, Laura and Jena walk outside with plates in their hands. Before Laura is able to sit down, Rusty jumps up on her. He knocks her down on the porch, smears pumpkin pie over her dress and devours her favorite dessert. She runs screaming inside the house. Jena sits on the porch step, calmly eating her pie, with her furry friend laying close by her side.

"You're in big trouble now, Rusty," she whispers in the dog's ear. He wags his tail as she feeds him the last morsels from her plate.

Laura wears a clean dress seated at the kitchen table with a fresh piece of pie. There will be no more struggles with Rusty for her.

A scenic winter follows a brisk fall. In cold weather there are difficult chores for the two older children. After Phil helps his father chop wood for the stove, Rita and her brother carry it into the house. Hard work is followed by fun times with snowball fights and sled rides for all the children.

Home alone during the week, Sarah and Jena sit at the window admiring the beautiful woodland. Trees are covered with layers of snow. Tiny flakes slip intermittently from branches to snow-covered ground. Bright red cardinals, brown sparrows and brilliant blue jays fill the yard like a colorful design on a white patchwork quilt. They flutter toward bird feeders hung in the back yard. Regardless of difficulties, it is with sadness Al, Sarah and the children watch their second picturesque winter fade from sight.

The seasons change rapidly from a short spring to an early summer. It is a very hot, humid day. Jena follows her fourteen-year-old sister outside. Shiny brown hair and dark eyes are the only things the two have in common. Rita carries two metal buckets to the pump. The device mystifies the small girl every time she looks at it. She stands close to Rita as the tall, slim girl swings the long handle up and down, up and down. Cool, clear water gushes from the spout. Tiny bubbles leap over the rim of a bucket and pirouette on hard ground.

Unable to restrain her curiosity, the wide-eyed tot asks Rita again and again, "How does the pump work? What makes the water come out? Why does the water stop when you drop the handle?"

Exasperated by her sister's incessant chatter, Rita blurts out, "No more questions, Jena! If you want to know all the answers, put your finger under the handle. You'll find out."

Without a moment's hesitation Jena pokes her finger in the hollow space beneath the long handle. Rita swings the heavy bar downward. Hard metal meets a fragile finger.

"Crack." The gruesome sound lasts but a second.

A shrill scream punctures the crisp air like the onslaught of a sharp dagger.

At the sound of Jena's outburst and Rusty's ferocious bark, Rita runs into the house. Al and Sarah dash outside. The father takes a white handkerchief from his pocket and wraps it around his daughter's mangled finger. Moments later he carries Jena, screaming, into a taxi. Ten minutes later the pair are at the doctor's office.

Sarah decides not to question Rita about what happened. "I'll let your father handle this when he gets home. You go outside and bring in some more water."

When the girl opens the door, Rusty runs up on the porch and growls at her. "I can't go outside now," she wails. "Rusty won't stop growling at me."

"Down Rusty. Stay down," Sarah commands.

In the kitchen, Rita empties water from buckets into two large tubs. They are placed together on a bench, near the side of the room. One tub holds hot soapy water. The other holds cold rinse water. A hand-cranked wringer, attached to the sides of the tubs, is used to squeeze water from the clothes. Rita stays in the house, away from the dog. Her mother hangs laundry on lines stretched between metal poles in the back yard.

When Al arrives at the doctor's office he takes Jena to the side door. Her shrieks can be heard inside before the door is opened.

Doctor Mueller, a short, elderly man with light

brown hair and a stern face, is in the office today. He is not Jena's favorite when she comes here. His assistant, Doctor Saunders, is in direct contrast to his boss. The young doctor is a tall, blonde, handsome man just out of medical school. Jena likes the doctor with a nice smile and soft voice.

"It looks like you put your finger in a meat grinder," the doctor tells Jena. He turns from the girl to her father. "What happened to her, Al?" he asks in a blunt, gruff tone.

"She had an accident at our water pump."

Miss Winters, the nurse, takes an X-ray. She is a young, slim, blue-eyed blonde. Jena likes her low, soft voice.

The doctor studies the film. "Your daughter's finger suffered multiple breaks. It needs to be set and put in a cast."

After the finger is set, father and daughter turn toward the exit door. "You be careful not to get that finger wet until I remove the cast," the doctor tells Jena. He remains somber. He does not smile when he remarks, "I'll see you in six weeks."

A cast and medication ease the pain. Jena cries softly. Al carries her from the cab, to the front steps, into the house. He returns home in a furious mood and confronts his oldest daughter.

"Rita, what the hell did you do to your sister?" he yells.

"I didn't do anything. She did it to herself."

"How could she break her own finger like that?"

"She always stands by me at the pump. She asks the same dumb questions over and over again."

"You could have answered the kid's questions."

"I let her see for herself how it works. She stuck her finger under the pump handle. Maybe she'll let me alone now."

"How could you let such a horrible thing happen?

You should take better care of your sister. She's only five years old. A girl your age should know better. You should have more sense than to let her do such a stupid thing."

He glares at Rita. "I don't want anything like this to happen again. Do you understand me?"

She looks him in the eye. "I hear you." Her voice is sarcastic. "Jena learned her lesson. It won't happen again."

"You aren't to tell anyone how your sister got hurt."

He turns to Sarah. "You tell the other kids this is to be kept in the family."

"Doctor Mueller took care of me today. He'll take the cast off in six weeks." Jena wipes her tears away as she talks to her mother.

Following the pump incident, Rusty barks at Rita every time she goes outside. His growl scares everyone who gets near Jena. She and Phil are the only ones able to approach the dog without fear of him growling at them.

The following Saturday, Jena goes to greet Rusty. She sees her father pound a heavy wooden post in the ground. A long, thick metal chain lays on the grass nearby. She realizes her friend is about to lose his freedom. Sarah stand helpless at the kitchen window. She watches Jena sit on the porch with her arms around her beloved pet.

For the remainder of the summer, Jena takes food and water to Rusty. Every afternoon she sits on the rope swing Al hung from the tall oak tree beside the dog house. She and Rusty have quiet "conversations" together.

"You're such a good dog. I love you Rusty."

The tiny tot gives the big dog a hug. He jumps up and licks her face. Jena giggles. She listens to his soft bark.

"I know you love me too," she agrees.

It is another hot Saturday. Phil's friend, Barry, comes to the Bordeau house. He finds the dog alone in the yard. The twelve-year-old bends over to pat him. Rusty growls. Barry jumps away. But he doesn't move fast enough. Rusty nips his arm. Barry yells and runs to the porch. Sarah runs to the door and sees a few drops of blood and teeth marks on the boy's arm. She cleans the small wound with antiseptic and covers it with a gauze bandage.

When Al comes home from work he sees his wife's red eyes. He looks at the patch on Barry's arm. There's no need for him to ask Sarah any questions. He can figure out for himself what happened today when he was away. Al makes an instant decision. The look of anger on his face could tell a story all its own. He has a plan. This evening, when the kids are in their rooms, he will tell his wife what he intends to do.

Al makes his announcement to Sarah when they are alone this evening. "We have to get rid of that dog. He's too mean. I'm going to take care of him before something serious happens to someone. I don't want another person to be attacked by him. The dog has to go. Tonight," he states, in no uncertain terms.

"Oh Al, Barry didn't know Rusty would bite him. I'll make sure no one goes near the dog again. It will break Jena's heart if you take him away."

"This is no time to worry about how she feels. First, you're upset because he takes Jena in the woods. Then he attacks Laura for her pie. Even though he's chained, Rita's afraid to go out to the yard. Now he attacks Barry. Phil and Jena are the only persons the dog doesn't growl at."

"Al, please don't take him away. For Jena's sake."

"I'll not listen to any more of this nonsense. Tonight I'll make sure we're through with the animal for good. Tonight, the dog goes. Don't tell Jena what happens to him. Then she won't feel so bad."

Al waits for the girls to be asleep. He takes his gun to the yard. He aims it at the dog's head. Rusty jumps up and growls.

"Bang!" The dog makes a dreadful howl. It becomes a whimper as he falls to the ground.

The shot shatters the serenity of a lovely summer night. Al steadies the weapon. He pulls the trigger once more. "Bang!" Rusty lies still. The shots rupture the stillness of night. Like bursts of thunder, the horrid sounds echo through a peaceful sky.

Silence once more embraces the night.

The girls remain asleep as father and son prepare a burial place for Rusty. Phil walks beyond the trees with a shovel in his hands and tears in his eyes. Al follows with a lifeless dog in his arms.

A short time later, they return. A spotlight illuminates an empty yard. Rusty lies at rest in Jena's beloved woodland.

In the morning, a cheerful child runs out to greet her faithful companion. She sees the empty chain near the dog house. She screams. She runs back to the house.

"Mother! Mother! Rusty's gone. He's not in his house."

"Your father took him away last night. We couldn't let him hurt anyone again. Your dog's safe. You don't have to worry about him."

"Oh, Mother," she cries, "he won't be happy without me. He'll be back. Rusty will come back to me."

"No, Jena. He won't be back. He's gone forever."

"Rusty. Rusty. Come back Rusty," she calls. She runs frantically through the yard. She sits on the swing, under the giant oak tree. All day she waits outside. At mealtimes, she doesn't eat. She sits outside. She waits for Rusty to return.

Early the next morning she resumes her lonely vigil. She swings back and forth. Her shoes draw lines in the soft earth as she drags then along the ground. Her head droops. Tears run down her pale cheeks.

At the end of day, Sarah hopes to console her daughter. "Jena, you mustn't wait any longer for Rusty. Remember all the happy times you shared. It will help you feel better."

Her words fall on deaf ears. Jena sobs as she dresses for bed. The distraught girl does not want to hear empty words; she wants to hear her beloved friend bark again in the yard.

Tonight, Sarah stands in the doorway and listens to Jena say her prayers. The small girl kneels beside her bed. She closes her eyes, folds her hands toward heaven, and talks to the only One who can work miracles.

"Dear God, take care of Rusty, wherever he is. Keep him safe. Let him come back to me. Amen."

She brushes tears from her cheeks and slides into bed.

Jena does not see the tears roll down her mother's face.

Oh, for the faith of a child, Sarah reflects, *to believe God will grant the impossible*. She knows how much her daughter hurts. She shares Jena's pain. Sarah loved the dog, also.

Since the loss of her pet, Jena never wanders from the yard. Her wondrous woodland has lost its enchantment.

The family endures many hardships living so far from town. In the winter, groceries must be lugged up the front steps through deep snow. Water must be carried to the house in frigid weather. In the summer, groceries must be toted a long distance on hot humid days. As this summer draws to an end, Jena still grieves for her dog. But there is one bright spark of light for her; tomorrow the cast gets removed from her finger.

The morning is sunny and warm. It is a nice day for Sarah to take her daughter to town. Miss Winters opens the office door. Jena is happy to see young Doctor

Saunders. She sees his bright smile and is sure everything will be all right.

"How does your finger feel, Jena?" She relaxes at the sound of his soft, low voice.

"It feels good. I'm glad to get this thing off. I couldn't play with anything. I was afraid it would get hurt again."

"I'll take care of that right now." He smiles as he removes the cast. His happy expression soon turns serious. "I'll have to take another X-ray. I don't like the looks of this finger." After a few minutes he gives Sarah the bad news.

"Jena is going to be disappointed. This bone was so badly mangled it has not healed well. I'll have to break it and reset it. If it isn't repaired now, it will never heal right. I'll give her medicine. She won't feel any pain."

As soon as Jena hears the words, "break it and reset it," she gets hysterical. "I don't want my finger broken again. Don't do it Doctor. Please don't do it," she cries.

"Jena," he explains in a calm voice, "you don't want to go through life with a crooked finger. Do you? I promise you, it won't hurt when I fix it this time."

"I don't care if it is crooked. I don't want you to break it again," she bawls.

"Doctor, give us some time to think about this. If she decides to have it fixed again, we'll come back," Sarah says.

"Mrs. Bordeau, it has to be done right away. Otherwise, it will be too late to repair it."

"I can't have this child hurt again. She just lost her dog. I can't make her go through something painful again. Not now." The woman remains firm in her decision.

"I'm sorry you won't agree to the treatment. I want to help the child." The expression on his face confirms his regret.

Sarah's words were ignored by her daughter one other day. Today, Doctor Saunder's words are disregarded by Sarah.

Life on the hill becomes more burden than delight as weeks pass by. Still, Sarah is not prepared to hear Al state at the dinner table tonight, "Fall is almost here. Before another harsh winter arrives, I've decided we'll move back to town. It will be more convenient for all of us. Tomorrow, I'll post the house up for sale."

Sarah drops a fork on her plate. Her eyes open wide. She stares into space. It takes several moments before she can speak. Her bewildered expression reveals to the children the move is a surprise to their mother as well as to them.

"Where will we live after the house is sold?" Her voice rises to a feverish pitch at the end of her question.

"We'll rent until we can buy another house. There's nothing for you to worry about. I'll handle it."

Several weeks pass. In the brisk air of a cool autumn morning, Jena and Phil saunter through dew-covered leaves. They take a final journey through their beloved woods. Crisp leaves crackle beneath their feet. Phil avoids the spot where Rusty is buried. For him, the woodland holds a terrible secret. But for Jena, it will always be her special paradise. It will remain a mystic garden filled with bouquets of precious memories.

It is late afternoon. The Bordeau family travels by taxi, behind a large moving van, toward their new home. Jena looks through the back window as they pull away from the big house. They ride past the Kale house. She departs from her rustic life on the hill, anxious to experience more exciting adventures to brighten her life in a new home in town.

CHAPTER 2
A MOVE BACK TO TOWN

The Bordeau family settles in a house on a street with neat homes and well-kept lawns. Jaunts to an outside privy in snowy, frigid winters and rainy, humid summers now become an obscure memory. With indoor plumbing, warm luxurious baths in the privacy of a closed room are a pleasure. Even Laura and Jena appreciate the comfort it provides.

Sarah initially resists the electric washer Al buys. But soon she discovers the time and energy it saves and the appliance becomes a blessing. New adjustments are difficult for the frugal woman. Financial concerns are paramount with her. Al enjoys some prestige that accompanies his job, but not the modest income he receives for his diligent work.

The trolley that runs past the house takes Al to work and Sarah to the mercantile and grocery stores. Now the family can ride to church when bad weather makes it difficult to walk.

School is a mile from home. In September, Jena and Laura travel to school together. Phil walks with them the first day. He takes a short-cut the final three blocks. He leads the girls along a stretch of deserted railroad tracks. When Jena lags behind, he picks up the weary girl. He sets her on his shoulders.

"I'll carry you the rest of the way, Shorty," he laughs.
"Good," she giggles. She bounces when he runs with her.

Small, patent leather shoes bump against his chest. The shoulder ride ends at the concrete school yard.

Jena wrings her hands as she stands beside her older sister. "Will you be going to the same room you were in last year?"

"Yes. I was absent so much when I had the measles and mumps. Then I got those stupid sties." Laura frowns. "I missed too many days. Sister Claude told Mother I would have to stay in second grade again this year."

Sarah has the girls dress alike for school. Today they wear floral cotton dresses. A small round button holds a thin strap across the front of their new shiny black shoes. Jena rubs the smooth soles over the rough concrete.

A short, red-faced nun in a heavy black dress, sheer black veil and white wimple stands outside. The school is an old three-story brick building. The girls stand and watch as the nun swings a large, glossy brass bell high above her head. A loud clatter vibrates in the morning air. Jena covers her ears with her hands. Students scurry to form long lines at the doors. Jena stares in awe. This is the first time she has seen so many children together.

"All the boys and girls going to first grade form a line to the right," the chubby nun calls out.

"I'll see you at lunch time," Laura calls out, as she rushes toward the line to the left of Jena.

Jena's eyes open wide with curiosity. She passes through an open red wooden door. She, with other children, walks along a huge hallway into a bright, sunny classroom.

A tall, thin nun stands in front of the class. Only Sister Vincent's clear, smooth face and long delicate hands are visible from beneath her habit. She places Jena in a front-row seat. The young nun's clear blue eyes twinkle as she watches the small girl's legs swing back and forth beneath the desk.

The day ends too soon for Jena. She rushes home

with Laura. She is anxious to tell Sarah all about her new adventure.

"Mother," she blurts out, "on the way to school, Phil sat me on his shoulders when we took a short-cut by some railroad tracks. A lot of kids were in the school yard. There were too many for me to count them all."

Jena waves her hands in amazement, then continues with her story.

"A short nun with a red face stood outside a big door. She swung a metal bell. The loud noise hurt my ears. All the kids ran into long lines. Then we walked into school. We passed through a long hallway to get to our rooms." Jena stops briefly to take a breath. "I have a nice, pretty teacher. Sister Vincent smiles a lot. She gave me a desk in the front row. I sit next to Sister's big desk. Look." Jena shows her mother a small book. "She gave the class this to take home."

Dick, Jane and Spot is printed on the cover. There is a picture of a small boy and girl and a furry dog running together. "It looks like a nice story," Jena exclaims. "I'm going to ask Phil to read it to me."

"You can talk to your brother about it when he gets home. Now go upstairs and change into play clothes."

This evening after dinner, Sarah sees her five-year-old daughter and twelve-year-old son together on the living room sofa. Jena listens intently as her brother reads the story. She remembers when she, Phil and Rusty shared happy times together on the hill.

Jena looks forward to school. On brisk days she and Laura skip through piles of crisp leaves. Autumn remnants rustle and snap beneath their shoes. Jena gathers up bright-colored leaves to take home to press between waxed paper. Some days, Phil walks with her and sits her on his shoulders as they travel along the train tracks. Her melodious laughter echoes in the cool fall breeze.

Early, one Saturday morning, Al's brother Ray and his wife Peg stop at the Bordeau house. The thin, dark-haired man wears jeans and a blue flannel shirt. His short, brunette wife has on a plaid house dress. Soft staccato rhythms from the percolator bounce in the background. The couples sit at the kitchen table and sip fresh-brewed coffee.

"It's unusual for you two to visit before lunch time. Is there something wrong?" Sara asks.

"I'm taking Peg to a jamboree in Longhill tonight. We want you to come with us. It's about time the two of you get away from the house and enjoy some time together."

"That would be great," Al agrees. "We've never been to a jamboree, Sarah. Let's go with them tonight."

"It will take an hour to drive each way. The children will be home alone too long. We won't get home till after midnight."

"We never get out together. You don't ever want to go away or do anything here in town. Ray's right. It's time for us to get out and enjoy ourselves."

"We should wait until the girls are older before we go that far out of town. What will they do if something serious happens while we're gone?"

"When they're older you'll find another reason to stay home." He looks at his sister-in-law. "Peg, you try to talk some sense into her. Maybe she'll listen to a woman."

"Sarah, Al's anxious to go with Ray and me. Please say you'll go. It will be good for all of us."

"It isn't safe for children to be alone so long," Sarah repeats. "Why did you drive all this way? You could have asked us this over the phone."

"We thought you might come if we talked to you here. Just think about it. We have children, too. Kory watches the three younger girls when Ray and I go out. Both she and Rita are fourteen. They're old enough to take care of the others."

"You may be right." Sarah ponders. "Dinner will be finished and Rita can put the girls to bed. They'll be asleep most of the time we're away." Sarah hesitates. "Ray, what time will you be here this evening?"

"We'll stop by the house at six-thirty."

Several hours later, Ray and Peg arrive as promised. Sarah wears a brown gabardine dress and brown high-button shoes. Her shiny black hair is combed back from her face. Her soft skin glows with cheeks covered with rose-colored rouge. There is an unusual gleam in her brown eyes. Al stands by her side in the living room. He is handsome in his navy serge suit and dark blue rayon tie. His blond hair and blue eyes are a striking contrast to Sarah's dark hair and eyes. His wife gives final instructions to Rita.

"Be sure to have the girls in bed by nine o'clock. And I want you and Phil in your rooms by ten." The parents bid them good-night then go out the door.

The children see Uncle Ray's light-blue, Ford sedan pull away from the curb. They watch as the car rolls along the smooth brick road. In the early dusk it disappears into the evening mist.

The four children scamper to the kitchen. Phil, Laura and Jena fidget at the table. Rita pours sugar, milk, chocolate and corn syrup into a sauce pan. On the stove the mixture boils. Rita stirs in butter and vanilla until it's creamy and smooth. She empties the fudge into a buttered dish. The four of them anxiously wait for it to cool.

After a few minutes pass, Laura coaxes, "Rita, can we eat a piece of it now?"

"Not yet. It's not cool enough to cut. We have to wait a little longer."

Phil reaches behind his older sister. He dips a finger into the mixture cooling on the kitchen table. Laura laughs. She whispers to Jena, "Phil fooled Rita. She doesn't know he took some of it."

Rita cuts the candy and turns to the girls. "Now that Phil's had his sample we can take a piece for ourselves."

"How did you know I swiped some?" Phil asks.

"Mothers know everything. They have eyes behind their head. I'm taking Mother's place tonight." She smiles with delight.

When the candy is eaten, Jena asks Rita, "Will you make us another treat the next time Dad and Mother go away?"

"Only if you go to bed and right to sleep."

All the children are in bed and asleep as Sarah ordered. The downstairs hall clock strikes midnight. The clamor of sirens awakens them from a deep slumber. Phil and the girls run to the front window in Rita's room. They see orange flames leap from a second floor window of the building across the street. Smoke billows from it. Men in heavy yellow slickers, white helmets and high black boots aim a hose at the flames. A firefighter uses an axe to break open the front door of the burning house. He runs up the stairs. Within minutes he appears with a silver-haired woman in his arms. The children watch, petrified. The ambulance drives away with the woman inside. They listen to the shriek of the siren. It echoes through the cold, damp night air as it speeds down the street.

"Rita, our house will burn," Jena cries. "I want Mother to come home. I want Mother here now!"

"The fire can't reach us. We're safe over here," Rita tells her. She tries to calm her little sister, but Rita trembles herself as she speaks.

"The firemen will have the fire out soon," Phil announces. "Don't cry, Shorty. The fire can't touch our house."

People with coats thrown over night clothes gather in front of the Bordeau house. They watch firemen toss a burning mattress from the window to the ground. A thick column of black smoke spirals into the air.

Water spills down the steps and out the door. A fireman soaks the mattress. The fire disappears.

"The fire's out," Phil declares. "It's all over, Shorty. Don't cry. We're safe now. Everything's all right."

Firemen remove the hose from the hydrant. The red fire truck rolls down the street. People rush back to their homes.

Laura looks at Jena. She grins. "Why were you so afraid over here? A dumb old mattress caught fire. That's nothing to cry about."

Phil looks at Laura. "You were too scared to even talk."

"It was okay to be afraid and cry, Shorty," Phil tells Jena, as he walks her and Laura back to their room.

It's past one o'clock before they all fall asleep again.

A short time later, Ray's car stops in front of the house. Al and Sarah see the burned building. They jump from the car.

"Good Lord! There's been a fire here," Sarah shouts.

"Don't you two get all upset about this. Everything seems to be under control," Ray remarks. He glances at the darkened Bordeau house. "The kids must be asleep. Things couldn't have been too bad here." He turns to Peg. "We have to get home and check on our girls." Ray closes the door and drives away.

Sarah's face is chalk-white. "I have to see if the kids are all right," she gasps. Al grabs his wife's arm. He tries to calm the panic-stricken woman. The odor of pungent smoke fills the couple's nostrils. Sarah pulls away and runs to the front door. She rushes upstairs to Rita's room. Their mother's frantic voice wakens the bleary-eyed children. Once again tonight, they gather in the front bedroom.

"What happened across the street?" Sarah's voice shakes as she cries out.

"There was a fire," Phil offers.

"I can see there's been a fire," Sarah exclaims. "I want to know what happened over here during the fire."

The burned mattress on the ground, charred windows and black marks on yellow bricks reveal a terrible tale.

All at once, four children blurt out stories about the calamity. Finally, Rita relates the entire incident to her parents.

"It was a big fire," Jena adds. "I was afraid it would jump over here. But Phil told us we were safe." She takes a deep breath and sighs, "I'm glad you're home now."

Sarah knows it's been a scary night for the children. She feels guilty she was absent when they needed her.

Downstairs, she complains to Al. "I told you we shouldn't leave the kids alone. Look what happens when we go away."

"Sarah, everything's all right here. Rita took care of things. Don't ruin our good night out by fretting about what could have happened. We need some time together away from this house. I work hard at the bank. You tire yourself out being constantly busy here at home. The nuns at the orphanage taught you too well," he grumbles. "Every Saturday this house smells of Murphy's oil soap and disinfectant. It's so spotless, we could eat from the floor."

Al's protests have no effect on Sarah. Every time her husband suggests they go out for an evening she continues to rebel. "I'll stay home until the girls are older. We'll both have more time then. We will enjoy ourselves when we don't have to worry about spending money we can't afford."

Al continues to work hard at the bank. The business gradually grows stronger. He hopes to advance within a few years. For now, his work is his prime concern. *It's possible Sarah is right about our finances. We don't have any extra money to toss around. We need to save for a down-payment on another house of our own.* After many years of marriage, Al finally begins to reflect on, and appreciate, his wife's prudence.

CHAPTER 3
A GLORIOUS CHRISTMAS

It is Jena's sixth birthday. The family celebrates with her favorite treat, devil's food cake with yellow icing. Sarah writes the customary, 'Happy Birthday Jena,' on top.

"Make a wish," Laura urges. "If you blow out all the candles your wish will come true."

Jena bends over the cake. She takes a deep breath, then exhales a strong gust of air. Tiny trails of smoke rise from the burnt out candles. "Now I'll get..."

"Hush Jena," Laura exclaims. "You can't tell us your wish. If you do, it won't come true."

Soon the cake and ice cream vanish. An anxious child rips open her present. Inside the box is a beautiful doll. It has small dark eyes, thick curly hair and a smile on its chubby black face. The twelve-inch doll wears white lace panties beneath an orange and white checkered dress. On her feet are lacy anklets under shiny, white patent leather shoes.

"Laura, Mother took me to the store last week. We saw a lot of dolls on a toy shelf. Some were little, some were big. But there was only one black doll. I told Mother I wanted that one." She sighs. "I blew out all the candles. I got my wish." Her eyes glow as she hugs her doll.

Tonight Jena enters dreamland with Mandy cuddled in her arms. Visions of the impending holidays fill her dreams.

It is a cold, snowy Thanksgiving Day. Dinner includes the traditional roast turkey with stuffing, baked yams, green beans and mashed potatoes with gravy. Rita helps prepare the stuffed celery and cranberry sauce. The aroma of baked rolls, pumpkin and minced meat pies floats throughout the house.

After the big meal the family plays their usual games on the dining room table. Sarah wins at domino. Rita is masterful at Chinese checkers. Al wins the 500 rum game.

Early Friday morning Sarah prepares for her annual trip to Bridgeport. This is the day she shops for Christmas gifts. On her list is a carefully thought out gift for Al. She plans one present for each of the children. In the past, Phil and the girls received games they could share with one another. The selection becomes more difficult as the children grow older.

Today is the first time the younger girls accompany their mother Christmas shopping in the big city.

"How can you hide gifts from the girls when they are there beside you?" Al questions Sarah in their room. "Jena won't believe in Santa any more if she sees you buy presents and carry them home."

"I'll have a salesclerk set things aside for me. She can schedule them to be delivered on a school day. The girls will be too excited with Christmas decorations and toys to notice what I do in the store."

After breakfast Sarah and the girls bundle up in Sunday dresses under heavy wool coats. They put on wool knitted hats and gloves. They depart into frigid weather. It's late in the morning when Sarah and her daughters step from the Greyhound bus. In front of a lofty Gimbel's department store stands a giant pine tree. On its branches are huge red bows, large colored bulbs and strings of bright lights.

"Mother, how can these buildings stand up so high?" Jena asks as she stares at the conglomeration of giant structures.

"The skyscrapers are designed and built in a way that they won't topple over, even in sever wind storms."

"Look at the beautiful tree," Laura shouts. She tries to be heard above the chorus of *Jingle Bells* that blares from a loud speaker outside the store.

Sarah listens to "ohs!" and "ahs!" as the pair admires the holiday splendor. Inside the store they head for Toyland. The three enter an elevator crowded with other children eager to talk with Santa. Jena stares at a man in a blue uniform. A matching cap covers the top of his thick gray hair. He smiles as he closes the door.

"What floor, please?" the operator asks.

"We want to visit Santa," Jena announces.

"That will be the fourteenth floor."

"Fourteen floors!" Jena squeals. She squeezes her eyes shut. The elevator races up, then stops. Jena opens her eyes.

"Toyland," the man calls out. "Everybody out for Toyland."

As she steps from the elevator, Jena sees Santa in his red suit. He wears a wide black belt around his big belly and high, shiny black boots. His white bushy curls, beard and mustache cover most of his rosy-red cheeks. A young boy sits on Santa's lap. He whispers something in the jolly man's ear.

"Mother," Jena shouts, her brown eyes round as silver dollars, "Santa looks just like all those pictures I cut out from newspapers."

Laura gives her mother a swift, furtive glance.

Jena's eyes dart all around the room. She stands in awe in a long line that leads to Santa. She stares at a giant fir tree. Bells, glossy bulbs and strands of colored popcorn hang from its branches. The scent of pine saturates the air. A model train runs on tracks that circle the base of the tree. A headlight shines from the center of its locomotive. The black engine pulls colored boxcars, gondolas, flatcars hauling logs, oil tankers and a little red caboose.

Jena's eyes dart from one object to another. She stands mesmerized. She watches the train go over trestles and bridges. The locomotive puffs small circles of smoke into the air. The train circles small farm buildings and tiny houses. Sharp blasts from the steam whistle rise above children's laughter. Jena presses her hands to her ears to block out the shrill sound.

A dainty elf motions for the girls to move ahead. "It's your turn to talk with Santa. He's waving for you to go up."

Laura gives her mother another sly, shrewd look.

As the girls approach Santa's large chair, they stop, stunned. The lid on an enormous jack-in-the-box pops open. Out jumps a laughing clown. They laugh at the silly surprise and hop onto the jolly-one's lap. They rub a hand over their cheeks as soft fuzzy whiskers brush across their face as he talks.

"Laura, what can I bring you for Christmas?"

"I want some jigsaw puzzles or a monopoly game," she grins.

"And what do you want for Christmas, Jena?"

"I want another doll." She gazes into his eyes. "Mandy needs someone to keep her company when I'm at school."

"And who is Mandy?" he bellows with a hearty laugh.

"She's my favorite doll," she beams. "I just got her."

"Ho! Ho! Ho!" he roars. "You want a doll to keep Mandy company. And have you both been good for your mother?"

"Yes, Santa. We've been good," Jena declares. "And on Christmas Eve we'll put milk and cookies on the table for you."

"I'll look for them. My reindeer like them, too. Remember, I'll need time to take toys to all the good little girls and boys. You must go to bed early on Christmas Eve."

"Oh, we'll be asleep when you come," Jena gushes.

Santa lifts Laura and Jena from his lap. He gives a hearty, "Ho! Ho! Ho! Merry Christmas!"

"Merry Christmas to you, Santa," Jena shouts and waves.

Sarah leads her daughters on an excursion through Toyland. Large glass shelves along the wall hold every kind of big and little doll. Scattered around the enormous room are bright-colored tricycles and two-wheeled bikes. They watch boys admire basketballs, baseballs and footballs. Stacked on corner shelves are wooden blocks, plastic bricks and rustic Lincoln logs. In the toy palace sit stuffed dogs, teddy bears, wooden soldiers and miniature pianos. As they stroll through this magic land, Jena and Laura discover so many games and puzzles. It's impossible to look at them all. Never in their wildest dreams could the youngsters imagine so many marvelous toys existed in all the world.

"Toyland's a magic Wonderland," Jena blurts out. "What happens to all these toys, Mother?"

"Santa delivers them on Christmas Eve."

Sarah hopes Laura will refrain from any more devious looks.

The trio exits the land of enchantment. In the elevator, the operator closes the door and pulls down a metal lever.

They descend at a rapid speed. Jena, breathless, squeezes her eyes shut again. She quivers as butterflies seem to fly in the pit of her stomach.

"First floor," the man call out. "Everyone out."

Sarah leads the way to the cafeteria. The happy travelers drape their coats over the back of their chairs.

Beneath her long gray wool coat the woman wears the brown dress she wore to the jamboree last fall. But this afternoon, there is no rouge to bring color to her glossy cheeks.

Sarah orders three hot beef sandwiches with gravy. All three choose warm peach pie for desert.

After a pleasant lunch, they continue to look at decorations throughout the store. Amid this holiday grandeur, the youngsters never notice their mother talk to a salesclerk. Sarah places money in the lady's hand. She arranges for a day the packages will be delivered and puts a receipt inside her purse.

Outside, the girls are in awe of sparkling lights, bright red and gold bulbs and silver bells that decorate giant buildings and tall Christmas trees. They listen to carols flow from loud speakers as they walk to the bus depot.

Another long bus ride takes the tired adventurers home. At the dinner table, Jena tells all about her great day.

"You must go with us next year, Dad. Santa's chair is beside a giant Christmas tree. A train runs all around it. And there are so many toys. We couldn't look at all of them."

Jena chatters on and on, as though no one before her has ever experienced the pleasure of these great wonders.

"Dad," she continues, "Toyland's on the fourteenth floor. Laura and my stomach did flip-flops when the elevator took us down so fast. And there are giant, decorated trees everywhere. And Christmas music plays in all the stores. There are even speakers on the buildings outside. And everything smells like pine. Bridgeport is a beautiful, magic Wonderland.

"Did you tell Santa what he's to bring you?" Al asks.

"Yes. And I promised to go to bed early too."

Four weeks seem like an eternity. Jena grows impatient. She wants to hear the sound of reindeer arrive. When the big night finally comes, Sarah reminds Jena of her promise. "You told Santa you would go to sleep early tonight. Now, hop in bed before he gets here."

Jena lies awake, too excited to sleep. Soon she hears strange sounds coming from downstairs. With Mandy in her arms, she creeps half-way down the stairs. She sits there motionless. With her cheeks pressed against the banister, she listens to the rustle of crisp paper. She hears bells jingle from behind the closed living room door.

"Tinkle! Tinkle! Tinkle!" echo the bells.

"Oh my gosh, it's Santa Claus," she gasps.

She runs up the steps and scrambles into bed with her sister. "Laura," she whispers. "Santa's here."

"He's not here." Laura yawns. "You were dreaming."

"He's here now. I heard him in the living room."

"Oh, be quiet. Just go to sleep," Laura hollers.

Jena pulls the covers over her head and squeezes Mandy in her arms. Within minutes, both girls are fast asleep.

Early Christmas morning Jena jumps out of bed. She rushes to the living room. In the corner she sees a tree with a white lace angel on the highest branch. It reaches the ceiling. Dotted among glistening bulbs and brilliant strings of lights, tiny silver bells dangle from the ends of prickly branches. She shakes a bell and hears a familiar jingle. She races to the kitchen and shouts, "Mother, I heard Santa here last night. I listened to the bells while he hung them on the tree. And he brought everyone a present."

She looks around and sees an empty dish and glass.

"Look. He ate the cookies and drank the milk. Santa *was* in the living room last night."

After Mass, the family opens presents. Jena rips open her gift and finds a pink, chubby doll. Laura gets a monopoly game.

"Santa remembered what we asked him for," Jena chuckles.

Phil gets a silver harmonica; Rita, a pair of white ice skates. A gold-plated pocket watch delights Al. Sarah opens a popular hand-mirror, comb and brush set. She takes her gift to the master bedroom. She carefully places it in the center of the dresser. As she stands before the large mirror she admires the reflection of a slim, beautiful woman. Her brown eyes sparkle, her soft skin glistens. The wisp of a smile spreads across her face. Sarah gently runs soft bristles through her wavy, jet-black hair.

This is a Christmas that weaves wonderful memories, especially for Jena. As her mother returns to the family gathering, there is a warm glow on her face. It is evident to all that this is a special day for her, also.

Jena sits with Mandy and her new doll cuddled in her arms. She enjoys the special delight of a Christmas she will always treasure; the rapture of passing through a magic wonderland in the big city. This is an extraordinary time when the entire family shares happiness and love.

CHAPTER 4
CONFLICT OF INTERESTS

It is the first Tuesday of the New Year. The doors of Sage Bank will open in thirty minutes. Al Bordeau is summoned from the teller's window to the manager's office. The young, handsome man walks cautiously to the door. His blue eyes glance from the elderly man's face to the papers piled neatly on his desk. Al takes a seat facing his boss, a tall, robust, gray-haired man.

"How was your holiday?" John Grason asks.

The friendly greeting helps Al relax. "It was nice for the family. Sarah took the two younger girls to Bridgeport the day after Thanksgiving. That's all Jena talks about now. How was the holiday for you and Mona?"

"It was a quiet one for us. With both children away at college, there wasn't much excitement in the house."

He snuffs out his cigarette in a crystal ash tray.

"Al, several years have passed since the Black Thursday stock market crash. This past year our bank has achieved a substantial increase in new accounts. I credit it to the fine workers in this office. Friday, I'm to attend a board meeting in Bridgeport. I'm to give a progress report on all my employees. I need to know your thoughts on the work you do. What are your personal expectations for the future?"

"I find great satisfaction in the work I do. I anticipate an advancement within the company in the distant future."

"How would you feel about returning to books

again? You've never been to college. Any promotion would require courses in advanced math. You would need extensive study in the field of business finances."

"That would not be a problem. I'm certain Sarah would not object to me studying evenings and weekends. In fact, it would please her if it included a salary increase. Our two oldest children will be ready for college in a few years. And you know what that entails financially."

"There are rumors of changes about to take place within our region." John Grason removes a silver cigarette case from his breast pocket. He lights another cigarette with a silver lighter. "I'll learn more about this on Friday. We'll discuss this again after my meeting."

The following Monday, Mr. Grason calls Al to his office. "I've good news Al. In a few months, I'll advance to regional manager. But first, I must train a replacement for my job here at Sage Bank."

"Congratulations, John. It couldn't happen to a better man. You deserve the promotion. You will be missed here. Who will be our new manager? Is he someone we know?"

"The board members insist that only our most respected employees hold management positions. The record shows you are a good family man and a diligent worker. I'm proud to say you have been chosen to be my successor. Congratulations, Al."

Al is taken by surprise. He is not prepared for such good news at this stage of his career. It takes several moments before the initial shock wears off.

"Thanks John. I appreciate your confidence in me. And I'm grateful for all you've done for me. This promotion comes much sooner than I ever anticipated."

"Your work shows you're capable of performing the job. You'll not have much time to spend with your family while you take the management courses. I hope they will understand. I wish you all the best."

The men exchange a firm handshake.

"I know you'll be successful at your new position, also. Congratulations again, John."

Al is exhilarated when he arrives home. He is anxious to tell his wife the good news.

"Sarah, John's been promoted to regional manager," Al says hesitantly. "His new work will start as soon as he trains a successor for his present job."

"You'll miss him when he transfers," she comments.

Al twists his hands together in front of him. He beams with a broad smile that lights up his face. "I can't wait any longer to tell you this, Sarah." Suddenly words rush from his mouth. "I'm to be the new manager at our office. The executive board choose me to replace John."

His face glows with pride.

"That will mean a salary increase. It's a blessing. The extra money will help when you put a down-payment on another house." Her calm voice lacks any sign of emotion.

Her reply is the second shock Al gets today. The first was a boost to his morale. But this lack of concern from Sarah kills all his elation. It crushes his spirit.

"My God, Sarah, my pay check seems to be the only thing you care about." The hostility is apparent in his voice. "Don't my ambitions or success mean anything to you? This is a great honor for me. I believed you would be as happy about it as me."

"I think it's good that you got the advancement. It shows that your boss notices how hard you work."

The lack of enthusiasm in her kind words only serves to accelerate the anger that begins to eat at him.

"Let's ask Ray and Peg to go out to dinner. Then we can stay for the Saturday night dance. The four of us can celebrate my promotion. Maybe then you will see that a raise in pay can be good for both of us. It will let us get out once in a while."

"It will be months before you begin the new job. It

would be better if we wait and celebrate later."

Sarah's indifference deflates her husband's pride like a sharp pin bursts an inflated balloon. The thrill of his promotion loses its luster when his wife refuses to share this honor with him.

Al phones his brother Ray with his good news.

"I'm to be promoted at work in a few months. I wanted to take out you and Peg this Saturday to celebrate with Sarah and me. But she won't go until my pay raise goes into effect."

Sarah leaves the room. She does not want to hear what else her husband has to tell his brother about how she feels.

"Let's take Kory and Rita to the races Saturday."

"Won't Sarah be upset if you spend money there?" Ray asks.

"What she doesn't know can't hurt her," Al grumbles.

Ray arrives Saturday morning. He drives Al, Rita and Kory to Longhill.

At the end of the third race, Rita sees her father put fifty dollars in his wallet.

"I bet on a winning horse," he tells her. He has a smug look of satisfaction on his face. He puts the wallet in his back pocket and strolls over to another betting window.

After the fifth race Rita runs up to her father. "Look Dad." She shows him ten crisp one-dollar bills. "Uncle Ray took Kory and me to the window. He placed bets for us. I picked a horse that won, too." The fifteen-year-old clutches the money in her hand. "I won this with the dollar you gave me."

"You'd better not let your mother know you played the ponies. If she finds out, this will be your first and last trip to the races."

Ray takes Al and Rita home as the sun settles on the horizon. Kory says goodbye and waves from the front seat.

At the table tonight Rita does not mention the money she and her father won at the races.

On weekdays Al gets home from the bank in time for dinner. His training courses fill his evening hours. Saturday mornings he and Jena work in the yard. She follows lines from the lawn mower and walks close behind with a wire rake. She gathers clippings and piles them in a corner of the yard. When fall weather arrives, father and daughter rake leaves. They use them for mulch around outdoor plants. The two of them talk together as they go about their work.

One Saturday morning a load of coal is delivered. The truck driver empties the large lumps in a corner beside the front steps. Phil and Al shovel the black cubes into the square open doorway beneath the porch. The coal cellar is almost full when they finish the job.

"We'll have all the fuel we need to keep us warm, no matter how severe this winter may be," Al tells his son.

"I'd rather shovel coal than chop wood," Phil answers.

A fresh snowfall creates a wonderland of beauty. Jena watches trees bend their branches as thick snow lays heavy on their sturdy limbs. She admires the lovely sight as cardinals and blue-jays cluster on the white branches. They eat suet and bird seed from the homemade wooden bird-feeder. On days like this she thinks about her beloved woodland on the hill.

All the children share the burden of snow removal from porch steps and sidewalks. They take turns with snow shovels after school. On weekends, Laura and Jena spend hours on their sleds. Winter days, when the snowfall is heavy, the town council closes off a side street near the Bordeau home. Children, and some adults, enjoy rides down the steep slope. Phil takes walks up the hill to his old neighborhood. He visits his friend Barry.

Rita often goes ice skating with her friends. She

returns home one blustery afternoon with snow-covered skates. Jena takes a cloth and wipes the shoes and blades for her sister.

"How do you stand in these things?" the youngster asks.

"It's easier than with roller skates. Try them. You will see how easy it is."

Rita hands the small girl her skates. They are too big for little feet. Rita stuffs paper in the toes of the shoes. She ties the long strings around Jena's ankles. Rita holds her sister's shaky hands. She leads the hesitant youngster across the carpeted floor. Jena wobbles. She grabs onto a chair.

"I don't know how anyone can stand in these."

"You can learn real quick."

"Not me," Jena disagrees. "I'll just fall and get hurt."

"You should try them on ice. It's a lot easier. You can go with me tomorrow when I skate."

"These things aren't for me. You can keep them. I'll use my roller skates. They're safer."

She removes Rita's shoes from her feet and hands them back.

Outside, the snow continues to billow. Large, soft flakes cover the ground with a fluffy blanket.

"Let's go make a snowman, Phil," Jena urges her brother.

Bundled like Eskimos, with only their faces exposed to the cold, Phil and the younger girls roll small clumps of snow into big, firm balls. Soon there's a torso and head. They add a long carrot nose, coal-chip eyes and pink button mouth. Twigs for arms and an old black hat complete the snowman.

The children admire Frosty as he stand in the front yard.

"It's time for you kids to come inside now. You've been out long enough," Sarah calls from the door.

Inside the house Sarah sets on the table cups of hot chocolate topped with mounds of marshmallow. It is a treat the children look forward to after hours of fun in the snow.

As the long winter lingers, Phil takes the girls for rides on a wooden toboggan. Laura's blond hair and Jena's short brown bangs peak from beneath woolen caps as Phil pulls them through the glistening snow. The girls' cheeks are cherry-red. Jena's wide eyes sparkle as a big brother twists and turns her and Laura along icy paths. Hearty bursts of laughter float through the crisp, frosty air.

This long joyful winter takes its predestined flight. A brief spring bids adieu when summer makes an early arrival.

On a bright sunny morning, Sarah takes the girls on the trolley to the town's largest grocery store. The clang of the bell pierces their ears. Laura yanks a thin wire from above the window. A buzzer sounds. The conductor stops the trolley in the center block of Main Street.

Mother and daughters pass a dairy store. The promise of sweet, freshly made ice cream tempts their taste buds. A short time later, grocery bags filled to the top rest on the floor in the small store. The shoppers sit at a white metal table and enjoy triple-scoop ice cream cones, their weekly treat before the trolley ride home.

These hot summer days Phil heads for the woods with two empty pails. Hours later he returns home, his pockets bulging with sassafras bark. In his hands he carries one bucket full of fresh raspberries, another with plump blackberries. Sarah fills pie dough with juicy blackberries then pops them into the oven.

Jena and her brother sit on the back porch steps. Blues songs flow from his well-worn harmonica. They sniff the pies cooling on the kitchen window sill.

"Hey Shorty, let's go inside and make some sassafras tea. Maybe it'll help you grow." He laughs. His blue eyes sparkle.

"I like you to call me Shorty. You never call Rita or Laura by any nickname." Pause. "But I don't like your smelly tea."

In the kitchen, their mother pours boiling raspberry juice from a big kettle. It flows through heavy gauze Rita holds over a metal pot. Drops of perspiration gather on their foreheads. The hot liquid flows into sterile bottles. Hot paraffin seals the jelly. As jars cool on the table, Phil and Jena eat a bowl of fresh blackberries smothered with sugar and cream.

"I'll get some tea later," Phil tells Jena. "I'm going down and take a swim across the river. It'll cool me off."

Deer River flows along the west side of town.

"Why don't you go to Franklin Park? The pool's safe and the water's clean." Jena trembles every time Phil ventures to the river. "Some day you may get too tired. I'm afraid you'll drown before you can swim back."

"The river's clean. The only things in it are fish. It's not even a half-mile wide. It's easy for a thirteen-year-old to swim across. When you're older, Mother will let you go swimming in the pool. The river's safe for guys, but not for girls," he teases.

Hours later, Phil strolls along the railroad tracks. From cupped hands deft fingers fly over his harmonica. Back and forth it slides across his mouth. Lilting strains of "Suwannee River" drift on the calm breeze.

Jena looks down the street. She listens as the music gets closer. As he comes into view she sees a towel and swim trunks tossed over his broad shoulders. She watches his every step as he strolls toward the house.

"Phil's home. He made it safe across the river," Jena calls to her mother. "I'm glad summer's almost over and he won't be able to swim in the river 'till next year."

School vacation comes to an end. The family rises to a bright sunny morning for the Labor Day town picnic.

Rita helps her mother prepare potato salad and fried chicken. The food is placed beside hot dogs, buns, baked beans, cookies and fruit in a large wicker basket. The family arrives at Franklin Park as field games begin.

None of the girls win water-balloon or egg tosses. Phil and Barry hobble across the field with one each of their legs tied together in a burlap sack. The family cheers with the crowd as the two boys bounce across the finish line to win the race.

Near a long picnic table, Al makes a fire on a park grill. At meal time, Sarah leads the family in their familiar prayer. "Lord, bless this food, our family, and all we receive through Your bounty. For all these things we thank You. Amen."

At dusk the band enters the pavilion. Phil wanders away with his pal, Barry. Al, Sarah and the three girls follow the crowd toward the music. Jena and Laura sit at the wall and watch their parents dance on the crowded floor. Several young boys take turns twirling fifteen-year-old Rita around in circles as the band plays on. The final dance is a long-lasting polka.

When the music stops, Jena says, "I hear thunder."

"That's not thunder, dummy," Laura tells her. "It's the start of the fireworks."

Hundreds of persons sit on blankets spread over the warm ground. The family sits among the crowd and watches brilliant sparks erupt in the sky. Gigantic umbrellas of bright red, blue and white explode. They light up the vast dark heavens.

"Boom! Boom! Boom!"

Thunderous tremors resonate through the crowd. The night air echoes "ohs" and "ahs" from excited observers. The brilliant display lasts almost a half-hour.

"Boom! Boom! Boom! Boom! Boom! Boom!"

Jena covers her ears as she watches the grand finale.

Barry and Phil part company at the park entrance. Barry heads for his home on the hill. Phil rejoins his family as they walk from the park. Melodious strains from his harmonica float soft and clear beneath a star-filled sky. Al holds his youngest daughter in his arms. They are six blocks from home.

The group arrives at the house just before eleven o'clock. A happy father carries his sleepy daughter to her room. The weary child wakens momentarily, then falls fast asleep the moment her head touches the pillow. Tonight summer ends. Tomorrow, another school year begins.

CHAPTER 5
THE DARK CLOSET

Jena is excited to be in second grade. She looks forward to May, when the class receives First Holy Communion. Her new teacher is well liked. Sister Claude is young and petite with blue eyes, skin clear as crystal, and a friendly smile.

"This year you will receive the Body of Christ," she instructs the class. "First, you will study the Ten Commandments. You will learn what is good and what is evil, according to the laws of God." Sister speaks with a soft voice. "You will visit the confessional. Father Karl will hear your confession the Saturday before you receive the Sacrament of Holy Communion."

It is a difficult task to explain the gravity of confession and penance to children. Sister Claude impresses upon her students the sacredness of the sacraments. The nun wishes to make this a pleasant and blessed experience for her students.

Jena is not her jovial self this warm spring afternoon. When she returns home from school her cheerful smile is missing. Her eyes are sad. A frown covers her face.

"What happened today, Jena? Why the gloomy face?" Sarah asks. "What kind of trouble did you get into at school?"

The young girl lowers her eyes. She looks at her feet. *What can I say? How can I tell her why I was afraid in church today?* she wonders.

"I didn't get into any trouble. And I didn't do anything wrong, Mother."

"Then why do you look so unhappy?" Jena lifts up her head. She looks into her mother's eyes.

"Sister Claude is so nice. But some of us were afraid when she took us to church today."

"How could anything scare you in church?" There is a hint of disbelief in her voice. "You go to Mass every Sunday. What could frighten you in church, especially when Sister is with you?"

"She showed the class the confessional. She told us we must whisper when we're inside." Jena pauses.

"This is true," Sarah tells her. "It is so no one outside the door can hear what you say. I don't understand why having to whisper your sins would frighten you."

She watches her daughter wrench her fingers and totter from one foot to the other.

"That's not what frightened me." She emits a deep sigh. "Sister had each one in the class go alone inside. I got scared after I closed the door." Jena shudders. "It was so black in there. It was like a small, dark closet. I couldn't see the kneeler. I couldn't see my hands in front of me," Jena cries.

"Nothing in there can harm you. It takes only a few minutes to talk with the priest. After you confess, you'll feel good your sins are forgiven. You'll be happy when you come out."

"I was glad to get out of there today. When I opened the door the lights in church were so bright. I had to blink my eyes before I could see." Tears fill her eyes. "Why is it so dark in there?"

"So the priest won't see the person who confesses to him." Sarah explains the obvious to the worried girl.

"Sister told us we must think hard tonight. We must try to remember all the sins we have ever committed.

"What happens if I forget to tell something I did wrong? Will I go to hell?"

An anguished look appears on the young girl's face. "No, Jena. God knows what's in your heart. He'll forgive all your sins. I'm sure Sister explained this to you."

"Yes, she did. But there's so much to remember. I worry that I'll forget something I'm to say when I'm in there."

The next day, Jena's heart beats fast as she kneels in her "dark closet." After she confesses, Father says, "Go in peace, your sins are forgiven." She breathes a sigh of relief. There is a smile on her face as she returns to the pew.

Later that day, Sarah sees Jena skip up the sidewalk. A smile lights up her face. The child's dark closet no longer is an ogre to fear. She is prepared to receive the Lord tomorrow.

Sunday morning is bright and sunny. The girls wear sheer white dresses and lace veils. The boys have on white suits and ties. In the classroom, a girl and boy stand side by side. The pairs form a line. Thirty-two children march from school to church. The organ plays soft strains of "Ave Maria," as the class walks down the long center aisle. They occupy the front pews. Parents and family sit directly behind them.

The Mass begins.

For the Communion service, girls walk in one row, boys in another. One after another they enter the sanctuary and kneel on a white satin-covered faldstool. On each tongue, Father Karl places a white wafer and prays: "Corpus Domini nostri Jesu Christi custodiat animam tuam in vitam asternam. Amen." ("The Body of Our Lord Jesus Christ preserve thy soul unto life everlasting. Amen.")

As the Mass ends, communicants and parents return outside. The remaining congregation follows behind them.

Uncle Ray and Aunt Peg, and Jena's God-parents, Bill and Marie Reinor, join the Bordeau family for dinner. Before the meal, Jena receives a white pearl rosary and a white leather prayer book trimmed in gold, gifts to be treasured as keepsakes of this blessed event.

During dinner, Al announces to his family and guests that his promotion to bank manager takes effect in one week.

Later this evening, Al, Sarah, Ray and Peg sit together in the Bordeau living room.

"Sarah, let's plan now for the four of us to go out to dinner next Saturday. We can celebrate my promotion. Aristo's Restaurant has a band on week-ends. We can go to the lounge and dance after we finish our meal."

"Only if you get us a place in the dining area with the bar out of sight. We can be home in ten minutes if Rita phones with a problem while we're away."

Al is pleasantly surprised at his wife's prompt acceptance of his proposal.

When this special evening arrives, Al is relieved Sarah has not changed her mind. When Ray and Peg arrive, Sarah is wearing a tailored navy-blue dress and navy pumps. Her black wavy hair reaches her ear lobes. She wears a tinge of rogue on her cheeks. Al wears his familiar navy serge suit.

"You look beautiful, Sarah." Al smiles. There is a rare sparkle in his eyes. "You're still as lovely as the day we married." Through her light layer of rogue he can see a blush appear. Sarah lowers her eyes and slowly turns away.

The parents leave the house. Rita and the younger girls set tiles on the dining room table for a game of domino.

"Will you make us a treat tonight, Rita?" Laura asks.

"After we finish a game. Now get into your bed

clothes. I'll make popcorn and we'll have some of Mother's home-made root beer."

Rita wins most games when she plays with the girls. But this time, Phil joins them. By the end of the second game, the popcorn disappears along with the domino pile.

Phil challenges his oldest sister. "You can't win them all. We'll play another game so I can win one."

Rita is not happy when her brother wins a game. "Jena helped you with the tiles. That's why you won," she grumbles.

The younger sisters are sent up to bed. Downstairs, Rita taunts her brother. "You won't win now. Jena's not here to coach you any more."

The two siblings are near the end of the game when their parents return.

Judging by the tone of voices in the hall, it was not a good evening for the couple.

"We could have stayed and danced longer," Al argues. "Ray and Peg are still there having a good time dancing."

"I can't enjoy myself when I see women smoke cigarettes and drink liquor. It's shocking. Couples are actually allowed to smoke and drink in the dining area now. I'd rather stay home than be out among those brazen women."

"Tonight was to be a celebration. Can't you put your judgmental opinions aside, just once, so we can have a good time together?" Al's face gets red as he discusses it.

"I won't associate with those women."

"We can't live like hermits, Sarah, just because you disagree with how other people behave. There's nothing wrong with anyone having a drink or two. Even you drank a glass of beer each night after you had Laura and Jena."

"You know Doctor Mueller ordered it. He wanted me to gain back weight I lost after the girls were born. And I only used it in the privacy of our home. I never drank at a bar like those women did tonight." Sarah wipes tears from her cheeks.

Hurt and outraged that his wife ruined his long-awaited celebration, Al ignores her rebuttal.

Ray and Peg remain at Aristo's. But there is no joy in the Bordeau house tonight. Rita goes to bed with a deflated ego; Phil won the final game of domino with her. Al goes to sleep demoralized; his wife ruined this special evening out with him. Tonight's celebration turns out to be more chaos than glorious occasion.

Lying in bed beside her slumbering partner, Sarah softly weeps. What began with praise of her beauty ends as a letdown for her. The festivities for Al's accomplishment in his profession becomes a bitter fiasco for him.

Their guests enjoy food and cheerful music as they dance the night away. But only sad songs fill the hearts of Al and Sarah tonight.

CHAPTER 6
SUMMER ADVENTURES

It is six months since Al's promotion to bank manager. He obtains a mortgage on a house in the center of town. The Bordeau family moves into the red-brick, seven-room building on a cool fall day. The first floor includes a large living room, dining room, kitchen and master bedroom. From the front door one enters a long hallway. A winding staircase leads to three bedrooms and bath on the second floor. A powder room is opposite the laundry in the basement.

An apple, peach and huge cherry tree stand dormant in the back yard. A red-brick walk runs beneath a grape arbor. It leads to a wooden shed in the corner of the yard. A small, enclosed back porch leads to a cement patio. The front porch runs the width of the building.

As furniture is placed in the rooms, Jena watches a small furry creature run under a living room chair. She kneels with her elbows bent on the floor as she peeks at the intruder.

"There's something small and fuzzy here," she tells Sarah.

Her mother stoops down to look at Jena's discovery. She pulls her daughter up by her arm. "That's just a mouse. Stay away from it before it bites you."

When all the furniture is placed in the appropriate rooms, Al puts slivers of cheese in mouse traps. He sets them in the living room, bedrooms and basement.

Before going to bed Jena checks the traps. In the living room she finds a metal wire pressed over the mouse's neck.

"It's a cute little thing," she giggles.

"It's good your father caught it and we are rid of it. Don't touch him. He's full of germs," Sarah tells her.

This is Jena's first encounter with death. She does not understand what happened to the rodent. "It looks like it's sleeping," she exclaims.

"It's dead Jena. Your father will put it in the garbage. Now move away from it."

Several weeks pass and the family settles in the new house. Jena looks forward to the Christmas holidays. As the season nears, she listens to classmates discuss what gifts they want from their parents.

"These dumb kids talk like they don't know Santa brings them gifts," she tells Laura. "Mother took us to see him. We talked with him in Toyland. I even heard him in our house."

The Friday before Christmas, the Jolly Old Man enters the classroom with his familiar, "Ho! Ho! Ho! Merry Christmas!" He passes out small oblong boxes of holiday candy. Jena can see he is Nick, the school janitor. His voice, eyes, shoes and false beard reveal her treasured belief to be a myth.

As the girls lay in bed tonight, a disillusioned child asks her older sister, "When did you learn Santa's not real?"

"I knew before we took our trip to Bridgeport."

"Why didn't you tell me it was all make-believe?"

"Mother told me not to ruin Christmas for you, that's why."

Jena looks at the tree Christmas morning concerned only with what is inside the packages beneath it. After Mass, the family opens presents as usual. The tag marked:

TO JENA - FROM SANTA, holds no mystery now. She knows it is her mother who buys and wraps the presents piled under the tree Christmas Eve.

Jena watches in silence as gifts are opened. Her father gets a brown leather wallet. Her mother's eyes light up. A wide smile spreads across her face as she opens a small square box. Inside is a ruby, solitaire ring from Al. Rita gets an oval wrist watch. Phil struggles to open the box that holds a 200 pounds weight-lifting set. Al carries up a two-wheeled bike from the basement for Laura. She squeals when she sees her present. Jena is happy with new roller skates and miniature piano. She is sad to lose the holiday magic of Santa and his reindeer, but content to remember the past Christmas. It fills her with warm, joyful memories.

Shortly after the holiday passes, Jena returns home from school one afternoon with tears in her eyes. "What happened now?" her weary mother asks.

"Sister Maria is sick. We have a mean old lady for our teacher while Sister is away. She doesn't like how I write. She hit my hand with a ruler," she cries. "When I told her about my crooked finger she told me to be quiet and hit it again."

"She doesn't know it was broken and never healed properly. I'll write her a note and explain this to her."

"I won't go back there until Miss Moore leaves and Sister Maria comes back." She stands rigid and stares at her mother.

"All kids must go to school. It's the law. It will be all right when your teacher reads my note." Sarah places her hands on Jena's shoulders and looks into her eyes. "She won't hit you again. You must believe me Jena."

For two weeks the sullen girl shuffles off to school. This Monday afternoon, she runs through the back yard, into the house.

"Mother, Sister Maria's back," she shouts. "That mean

old Miss Moore is gone."

Sarah smiles, happy this latest crisis is over.

Winter fades into spring. Jena tags along beside her father as he plants flowers and seeds the lawn. The trees bloom with fragrant, delicate blossoms. Hard, tiny green grapes cling to the vines winding around the trellis of the arched grape arbor. With the onset of summer, green cherries turn deep red. Outside Rita's window huge limbs of the giant cherry tree hang over the back porch roof.

It is a hot summer day. Jena takes a pan and climbs out the window onto the roof. She pulls down a heavy branch and samples one of the ripe cherries. Her agile fingers quickly pick the sweet, juicy fruit until the pan if almost full.

Inside the house Sarah hears noise come from the roof. She goes to the back yard and sees Jena busy at work.

"Jena!" her mother yells. "What are you doing up there?"

"Picking cherries for you. The pan's almost full."

"You get back in the house right this minute before you fall from there."

Jena climbs back inside. She slides the pan beside her and carries it down to the kitchen. She is rinsing the fruit in the sink when Sarah opens the screen door. The woman walks over to her daughter. There is a stern expression on her face. Her hands are clutched tightly on her hips.

"You should thank the good Lord your father didn't see you up there. If he ever catches you on that roof he'll tan your bottom."

"I'm not afraid out there, Mother," she grins. "I won't fall. The birds can't eat all that good fruit."

"Forget about what the birds eat. You are not to go on that roof again."

Several days later, Jena takes another pan to the

roof. She fills it with forbidden fruit.

When Sarah goes to the refrigerator a short time later she sees a large bowl filled with cherries. She sighs a silent prayer: *Grant me patience to deal with Jena, Lord. Please, give me patience.*

The small girl walks beneath the grape arbor. Her hands are filled with the lush delicacies. She stops outside her brother's door.

Phil spends Saturdays in the 9 by 12 foot building. He has replaced hinges on two square wooden panels that serve as windows. Cobwebs have been wiped from the walls and floor. A padlock is placed on the door when he is away from it. His sisters have never been inside his private domain. Jena is anxious to visit her brother in his mysterious hideaway.

On this balmy day the curious child hears Phil's weights bounce against the floor. She listens through the open windows.

"Hey, Phil," she calls, "I brought you some cherries."

He opens the door just wide enough to reach her hands. He takes the fruit.

"When can I come inside and see how you lift weights?"

She bends her neck to get a peek inside.

Her brother steps outside and closes the door behind him. The eight-year-old looks up adoringly at the fifteen-year-old who towers above her. His blond hair and blue eyes shine in the bright sunshine. He wears khaki pants and a tan shirt.

"Any girl who comes in here must be initiated."

"What do you mean? What's it like, Phil?"

"It's something like when you go to confession before you make First Communion," is his irreverent analogy. "It is a ritual you must go through. A girl must complete this ceremony the first time she comes in here."

"When will you initiate me?" Her eyes light up with

anticipation. Her words rush forth with excitement.

"I'll get things ready tonight. Tomorrow you and Laura can be initiated together."

"Can Rita come with us?"

"She wouldn't want to come. She's not interested in what I do. She just wants to be with her friends."

In the evening, Jena watches her brother carry a load of strange objects in his arms. He takes them to the shed.

"What's your brother up to?" Sarah questions her.

"He's going to initiate Laura and me tomorrow when we go inside his shed. Tonight he's getting things ready for the ceremony." A big grin spreads over Jena's face.

"He better not do anything that can hurt you girls."

"Oh, it will be fun. He won't hurt us."

The next day Laura and Jena stand beneath the grape arbor. Phil blindfolds them with an old towel. He leads them to the door, then guides them into the shed.

"The place smells musty," Laura complains.

The girls hear a mysterious "Click." They can not see the light go on. They feel something flimsy brush across their face. They raise their arms to brush the object away.

"Be careful not to break the cobwebs," Phil orders. "We'll have spiders all over the place if you do."

Jena's hands tremble. She holds onto Laura. Phil leads them through a labyrinth of webs. He stops in the middle of the room. First Jena, then Laura, feels a jab on her index finger.

"Ouch!" they shriek, one after the other.

Something warm runs down toward their wrist.

"What's that on my finger?" Jena asks. She squeezes her arm, lowers it, then holds it by her side.

"It's just a trickle of blood. You're now blood sisters to your blood brother. The Indians perform this ritual when they bond with one another." Phil's tone is serious.

The girls get a tight knot in their stomach. They

hear a "Click" once more when Phil pulls a long thin chain. He turns off the single light bulb in the middle of the ceiling.

"It's all over," he announces. He removes their blindfolds.

The girls open their eyes to a dark room. They hear the mysterious "Click" once more. A light comes on. They squint their eyes as they look up toward the ceiling. All around the shed are long, ragged, burlap sacks that hang from the rafters. On their finger is red wax. There is a snuffed out, red tapered candle laying on a long bench attached to the wall.

"Phil," Jena laughs, "you fooled us. There's no spider webs or blood. What did you do to our fingers?"

"It was just a little pinch. I used one of mother's sewing needles, that's all." He gives a hearty laugh.

"That was too scary for me. You can have your silly, smelly shed. I don't want in here any more." Laura frowns and goes outside.

"It was scary, Phil. But it was fun. It's a great trick you played on us." Jena gazes at her brother and giggles.

The young fellow uses a step-stool to remove the burlap maze from the rafters. Jena can see barbells and weights resting along the back wall.

Phil calls his sister by her favorite name. "Hey, Shorty, help me with these sacks." He motions to her. "Take them and the candle down to the basement."

"Sure, Phil, blood brothers and sisters have to do things for one another." She is excited he asks for her help.

When she returns to the shed, Phil is lying on a mat in the middle of the floor. He holds a metal bar, with round weights on each end, over his head.

"How can you do that? Could I ever get strong enough to lift just one of those things?"

He lowers the weights, goes to the corner and picks

up a pair of three-pound barbells. "These are your size. If you ever try to move any other weights you'll get hurt. Then Mother will never let you in here again."

He tosses one of the barbells to her. She catches it and throws it back to him. The missile travels between them, back and forth, back and forth....

"You're not so weak for a half-pint," he laughs.

A smile spreads from ear to ear across Jena's face.

"Maybe the workout will help you grow. You don't want to stay a little squirt all your life, do you?" Once again Jena hears his hearty laughter. She grins.

She watches as he twirls a thick rope around his long legs. It twists in circles as he jumps over and over through the large hoops. She sits and stares as her big brother exercises in his hallowed abode.

Jena rests her head against the wall. *Nothing can ever hurt me here,* she dreams. *I'll always be safe and happy as long as my blood brother is here to protect me.*

"Hey, Shorty," Phil calls. "Wake up. Let's go to the house and get lunch. I'm starved."

In the kitchen, Sarah confronts Jena. "What happened in the shed this morning? Laura didn't like what your brother did in there. She said you would tell me all about it."

"Oh Mother, just because Laura didn't enjoy it doesn't mean there was something the matter with it." Her vehement reply reveals her irritation over her sister's reaction to the happy event. "Laura thinks the shed is smelly and doesn't want to go back there again. We walked in the dark through some old burlap sacks. Then Phil dripped some candle wax on our finger," she laughs. "No one got hurt. He made Laura and me his blood sisters. He's our blood brother. We're bonded for the rest of our lives." She speaks rapidly, elated as she relives the event.

"I must agree with your sister. It seems like a very silly thing for him to do. But then," her mother ponders briefly, "when I think of some foolish things you get into, I can understand why you enjoy something like that."

This is one of the happiest days in the young girl's life. As she rests warm and secure in bed tonight, Jena reviews the day. *Phil and I shared a special time together. We are bonded forever, even though no blood passed between us.* With a smile on her face she drifts into peaceful reverie.

CHAPTER 7
RITA AND BOB

The change in her life excites Rita. A classmate takes her to see a movie this summer. This is her first date with a young man. Bob drives her to the theater. They see "Dark Journey," a story about British and German spies meeting and falling in love in Sweden, during World War I.

For ninety minutes they sit in the quiet theater. Not a word is spoken between them. As they walk across the street to the ice cream parlor, Bob asks, "Did you like the movie?"

"It was all right. I don't go to many of them. I would much rather bowl or go dancing."

For an awkward moment she glances at the tall, muscular fellow. "Winter is my favorite season. I ice skate at the rink in the park. In fact, that's what I enjoy most."

"Would you like to go bowling Friday evening?"

"Sure. That should be fun. Some of our classmates will be there. We can challenge them to a game."

Both Rita and Bob will be seniors this fall.

"I'm registered at State University," he tells her.

"I've been promised a job at the hospital as a nurse's aide after I graduate. If I like the work, I may enter nurses training. I sent in my application. Right now, I'm not certain what I'll do. There's a lot for me to think about before I decide."

Rita and Bob go out together several evenings a week. When school starts, they date on weekends. Each

Sunday he drives Rita home after Mass. Sarah lets them have breakfast alone in the Bordeau kitchen.

"It doesn't take Rita and Bob much time to finish their cereal, rolls and coffee. Why do you allow them to sit and talk at the table for over an hour?" This is the fourth Sunday Laura makes the same complaint to her mother. "What's so important about those two being alone for breakfast? They could sit in the living room and talk. Then the rest of us wouldn't have to wait so long to eat."

"You'll understand when you're older," Sarah answers. "Someday you'll want to be alone with someone you like."

"But I'll never make anyone wait to eat," she pouts.

Tired of Laura's constant protests, Sarah has a talk with Rita as they walk to Mass this morning. "You and Bob spend too much time in the kitchen together. The family must wait too long for breakfast. Beginning today, the two of you can join all of us for our morning meal."

Rita glances at her mother. She does not comment.

"It will give Bob a chance to know all of us better," Sarah suggests. "You two share evenings together when you go dancing or bowling. Bob's a nice young man. He should understand this."

Bob does not drive Rita to her house this morning. She joins the family as they walk home from church. "I hope Bob isn't upset. Will he meet you at the house?" Sarah asks.

"He didn't say much. But I can tell by how quiet he was after I told him; he's disappointed. He's going home to be with his parents. There will be less commotion with just the three of them at the table. Besides, his parents would like to spend as much time with him as possible before he goes away to college next year." Rita shows no emotion. It's just a matter-of-fact statement.

"Will he be taking you to the dance this evening?"

"Yes, Mother. He'll be here at eight o'clock. He wants

to keep spending time with me." She does not reveal how she feels about dating Bob. Sarah senses Rita's disapproval with the decision concerning breakfast alone with him.

Rita is unusually quiet at the breakfast table today. But Laura doesn't mind. She is happy her older sister will no longer dominate the kitchen every Sunday morning.

"It sure is good to eat soon after we get home," Laura tells her mother. They clear dishes from the table after the family leaves the kitchen. Rita goes to her room to be alone.

Bob continues to be absent Sunday mornings. He stops at the Bordeau house every week-end. He takes Rita bowling, dancing, or to an occasional movie.

The school year passes rapidly. Today marks the final day of classes for the younger girls. They arrive home anxious to see their big sister prepare for her Senior Prom.

When Bob arrives this evening he is wearing a stiff white shirt, black pants and jacket. He stares at the high gloss on his black leather shoes. He twists his fingers nervously as he sits alone on the sofa, not speaking. Beside him, in a clear plastic box, is an orchid for Rita.

Jena sits across the room from him. She stares at the young man. It is the first time she has seen anyone in a tuxedo. "You look good tonight," she smiles. "Wait until you see Rita. She looks real nice, too."

Bob does not look at Jena. His eyes focus on his shoes. He feels his face get hot. "I'm sure she does. How about going to see when she's coming down. It's almost time for us to go." There is a quiver in his voice. He clears his throat.

Jena runs upstairs to Rita's room. Sarah watches her oldest daughter look in the mirror. Rita inspects her long dress.

"Mother," Jena whispers, "Bob told me to come up and tell Rita it's time for them to go."

"You go and keep him company. Rita will be down soon."

Jena goes downstairs and repeats her mother's message. "Rita will be down soon."

Bob makes no reply.

"What are you going to do now that you're done with school? I think Rita is going away to be a nurse."

"I'll stay with my parents this summer. In September I'm to enter State University to study engineering." Bob squirms in his seat as he talks to her. He glances at the stairway. "I hope your sister comes down soon."

Upstairs, Rita stands before her vanity table. She runs her hands along the folds of her peach organdy gown.

"Are you sure the neckline is all right, Mother?" she inquires for the third time.

"You look fine. Don't worry so much."

Rita looks in the triple mirror. She pats her fingers over the ends of her soft brunette curls. "How does my hair look?" Her voice trembles. She checks her body from side to side and front to back. She smiles for an instant at her reflection.

"Your hair looks nice. Bob must be tired waiting for you. It's time for you to leave. Go to the prom and enjoy the dance. Don't worry so much. Everything will be fine."

In the hall, Bob's hands shake as he pins an orchid corsage on Rita's gown. Seated next to his girl in the car, he stares at her. "Wow! You look beautiful," he exclaims.

Rita feels blood rush to her face. She turns away from him and looks out her side window. The early evening air cools her fiery cheeks.

At the prom, there is no sharing his girl. Bob and Rita are together for every dance. He wants her all to himself tonight. After the orchestra plays the final tune, they linger on the dance floor. Bob talks with three other couples from his class.

"I'm taking Rita to Aristo's," he tells them.

"Why are you going there?" one of the fellows asks.

"If you were ever there you'd know why. They serve the best food in town. And there's a dance floor. It's the only place to go for a special occasion," Bob assures his friend.

All the couples agree to meet at the table Bob reserved. At the restaurant, the jubilant graduates enjoy fine food and continue to dance.

It is past one o'clock when Bob drives up to the Bordeau house. Standing on the porch he puts his arms around Rita. This is her first good-night kiss from him. She turns, frees herself from his embrace, opens the door and rushes inside. The house is dark and silent as she enters her room. When she looks into the dresser mirror she covers her cheeks with the palms of her hands. She does not like the red cheeks reflected back at her. She dresses for bed but sleep eludes her. She reflects on the evening. Strange feelings for Bob surface following his kiss.

After Sunday Mass, the graduation class gathers in the school auditorium. Rita's parents proudly watch her in white cap and gown, seated on stage with fifty classmates. It is the customary, routine ceremony. Father Daniels, the pastor, offers his congratulations as he hands each graduate a diploma.

Bob waits for Rita as fellow graduates slowly exit the hall. He sees her and Sister Monica engrossed in private conversation in a remote corner of the large room.

Several minutes later, he meets Rita at the door. His curiosity erupts as he drives her home. "What did you and Sister talk about in the hall? You both looked so serious."

"There are things to be resolved before I go away next fall. I must notify the nursing school by next month if they are to keep my registration on file. One of the things I discussed with Sister Monica is where I will go when I leave home."

"Let's not worry about that now. We can talk about it later. Right now, let's go meet our friends in the park."

He smiles at Rita as he drives away.

It is dinner time when she steps from Bob's car in front of her house. "I'll be back at eight o'clock," he calls out, then drives away.

Bob is punctual, eager as ever to see his girl. The three couples who were with him and Rita at Aristo's show up together shortly after Bob arrives. The four men move furniture and roll back the living room carpet. The couples dance on a hardwood floor. Records continue to spin on the turntable of a mahogany Victrola. Couples dance around the room. Soft music floats through every room in the house.

Two excited, wide-eyed girls sit on the stairs across the hall from the living room. Smiling faces are pressed against round spindles of the banister. They watch Rita and her friends talk and laugh as they dance.

As Sarah serves refreshments to the group, Laura whispers, "I can't wait to grow up so we can have parties like this. Maybe Mother will let us have one when we graduate."

"That's eight years away for you and nine for me," Jena answers. "That's a long time to wait for a party."

At ten o'clock Sarah scoots the girls off to bed. They lay awake and listen to the music. It is past midnight when three couples leave the house. Two curious youngsters strain to hear what Bob and Rita are talking about in the downstairs hallway. When it gets very quiet down there, Laura comments, "I wonder if those two ever kiss when they're alone."

"They probably do. They're old enough," Jena laughs.

The girls can't see Bob put his arms around Rita's waist. They are not able to watch how delicately she turns her face aside when he attempts to kiss her. Bob moves swiftly and gives her a long, firm kiss on the lips. Rita frees herself from his arms and turns away. When he attempts to kiss her again, she opens the door.

"Thanks for everything, Bob. It was a wonderful week-end. I'll always remember and treasure our times together."

"I'll be here next Saturday to take you bowling," he reminds her. "Good luck in your job tomorrow," he calls out as he walks from the porch to his car. She shudders as she watches him drive away.

Rita is overwhelmed by mixed emotions. She tosses in bed as she tries to put thoughts of Bob from her mind. She struggles with the decision she must make concerning her future.

Early Monday morning, Rita wakens from a restless sleep. She begins her job in Sage General Hospital. She and Bob continue to date throughout the summer.

This cool Saturday afternoon is the last time she will see him before he leaves for the university tomorrow. As they sit on a park bench, Bob urges Rita, "Let's write to one another at least once a week."

"I won't be able to write to you, Bob," she answers in a soft, calm voice. "I won't be at Bridgeport Nursing School."

"You can write to me wherever you go," he persists.

"On graduation day, you told me we could talk about this later. I've tried all summer, but I haven't been able to tell you where I'll be." She pauses. "I can't write to you from....

"I don't care where you go," he interrupts. "No matter how far away you are, we can write to each other. Let's promise to write every Sunday, no matter how busy we get."

"Bob," she repeats, "I can never write to you."

"You've been so quiet lately when we've gone out.

You must be seeing another fellow besides me."

"I haven't been out with anyone but you." She looks into his eyes. "I am telling you the truth, Bob."

"Well, there's a reason we always went out with a group. You never wanted us to be alone together. You always resisted when I kissed you. If you don't want to write to me, there must be someone else in your life."

"I've told you all along we are good friends. I never led you to believe otherwise," she reminds him. "We will always be good friends. But I can't write to you."

"But I want to be *much more* than your friend. You must know I want to marry you when I finish at the university. You must know I love you," he finally confesses.

"Bob, there is another man in my life. But he's no ordinary man." There is an awkward silence. The blood drains from his face. Bob stares at her. He is unable to speak. He sits there, stunned.

"I'm sorry it will hurt you, but I must tell you this." Her words flow soft and slow. "When I leave home tomorrow I'll enter the convent. That's what Sister Monica and I talked about after graduation. She's my sponsor."

Bob feels anger as the veins on his forehead pulsate dangerously. His cheeks seem to be on fire. He clenches the bench and stares at Rita. "Why are you doing this? I believed after school, when I have a good job, we would be married. But you want to enter the convent. Instead of marrying me, you want to be a bride of Christ."

He puts his hands on his head. He leans over with his elbows on his knees. "You a nun. No!" he shouts, and leaps from the bench.

Rita runs behind him. They reach the car together. She is inside before he drives away. Bob doesn't look at her. He remains silent as he takes her home.

He stops the car at her house. He keeps his eyes focused on the dashboard. This is the only time he does not open the door for his girl. Rita closes the car door. She leans her head inside and murmurs, "Good luck, Bob, and God bless you. I'll pray for you."

Bob stares out the windshield. Rita listens as tires screech. She watches as he races his red Ford down Elm Street.

Rita's news not only shocks Bob, but also her family. She makes the announcement at the dinner table this evening.

"Is this why you've been in your room so much?" Jena asks.

"You and Mother talked a lot with your bedroom door closed. You two kept this secret from us." Laura denounces both of them.

"You always said you want to be a nurse. Now you tell us you want to be a nun," Jena accosts her oldest sister.

Rita offers no explanation. She remains silent.

The youngest girl turns to her mother. "Why didn't you tell us Rita isn't going to Bridgeport tomorrow?"

"It's her decision to tell whomever she chooses. She wants people to find out after she leaves for the convent. She didn't want you or Laura to tell anyone outside the family."

Sarah glances at Jena. "Rita told me she will study to be a nurse after she finishes the novitiate."

"What about you and Bob?" Phil asks Rita.

"I told him this afternoon. He'll forget about me when he's at the university. He'll be too busy with his studies to think about me."

"Sarah," Al raves, "you could have told me about this."

"Rita knows how you feel that your sister became a nun. She thought you might try to change her mind."

"You're damn right I would. My sister died too young. Those heavy wool clothes she wore all summer were enough to kill any woman. Is that what you want for our daughter?"

"Neither sun nor heavy clothing had anything to do with Sister Elizabeth's death. It was God's will. Rita didn't want us to keep arguing about this before she left. That's why she waited until today to tell you."

Sarah turns toward Rita. "It seems she made the right decision."

"You allege to be the strong Christian in this house. Time will tell what happens to Rita, and how God protects each of our children." He turns his back to his wife and walks to the front porch.

After Sunday Mass, Rita shares her final meals with the family. It is early afternoon. A taxi arrives and drives Sarah and Rita to the priory. At the door, Rita picks up her suitcase, kisses her mother good-bye, and follows a youthful nun inside.

Following lunch with his parents, Bob places a small trunk and suitcase in his car. He bids his mother and father good-bye and drives away. As he travels down the road he thinks about Rita. He imagines her walking through a convent door this brisk September afternoon. He agonizes over her rejection to be his wife. Tears fill his eyes as he pictures the solitary life she has chosen. In a few years she will become the bride of Christ.

Now that his plans for marriage to the girl he loves have been destroyed, he resolves nothing, or no one, will ever ruin his plans again. *I will get my degree in engineering and make a successful life for myself,* he vows.

Bob's journey is bittersweet. It is with mixed emotions he travels along the interstate to begin a new life at the university.

CHAPTER 8
REEL MAKE-BELIEVE

Nature reveals her magic with the arrival of autumn. The soft brush of frost transforms green leaves to palettes of radiant orange, red and gold. On this bright fall day, Laura and Jena sit at the dining room table about to begin a game of checkers. Phil takes a seat across from Laura.

"Are you going to join us in a game?" Jena asks him.

"Sure. Now that Rita's gone, I'll be the one to win all the games."

Laura takes away the red and black checker board. She replaces it with one for Chinese checkers. Phil's home point is first to be filled with blue marbles. Laura has red ones lined up next. Jena is last to set her yellow marbles in place. The players concentrate on their moves as the game progresses. Phil has the best strategy. Blue marbles reach his opposite point before his opponents' red and yellow ones land in their safety zones. Soon all blue marbles are in place across from Phil. He is the indisputable winner.

"I told you I'd beat you at this," Phil teases.

"You're just lucky this time," Laura berates her brother. "You won't win two in a row. The next game belongs to me."

The second game nears an end. Phil and Laura are close rivals for the winner's spot. With no hope of winning herself, Jena shows her brother a strategic move. "Put your blue marble here." She points to an empty spot. "This move will fill your last space."

Laura jumps from her chair and hollers, "Don't you show him where to move!" She thrusts her arm toward her sister. Jena falls off her chair, onto the floor.

"My shoulder! My shoulder!" Jena yells.

Phil attempts to lift her from the floor.

"Don't touch me. I hurt," she wails.

Al rushes from his desk in the master bedroom, into the dining room. Sarah runs up from the basement.

"What in the world happened now?" Al roars.

"Jena showed me a winning checker move. Laura got mad and knocked her down." Phil answers as Jena lies panic-stricken.

Al lifts the screaming child from the floor. "Doc Mueller will have to take a look at her."

"You'll have to take her. I'm pinning lace curtains on the stretcher in the basement. I need to stretch them when they're sopping wet. If the curtains dry before I finish, they'll not be wide enough to fit the windows." Sarah looks at her daughter. "I'm sure Jena would like you to carry her there."

Sarah rubs her delicate fingers together. The sharp nails that encompass the huge wooden frame prick her finger tips. It is an unavoidable hazard when using the instrument.

"Try not to scream, Jena," she tells the distraught child.

Al regrets another emergency causes him to take his daughter to the doctor. They never spend time in the waiting room. Once again he carries Jena through the side door.

Doctor Mueller is in his usual cantankerous mood.

"What's the problem this time?" he asks Al.

"Jena fell at home. Her arm got twisted under her when she landed on the carpet." He doesn't mention what part Laura played in the incident.

Jena's cries can be heard in the next room as the doctor examines her. "I'll have to take X-rays," he announces in his ordinary gruff tone.

Tears run down Jena's cheeks. Miss Winters guides the child to a side room. Jena shivers as her bare chest is pressed against the cold plate on the machine. She sits sobbing in the dressing room. The doctor checks the film.

When Jena is dressed, Miss Winters guides her to the chair beside the doctor's desk. "You have another broken bone, Jena." She continues to cry. She sits in the chair listening to Doctor Mueller talk to her. "You're too energetic for a small girl. You're not as strong as a boy. You have to be more careful when you play."

Neither Al nor Jena offers a reason for the mishap. They just sit and listen to what the doctor has to tell them.

"The X-rays show a fractured collar-bone. You must keep this brace on for six weeks. You're to take it off only to bathe." He looks into her red, swollen eyes and waits for a reply from the frightened girl. "Do you understand me?" He insists on an answer affirming Jena will obey his instructions.

"I understand you," she tells him. Her words are barely audible between sobs. "But how can I go to school with this thing on?" she blurts out. She points to the contraption on her chest.

"You must be very careful not to bump into anything. Keep away from crowds. And don't play any more rough games," the doctor insists.

"Al, have Sarah keep a close eye on this girl. She's too reckless. I don't want her in here again with any more broken bones," he orders.

When Jena gets home, she sits on the sofa, afraid to move.

"How do you feel, Shorty?" Phil asks.

"I don't hurt so much with this thing on. The doctor

told me not to play so rough. He said I'm too careless and Mother should keep a better watch on me. Dad didn't tell him how I got hurt or that it wasn't my fault. He only said I fell on the floor."

Al repeats the talk he had with the doctor. "Sarah, Doc doesn't know Laura knocked Jena down. No one must find out what happened here. Tell the kids this is to stay within this house. I don't want people to think we have a war going on in our family." He lowers his voice. "Keep a closer watch on the girls. Doc was very insistent. He doesn't want Jena to be back there again with any more broken bones."

Jena goes to school on Monday. She is upset when some of her classmates ask about "that thing" she has on. Sister Marian moves her to the seat in front of the nun's desk. She informs the class no one is to bump Jena while her bone is mending. The weeks pass slowly. The restless girl suffers discomfort and embarrassment because of the brace she must wear.

Six weeks drag on too long. To the impatient girl it seems like several months since her visit to the doctor. On Saturday, Sarah takes her to have the brace removed. Doctor Mueller repeats the same instructions issued to Al. "Keep a closer watch on Jena. She's not to get any more broken bones."

When mother and daughter return home, Al has a surprise for them. "We'll celebrate that your brace is off. This afternoon I'll take you and Laura to the State Theater. It's time you two get to see a motion picture."

"Now I can sit down and not have that brace bother me. I can't wait to go." Jena jumps up and down. "Some of the kids at school go all the time. They told me the pictures are so big they fill the front wall. When are we going, Dad?"

"We must eat first. Then we'll leave."

After lunch, Al and the girls depart. The main road

is closed for repairs. The trolley tracks must be removed. When the road reopens there will be a bus route through town. Until then, they must walk ten blocks to the theater.

Al buys tickets at the outside booth. Inside the lobby a uniformed man takes the tickets. He hands the torn gray stubs to Laura. Al watches his daughters. They are fascinated by giant photos on the walls. They depict scenes from the movie they are about to see. The title is printed in enormous black letters, "HEIDI," with Shirley Temple and Jean Hersholt.

"It looks like a good story," Jena whispers to Laura.

At the concession counter, Al stands to the side as Laura buys a box of popcorn. He leads them to three empty seats halfway down the aisle. It becomes silent in the theater as the lights grow dim. Al glances at his daughters as they stare at the screen, mystified. The movie begins. They sit hypnotized by the huge pictures that move in front of them.

The first scene is the beautiful Swiss Alps. For six years Heidi, an orphan, lived with her wicked Aunt Dete, near the Black Forest in Germany.

One hot summer day, they travel to a mountain village. The woman leaves the young girl with stern, Grandfather Adolph. For many years he had lived a hermit's life in his isolated hut. He soon learns to love his granddaughter. He teaches her to milk goats and to read.

One day Heidi hands Grandfather his Bible. She is surprised that he knows, from memory, the parable of the prodigal son. The following Sunday, the pair walks down the mountain. The congregation is stunned when they enter the church. After the service the people welcome him back to the fold with open arms.

On Heidi's eighth birthday, Aunt Dete returns to

Grandfather's hut. He is out, gathering firewood.

Jena looks at her father and gasps, "Oh, no!"

The Aunt steals the girl and takes her far away to Frankfort, to the home of a rich man and his crippled daughter, Clara. A mean nursemaid pays Dete to let Heidi stay as a companion for the invalid girl. The youngsters become good friends.

Heidi works with Clara and the girl learns to walk again. On Christmas Day, Clara surprises her father when she walks away from her wheel chair.

Grandfather walks 100 miles in his search for Heidi. He finds her in Frankfort and they return together to their beloved mountains.

The following spring, the Pastor, his new wife and Clara travel to the mountain for a reunion with Heidi and Grandfather.

Outside the theater, Jena talks about the story. "Dad, can we ever go to the Alps?"

"I don't think any of us will ever get there. The movies are the only way most people get to see places far away. Besides, it costs a lot of money to travel."

"Are there people as mean as Heidi's aunt?"

"I suppose some people can be that mean. But I don't think there are many as cruel as she was."

"How did you like the movie, Laura?" Jena asks.

"It was good. I liked the scenery. All the other stuff is make-believe. You make it sound like Heidi and the other people are real. They're just actors, Jena. The only real thing about the movie is the scenery."

"When will you take us to another movie, Dad?" Jena asks.

"You girls know how to get here, buy tickets, and go

to the concession stand. The two of you can come together when there's another good movie showing."

Jena returns to the story. "Grandfather finally was kind to Heidi after she stayed with him for awhile. He learned to love her." She rambles on and on, talking about the movie. "I'm glad we have a good father. Not a mean person like Heidi's grandfather was at the beginning of the story."

Jena walks hand in hand with her father on their joyful journey home.

CHAPTER 9
TRANSITIONS

Al and his youngest daughter leave the breakfast table this warm June morning and walk to the back yard. The early morning sun has absorbed dew drops from blades of unruly grass. Al pushes the lawn mower back and forth across the yard. Jena walks close behind. She follows wheel tracks on the fresh cut grass, combs the clippings with a wire rake and piles them in the corner by Phil's shed. She looks forward to Saturdays, when she and her father share friendly chats. He enjoys answering her questions.

"Why do people deposit money in banks? Why do they borrow money?"

He answers these and many other questions. He tells her about honesty. He explains why integrity is an important quality in his employees and why persons who work in banks must possess strong moral standards. "We are responsible for other people's money."

"You have a hard job. You even do some of your bank work at home now."

"It's a good job. People respect me. It's an honor to be chosen for the position. I like the kind of work I do. Maybe some day you'll work in the bank, too."

"But you never have any fun. Why don't you take mother to a movie or something? It was a lot of fun when you took Laura and me there."

"Your mother doesn't care to go out much. She

believes women should stay home, clean house, and care for the family."

A wistful look appears on Jena's face. She observes her father's mournful expression. "If I ever get married I'll go out with my husband. I will want us to be happy and have fun together."

It is noon when the duo completes the yard work. After lunch Sarah clears dishes from the table. Al, Jena and Laura sit on the front porch. They relax on the glider and watch gusty winds blow in a summer storm. Huge black clouds roll across the sky. Long streaks of lightning crackle high above. The roar of thunder announces an imminent tempest.

Al and the girls glide back and forth, unperturbed, to the rhythm of a squeaky chain. Sarah tends to the customary ritual she performs with every storm that occurs. She lowers blinds throughout the house.

"Why is mother so frightened of storms?" Jena asks. "It's nice to watch the clouds drift high above and lightning flash through the sky. She misses all this when she goes to the basement to pray."

"Your mother was six years old when she boarded a liner to come to America. There was a violent storm at sea. Her parents died when an epidemic swept through the ship. For eight years she lived in an orphanage. When there was a severe storm, the nuns warned the children the end of the world was near. Your mother hid under her bed and prayed until the storm was over. She has never been able to conquer her fear."

"It must have been terrible living there," Jena remarks.

"She had to work hard. The girls had to keep the rooms neat and clean. That's where your mother learned to be such a good housekeeper."

They watch massive black clouds fill the sky.

"Now I know why you tell Jena and me about clouds and storms," Laura says. "You don't want us to be afraid like mother every time it storms."

"What I want you to learn is that storms are just another part of nature. What you must remember is to seek shelter when the weather gets bad. Never stand under a tree or near metal objects. These things attract lightning. Rain is something to be respected, not feared. It helps us grow food and provides water to keep us alive."

He points to the sky. "The dark, heavy clouds you see are called nimbus clouds. They hold the rain. Round woolly clusters of clouds, the kind you see on calm days, are called cumulus clouds. White filmy masses are cirrus clouds."

"Look how fast they're moving, Dad." Jena points to them.

"The rain should be here very soon," he tells her.

There is another sharp clash of thunder. A cloudburst sends a torrent of rain to the hot ground. A deluge flows down the street. When the rain stops the girls run across the sidewalk to the curb. They jump up and down in the cool fresh air. A stream of water gushes over their bare feet. Their small toes wiggle as bubbles ripple between them.

A trail of wet footprints follows the girls down to the cellar. Jena sees her mother pace around the worktable. The woman's hands quiver. She rubs a wooden rosary. One by one, small black beads slip through her slender fingers. "Lord, save us. Lord, help us," Sarah whispers.

Jena stretches her arms around her mother. Sarah stands still when the child hugs her.

"The storm's over, Mother. It's safe to go upstairs now."

The young girl learns about the weather from her father. She comes to appreciate the harmony of nature.

She listens to the trill of robins that nestle on tree branches in the yard. The feel of cool breeze brushing against her face delights her. She enjoys the pitter-patter of tiny raindrops that gently dance on solid ground. A creative spirit stirs within her.

The scent of cool, fresh air after the summer rain refreshes Jena. She wipes raindrops from a lawn chair. With pencil and paper in hand, she sits on the wooden seat and writes.

A ROBIN SINGS

You sit and sing your lilting song
high in the cherry tree
red robin, what a lovely sight
you make for me to see.
The sweet, soft warble of your voice
floats through the still, fresh air
and fills my heart with happiness
to hear you singing there.

Jena finishes her poem and walks to the shed. She goes inside. The sheet of paper is hidden behind her back.

"Phil, if you don't laugh, you can see something I wrote. Do you want to read it?"

"Sure, Shorty. Why wouldn't I?" His voice is sincere.

"Because it's a poem. You might think it's silly."

"Let's have a look at it." He reads it and smiles. "This is pretty good. It's not bad at all for a half-pint. I'll show you something I just finished. Tell me who you think it is."

He grins and takes a sheet of art paper from his bench.

Jena looks at the drawing he hands her. "This is Barry," she squeals. "Did you really draw this, Phil?," Her eyes pop open in surprise. "This is nice. Where did you learn to draw?"

"I had to do something for art class last year. I drew a dog then. The sketch pad was in here so I drew this today."

"It's really good. Now let me see the dog."

He reaches inside the bench again and brings out another sketch. Jena has a wistful smile as she looks at it. "This is a picture of Rusty." She sighs. "Oh, Phil, this is beautiful. Let's hang it up in here."

She stares at the picture as he pins it on the wall.

"What are you going to do after you graduate next year? Do you want to go to art school? You could be a good artist."

"No, Shorty. I'm going to college. I want to be a veterinarian. Having Rusty made me want to care for animals."

"Does this mean you'll go away in the fall?" She frowns.

"I've decided to leave after I finish school. There's a summer job I can get to help pay my tuition."

"I'll miss you, Phil. Who will be my friend if you go away? I'll miss being here and tossing barbells with you."

"We can write to each other. I'll try to come back for the holidays. We'll see one another then."

"But we won't talk together. And I won't hear you play your harmonica." Her smile is gone. Tears fill her eyes.

It is September. Jena begins fifth grade. She is unhappy this will be Phil's last year at home. It lifts her spirits to see chubby, rosy-faced Sister Patrick the first day at school. The cheerful nun creates a pleasant atmosphere in the classroom.

It is the second week of school. Sister Patrick tells

the class, "The district music supervisor will visit our classroom today. This will be her only visit this year. I want you children to show her how well you can sing."

The tall, robust nun leads the class in a medley of songs. At the end of her visit, she gives her usual instructions: "There are forms here for anyone who wants to take private music lessons. They explain about lessons, group theory classes and the use of practice rooms in the convent. Those of you who are interested can take a form home. Have a parent sign it. The papers need to be back to Sister Patrick by Friday."

Jena takes a paper home to Sarah, confident she'll be taking her first lesson next week.

"I can play a lot of songs on the little piano I got for Christmas two years ago," she tells her mother. "I would really like to learn to play a real piano. There are practice rooms in the convent. It costs only thirty-five cents a week. Before I can begin lessons, this permission slip has to be signed by you or Dad. I have to take it back to Sister by Friday."

Jena hands the paper to Sarah.

"Your father will never allow you to have piano lessons now. We have to pay for your brother's college expenses." She hands the slip back, unsigned.

Jena can not hide the look of disappointment from her mother. She lowers her eyes and turns to walk away.

"I would want you to practice at home so I could listen to you play. The family could enjoy the music, also. We can't afford to buy a piano now."

"It's important for Phil to go to college," Jena says. "I know he really wants to go away and study. And I can wait for my music." But silently she prays. *Maybe I can have piano lessons next year, God. I'm sure You will find a way for me.*

After several days of Indian summer, fall weather

returns. Time goes too fast for Jena. The family celebrates Thanksgiving and Christmas. The next five months rush by. Soon the school year ends.

It is the first week of summer vacation. On a hot Saturday morning, Sarah carries a basket of wet clothes outside to Jena. The girl, now ten, stretches to hang the last two pieces on the line. Her stomach feels strange. She runs to the powder room. In a panic, she rushes to Sarah in the laundry.

"Mother," she cries. "There's something wrong with me. I was pinning clothes on the line. I don't know what to do. There's blood on my underclothes." Jena is hysterical.

"There's nothing wrong with you, Jena. Come upstairs with me. I'll give you something to use."

Her daughter's rapid development has been a concern of Sarah's the past year. She was hopeful this problem would not present itself until several months from now, after the girl's eleventh birthday. *Thank God*, she silently rejoices, *this will be the last time I'll go through this with a daughter.*

The woman leads Jena to the bathroom. She explains how to use a belt and sanitary napkin, but does not explain menstruation. "You will feel comfortable with this on." The mother offers no information about the change taking place within the girl's body. Sarah believes knowledge of anything related to sex or having babies will make a young girl curious. She feels too much information will jeopardize her innocence.

"When this happens again, use napkins from the box. You are not to talk about this to anyone."

"When will it stop? When will it happen again?"

"It will happen every month and last about three days."

Jena returns outside to finish her work. She is

relieved nothing serious is wrong with her. What she doesn't know is that her mother and sisters experience this same thing.

After lunch she asks her mother, "Can Laura and I go to the movies this afternoon?"

"What's the name of the movie?"

"Snow White and the Seven Dwarfs." Dad said when something good comes to the theater you would give us money for the show and some popcorn."

"If your father said it's all right, you can go." *A movie might take Jena's mind off the shock she had this morning,* Sarah thinks. *The girl is too young to understand what it means. At least she can forget about it while she's at the show.*

Laura and Jena walk in a hot summer sun.

In the cool theater the movie appears on the giant screen.

The wicked witch talks into a magic mirror. She is angry to hear Snow White's the fairest in the land.

Their popcorn disappears as the girls laugh at the antics of the little men and watch animals run through the forest.

The Seven Dwarfs sing and whistle as they walk back home from work in the diamond mine. They love beautiful Snow White, who cleans their messy cottage.

Snow White eats the witch's poisoned apple and dies. Prince Charming finds her. His kiss brings her back to life. They marry and live happily ever after.

Jena obeys her mother's order. As the girls walk back home, she never mentions what happened to her that morning. It is the one secret she must keep from her brother, also.

This mysterious change in her body is not the only thing that upsets Jena today. She sees Phil prepare clothes he will take with him when he leaves for his summer job.

Sarah respects her son's wish for a quiet birthday and no graduation celebration. After dinner, she serves home-made cake with ice cream. He gets a new leather suitcase.

Jena and Phil visit his private sanctuary in the evening. "I'm happy no one made a fuss about my birthday or me going away. That would only make it more difficult to leave here."

"I'm going to miss you so much," she cries.

"I'll try to be back for the holidays. You can come in here any time you want while I'm gone."

Upstairs in his room she watches her brother pack his harmonica with his clothing. He uses the large brown suitcase he got just a few hours ago.

"You're leaving tomorrow morning, aren't you?" she pouts.

"Yes, Shorty. You take care of yourself when I'm gone."

After Sunday Mass, Jena watches her brother carry two heavy suitcases onto a bus. She sobs as he rides away to begin a new life for himself.

It is a long, sad week for the young girl. She is glad when Saturday morning comes. She follows Al and pulls the rake behind the lawn mower. Together they dump clippings in the corner of the yard.

"Let's look inside Phil's shed," she tells her father.

Al removes the padlock and opens the door. He sees the sketches of Barry and Rusty on the wall.

"Where did your brother get these pictures?"

"He drew them. He showed them to me one day I

was here."

"He never showed them to your mother or me."

"One day I wrote a poem and gave it to him to read. After that, he showed me his drawings. He doesn't think his art is important."

"His talent will help with his college studies," Al says.

"I miss him a lot." She feels her eyes fill with tears. "I wish he could work closer to home. Then we could see him on weekends."

"He should be home with us for a while at Thanksgiving and for the Christmas holidays this year."

"That's five months away. That's a long time."

At lunch, Al reminds Sarah about his first bank meeting out of town. "I'll be away next week. All the district managers will get to meet one another. I'll be home late Friday night."

The girls go outside. Their parents sit at the table and sip hot coffee.

"This morning Jena and I had a talk about her brother," Al tells his wife. "She wanted to see inside his shed. On the wall are sketches he drew. He did one in art class at school."

Sarah sees a look of disappointment on her husband's face.

"Phil told Jena things he never told us," he mutters.

"They were very close. She's so unhappy with him away. I hope she finds something to occupy her time."

"She always enjoys a movie. I'll take her and Laura to the State. That will take her mind off Phil."

A short time later the trio boards a bus. They get off in front of the theater. Laura buys tickets at the booth. She hands them to the man in the lobby. Al and his daughters look at giant posters on the walls and read the title, "THE MAN IN THE IRON MASK," with Louis Hayward and Joan Bennett.

"It looks scary," Jena tells her sister. She sits captivated as the story begins.

There are twin brothers. The good one, the true ruler to the French throne, has been in the bastille eight years. The insane one has locked an iron mask on his imprisoned brother.

Captain D'Artagnan and his three musketeers wander through beautiful country sides, luxurious chateaux and palaces of seventeenth-century France.

"Your grandparents came from this country," Al whispers to his daughters.

Ann of Austria, mother of the twins, keeps the birth of the second son a secret. Only the musketeer Aremis, then Bishop of Vannes, knows the true king was locked in prison on his fifteenth birthday.

Aremis has a plan to place the good twin on the throne. He secretly switches the men. Then one night at the palace, he brings the brothers face to face before their mother. Ann cannot tell which son is the true king.

Jena stares and lets out a loud gasp. Al picks her up and sets her on his lap.

Aremis has the evil twin locked in a mask and exiled to a desolate island. The good twin takes his rightful place on the throne and peace is restored to the country.

Outside the theater, Jena riddles her father with questions.
"Is this a true story, Dad? Why did Ann put her son in prison because he was a twin? Why did the prince have

an iron mask over his head?"

"Some people think this is the story of King Louis XIV of France. They believe Ann hid the twin because she feared news of his birth would cause the throne to topple. The mask was used to hide his identity from the jailer."

"Why did your parents leave such a beautiful country?"

"They were farmers. Priests opened a new abbey in America. They needed workers to help grow food and tend to the animals. My parents raised their family in a farmhouse near the abbey."

"Laura, do you think the movie was scary?" Jena asks.

"How can you get so excited about a silly story?" Laura laughs. "Movies are only make-believe. Everyone knows that."

"Dad, it's not much fun coming here with Laura. Will you bring us again some time?"

"I'll have a lot more bank work to do when I get home from my meeting. There's no reason for me to bring you girls. You already came once by yourselves."

"Dad, I'm happy you brought us today. Mother would never allow Laura and me to see such a scary story all by ourselves. Maybe she wouldn't mind if we told her it all took place in the country where your parents lived before coming here."

"It will be better if you don't talk about it at all. She might worry about other movies you want to see. If she feels some might frighten you she won't let you come back."

Monday morning, Jena wakens early. She has breakfast with her father before he leaves for his trip. It is the first time the family will be alone with no man in the house overnight. She walks with him as he carries his suitcase down the sidewalk to the bus. Al sits at the window and smiles. His daughter stands with a somber

104

face. She waves good-bye as the bus rolls away.

Dad will be gone five days. When he comes back Saturday morning, it will be a great day for me. We'll work together in the yard. Jena's tears disappear as she thinks about the coming week-end. A faint smile appears on her face as she strolls along the sidewalk on her way back to the house.

CHAPTER 10
THE AFTERMATH

Al arrives at the conference room of the Royal Hotel to find a large gathering of bank managers. Astonished by the grandeur of oak walls, 2-tier crystal chandeliers and plush red carpet, he pauses to admire his surroundings. He sees John Grason, a towering figure in a three-piece, gray pin stripe suit, separate himself from the group. Al's former boss walks toward him. He greets him with a firm handshake.

"Hello, Al. You arrived just in time for me to introduce you to all the managers," he remarks as they walk to a huge oak table.

"I was not aware there would be so many men at this meeting," Al remarks. "It took me by surprise as I entered the room."

"I told the managers from our larger branch offices to bring their assistants."

The men are seated. John Grason calls the meeting to order. The regional manager turns to the slim handsome man seated at his left side.

"Gentlemen." Pause. He pulls up his belt. "This is Al Bordeau." He turns to him. "Al is the man who replaced me at Sage Bank. He's a diligent worker and an exemplary family man. I expect we will hear great things about him in the future," be boasts. "Now let's hear Al."

His nervousness is evident as he stands. His legs, unsteady as he turns toward his mentor. "Thanks John, for those commendable words." He grasps the edge of the table to calm his shaky hands, takes a deep breath, then continues. "You've been a great boss and an excellent advisor. I feel honored to be chosen as your successor. I'm pleased to be here with all of you and look forward to many more such meetings in the future."

The five-day agenda consists of meetings after early breakfast and mid-day lunch. Following a late dinner, the men socialize in the lounge.

A fierce storm arrives just as Al is scheduled to depart for home Friday night. The turbulent weather continues into the early morning hours. He boards the bus when the deluge dwindles to a light drizzle.

Al arrives home at dawn. The praise heaped upon him at the meeting imbues him with glorious self-esteem and pride. *I hope feelings of elation and success endure a long time,* he reflects in the shower. The hot water only slightly eases his tense body.

Al looks forward to serene, restful sleep as he slides into bed. Instead, following his violation of Jena, the delight experienced last night ends with a jolt. Al finds himself tortured by guilt, remorse and fear. *Never in an entire lifetime could I imagine, that in such a brief period of time, my marriage, career, and entire future would be in jeopardy. How can I ever live with this agony?* he writhes in despair.

He tosses for hours, unable to sleep. Mysterious demons torture his soul. Not for one moment can he forget the diabolical crime he perpetrated on his innocent daughter this morning.

Bright sunshine warms the room. Al listens to the ripple of Jena's laughter flow from the yard through the open window. He agonizes over loss of her love and trust. *That damn storm brought all this about. If the bus had been on schedule last night, this never would have happened,* he grieves. *I will not let one brief moment of passion destroy everything I struggled so hard to attain. But how can I be sure Jena will keep this secret between the two of us? If Sarah, or anyone else finds out, it will destroy my life and this family.* Al rises. He stares at a bed that will never again bring him peaceful slumber. He stares at a bed that will remind him forever of the evil deed he committed this day.

The forty-three-year-old man is unaware his ten-year-old daughter connects this recent event to the start of her period.

Sarah is, as usual, at the sink when her husband enters the kitchen.

"The girls and I had our lunch. Do you want breakfast or should I make lunch for you?"

"I'll get myself a cup of coffee." He keeps his eyes anchored to the mug in his hand. "I want to clear the mess in the yard. I'll make something for myself later."

"I'll call Jena. She wants to help you."

"This job's too heavy for her. It's better that I do it alone. There's nothing for Jena or Laura to do at home now. Give them money for a movie. You won't need them until dinner time."

"You took them last week. They don't need to see a movie every week. It's too soon for them to go again."

"Sarah, let them go. We know where they are and they can't get hurt there. You should be happy they won't be here to bother you all afternoon."

The wife does not oppose her husband. He's the head of the house. She follows his instructions.

The yard work is finished before the girls return home. Al rushes through a shower and goes to the kitchen. He sits alone at the table and eats a bowl of soup and a sandwich.

He calls to Sarah in the living room. "I'll be at the bar. I feel like being with men. It's close to dinner time.

You and the girls can eat without me."

Jena and Laura return home. They notice there are only three plates on the table. "Where's Dad? Isn't he eating with us?" Jena frowns. She stares at her father's empty seat.

"He went out to be with men for awhile," Sarah answers. "He said the tree branches were too heavy for you to help with. It took a long time for him to clear the yard. He ate before he left. We'll eat supper alone."

The confused woman ignores the sullen look on Jena's face. The disappointed child eats her meal in silence. Sarah does not understand Al's odd behavior. She doesn't know how to explain his behavior to her daughters.

Al stands at the bar and pays for his drinks. The men beside him see two new, crisp, fifty-dollar bills in his wallet.

"These stay in here," he tells them. "They are from my first pay as bank manager. They're good luck tokens."

The girls are asleep when their father gets home. He walks through the hallway to the bedroom. The smell of liquor drifts to the living room where Sarah sits in the dark. She waits for her husband to fall asleep before she crawls into bed.

Al begins a new schedule the next day. He rises before the girls are awake and attends early Mass alone. Weekday evenings, Al secludes himself at his desk in the master bedroom. Saturday mornings he spends time at his office. Afternoons he sends the girls shopping with their mother while he works in the yard. After dinner he joins his men friends in the bar.

The girls attend a movie every other week-end. The ticket collector and ushers at the State and Strand Theaters now know Jena and Laura by name. The movies they see read like a litany: "Rebecca of Sunnybrook Farm," "Boys' Town," "The Wizard of Oz," "The Hunchback of

Notre Dame." The list grows longer every month.

When Jena returns from shopping with her mother or a movie with her sister, the lawn is always freshly mowed and raked.

"I would rather help Dad in the yard than go to the movies with Laura," she complains to her mother. "Why doesn't he spend time with me any more? He either works at his desk or is out with his men friends."

"He told us his new job would require time away from the family. He still takes advanced management courses. And there's a lot more office work for him now. He needs time away from his heavy work load." *How can I possibly answer Jena's questions,* Sarah worries. *I can't even understand why he is acting so strange. Something must have happened when he was out of town to cause this change in him.*

"Jena, I recall you once told him to go out and enjoy himself. Well, now he relaxes with the men Saturday evenings."

"Ever since he got back from his trip, we never spend any time together. Now he even goes to church alone."

"When he was a boy he always got up early to work on the farm. When he walks to early Mass he enjoys peace and quiet in fresh morning air." *It is difficult to watch Jena suffer because Al spends so much time away from home. I wish she would accept his new routine and not complain any more.* Sarah frets about how the change in Al affects the entire family.

It is the last weekend of summer vacation. The girls take a stroll downtown to see a movie. They are near the theater when Laura mentions the new event in her sister's life.

"When did you get your first period?" she asks.

"What are you talking about?" There is a look of surprise on Jena's face as she gazes at her sister.

"You know what I mean Jena. Your monthly period."

"How do you know about it?" Her eyes open wide. She stares at Laura. "Mother told me not to tell anyone. She's the only person I'm allowed to talk to about it."

"Oh, Jena," Laura laughs, "every girl does it. It's part of your body getting ready to have babies."

"Laura, what do you mean, having babies?" she raises her voice in disbelief.

"This makes a girl ready to have babies after she gets married," the older girl explains.

"How does it happen?" Jena is shocked by the idea.

"When a man and woman go to bed they get together. This makes a baby start to grow inside her. But it's a bad sin if they do this before they are married."

"That's not true. It's a lie. You made it all up."

Jena feels her body get stiff. She is angry that her sister could make up such a story. "You are a liar," she shouts.

"It's true, Jena. Really it's true," Laura insists.

"It's a damn lie, Laura. It's not true. It's a damn lie!" She yells and shakes her fist at her sister.

"I could never make up anything like this. Let's go visit Aunt Marge. She'll tell you all about it."

They walk in silence. They stop two blocks past the theater. Laura knocks on the door of a large yellow brick house. A woman opens the door.

"Laura and Jena, this is a surprise. It's been a long time since you visited me. Come inside."

The tall, robust brunette sits on a tan upholstered chair. The girls sit on a maroon sofa, across the room from her.

"Aunt Marge, Jena started her period. I told her how women have babies. She won't believe me. Mother didn't talk to her about it. Tell her what you told me when I started."

Jena sits frozen to the couch. Her face turns white. She looks at the wall as she listens to her aunt's deep voice.

"There's nothing to be afraid of Jena. All girls have menstrual periods. Your body changes. You become a woman. Laura told you the truth. You can have babies. This is God's way for men and women to create a family after they are married."

Jena still can't believe everything Laura told her is true. *I wonder, what if she's wrong about how a baby is made?*

"How does a baby get inside the girl?" Jena blurts out.

"When a man and woman marry they make love. When they get together, the man places his seed in the woman's body. It meets a tiny egg inside the woman. This is how a baby starts to grow. You must never let a boy touch any private parts of your body. Only the man you marry should do this."

Jena feels a chill rush through her body. It is almost like she is paralyzed. She leaves the house without saying another word. She remains silent as she and Laura walk to the theater.

The movie flashes across the big screen. Jena pays no attention to the story. She dwells on the warning from Aunt Marge. Lost in thought, she broods over how a man and woman make a baby.

The sun is bright as they exit the double doors.

This time it is Laura who asks the question. "How did you like the movie?"

Jena can't even remember the title. She has no idea what the story was about. "It was okay."

"Don't worry about your period, Jena. Mother, Rita and I have them. All girls do. You'll get used to it soon."

At home, Jena goes up to her room and closes the door. She takes a piece of paper from a box of sanitary napkins. She writes her name and address on the designated spaces and places the coupon in an envelope. She addresses it, stamps it, walks to the corner mail box and drops it in the slot. The pamphlet she orders, "What Every Girl Should Know," should arrive in four to six weeks.

Jena is quiet at the dinner table. She picks at her food then returns to her room. Behind the closed door, she tilts the large mirror on the dresser. She turns from side to side and inspects her body. She checks to see if her tummy has started to grow bigger.

"What's the matter with Jena?" Sarah asks.

"She's worried about her period," Laura answers blatantly.

"It's something we all must suffer with. In a few months she'll get used to it."

Jena remains in her room all evening.

She is speechless as she walks to Sunday Mass with her mother and Laura. After dinner Sarah enters the living room. She sees Jena sitting on the sofa in a fetal position. Her left hand holds an open book. Her right hand thumb is in her mouth.

Sarah stands motionless. A look of terror covers her pale face. "Jena!" Sarah gasps, "what are you doing? Stop this nonsense immediately. Take that thumb out of your mouth!"

The girl ignores her mother. She stands up and slowly walks to the hallway, up the stairs and into her room. She closes the door. Once again she tilts the mirror on her dresser. She checks the size of her tummy.

After dinner, Sarah finds her daughter curled up on the sofa. An open book is on her lap. Her thumb rests in her mouth.

Sarah is petrified. She has no idea what is wrong with her daughter. "Jena, take that thumb out of your mouth." Her voice is a harsh, angry tone.

The girl ignores her mother. She gets up from the sofa. Without a word, she goes up the stairs, into her room.

Throughout the week the distraught mother witnesses her daughter's abnormal behavior. On the way to the theater Saturday, Jena stops in front of the church. "You can walk the rest of the way alone," she tells Laura. "I'm going to stop in church for a little while. I really don't want to see a movie today."

Nothing Jena does surprises Laura now. "It doesn't matter to me where you go. I'll meet you at home later."

Jena covers her head with a thin, blue scarf. She enters the side door of the church. Laura strolls nonchalantly down the street.

The church is cool. The worried girl shivers in the dark. Candles on the side altar illuminate that small area. The terrified girl kneels in the back pew. She prays that God will give her strength to make a good confession.

Jena has a relapse. She sits in a pew with her head bowed. She is terrified to enter the dreadful "dark closet." Rays of sunlight stream through the colored stained glass window. She sits immobile, engulfed by fear. *How can I tell the priest my terrible sin?* She shudders at the thought of going inside the confessional.

She waits, terror-stricken.

Other parishioners complete their confessions. It is several minutes since the last person exited the church. Jena musters courage to enter the small stall. Her bent knees rest on the kneeler. She rests her folded hands on the small shelf in front of her. She trembles in the pitch-black darkness. The priest slides the small window open. She hears him breathe.

"Bless me Father," she whispers. "It's been four weeks since my last confession." Jena hesitates.

"Speak up my child, I can hardly hear you."

"Bless me Father," she pauses.

"It's been four weeks since my last confession."

She pauses once more. "I made a mortal sin," she whispers.

The priest strains to hear her.

"Go on my child," Father Kelly instructs her.

"I have committed a mortal sin," she repeats.

Father knows by the voice a young girl is speaking to him. "Why do you think it is a mortal sin?" This is the first time he hears a child confess to having made a serious sin.

"Because it is a bad sin." Tears fill Jena's eyes.

The priest hears her crying. Father Kelly is a young priest. This is his first assignment in a parish. But he realizes how children can be confused between sin and bad behavior.

"What sort of sin is it?" he asks.

Her entire body is shaking. She wipes tears from her eyes. She sighs. "A sin of impurity."

"Was it an impure thought?"

"No, Father." Jena does not know how to describe the sin.

"Was it impure speech?" The girl is a challenge for him. He searches for an answer. He has no way to know the severity of the transgression.

"No, Father," she whispers. She continues to cry.

Confused by her answers, Father asks the most improbable question. "Did you commit an impure act?"

Jena's body becomes rigid. The voice from the other side sounds impatient. She rushes to answer. "Yes Father."

"Were you alone or with another person?" he asks abruptly.

"With someone," she whispers.

Father Kelly expects the young girl was merely exercising childish curiosity. "With whom did you do this?"

The priest's voice sounds angry to the child. "With

my father," she sobs. Jena waits for him to condemn her for her sin.

He remains silent for a few seconds. Jena responds with such fervor, Father Kelly has no doubt the child speaks the truth. He now realizes the gravity of the child's sin.

"Do you know what happens when you do this act?" he probes.

"Yes, Father. It makes a baby."

"Do you want a baby?"

He asks this so quickly it frightens her. She does not tell him how she found out about having a baby.

"No, Father," she sobs.

"If you ever do this again I will not give you absolution."

Jena hears his stern warning. She is too overwhelmed to respond to his threat.

"Do you understand what I'm telling you?"

"Yes, Father," she whispers.

She is too scared to hear what the priest says next. She only hears his last few words. "For your penance pray one rosary. Now, make a good Act of Contrition."

The small door slides shut. Jena exits the "dark closet." She walks with her head bowed in the darkness. She rubs tears from her eyes and returns to the back pew. She repeats a set of one "Our Father," ten "Hail Marys" and one "Glory be to the Father," five consecutive times. The pearl beads slip between her fingers. They are a reminder of her First Communion three years ago.

Jena did not hear Father Kelly pronounce absolution. She fears her sin was not forgiven by the priest or by God. She returns home in a somber mood.

"Laura is at Megan's house. She won't be home for dinner. She told me you didn't want to go to the movie today. You went to church instead," Sarah says. "You were there a long time. Your father and I were just about to start dinner without you."

Jena sits across the table from her father. She stares at his bowl. She watches him stir small, white octagon crackers in his oyster stew. When his bowl is empty, Sarah places fried oysters, parsley potatoes and green beans on the dinner plates.

The despondent girl lifts her eyes. She shutters when she sees her father glare at her.

"Where did you go today?" he bellows. "Laura was home from the movie an hour ago. Your mother had dinner ready before you got here."

"I went to confession." She does not look at him when she answers. "It took a long time to say a rosary for my penance."

Al is terrified. *My God*, he fears, *what all did this girl tell the priest? It must be serious for her to have to pray a rosary for penance.*

With a scowl on his face he springs from his chair. He swings his arm across the table. His hand strikes a firm blow to Jena's jaw. The startled girl leaps from her chair. She rushes from the table. As she passes her father's chair, the angry man kicks his daughter on her back. She sobs as she runs to her room.

Shocked by her husband's sudden anger, Sarah exclaims, "Why did you do that to her? What did she do that was wrong?"

"I don't like the way she looked at me," he raves.

"She just started to eat dinner. She didn't do anything wrong."

Sarah leaves the table. She makes an ice pack and takes it up to Jena. The woman's face turns pale. Her daughter's jaw is red and swollen.

"Hold this on your face," she says. "It will help keep the swelling down."

Al is gone when Sarah returns to the table. She hears the front door close as her husband leaves the house.

Jena remains in her room all evening. She refuses to come downstairs to eat dinner. Laura is oblivious of the turmoil. Neither Jena nor her mother mention the trouble they had at home while she was at her friend's house.

Sarah goes to evening confession. The frightened woman waits until the last person leaves Father Karl's confessional. The short, kind man is easy to talk with. She finds solace in this small, dark cubicle.

"It has been one week since my last confession, Father," Sarah begins. "But now I need your advice about my family."

"What is the problem, dear lady?" His voice is soft and compassionate.

"Something is wrong with my daughter and it frightens me. It began when she and her sister came home from a movie one week ago." Sarah pauses, not sure how to tell him about Jena.

"Just tell me what happened."

"The next day, I found her on the sofa with her thumb in her mouth. Now she always sucks her thumb. She's almost eleven. It's as though she's a baby again."

"Could the movie she saw have frightened her?" he asks.

"She and her sister saw "Pinocchio." I doubt that would frighten a girl her age."

"Has anything unusual happened to her lately?"

"She had her first period several weeks ago. Her sisters were older when they started. It never was a problem for them."

Sarah pauses. She finds it difficult to talk to the priest about personal matters.

"Can you think of anything else that might have frightened her? Is there a problem at school?"

"She likes school. I would notice if she was having

problems there." Sarah begins to cry. She tells the priest what happened at home, before she came to church.

"You must try to forgive your husband for his cruelty. It sounds as though he acted impulsively. It probably will never happen again. You must pray for God to guide you in this matter."

"She and her father were always so close. Now he seems to be very angry with her. She's no longer a happy, carefree child. She looks like my daughter. But sometimes, she behaves like an infant. Lately, she seldom talks when she's home."

Sarah can't hold back her tears. She wipes her eyes with a delicate linen handkerchief. The priest waits for the woman to regain her composure.

"It's as though a stranger lives with us. I pray for God to help me, but each day it gets worse. How can I restore peace at home when I don't know what's wrong?"

"My dear lady, you must put your faith in the good Lord. Next Saturday, come back to church an hour before confessions are to begin. Bring your daughter with you. I will talk with you first. Then I'll have a talk with her. Perhaps I can find out what troubles the child. Then we may be able to help her."

Sarah returns to the house before Al gets home. She must wait a week before Father Karl talks with Jena. *It will be an answer to my prayers if Father gets her to talk with him about her problem. Please God, let our family live in peace once again,* the woman prays.

Jena goes up to her room when she returns home. This becomes her personal safety zone. She isolates herself from classmates at school. She is engrossed with reading. Books become constant companions. School is her refuge away from home.

This is the day the music supervisor makes her annual visit to the classrooms. This year, when she asks if anyone wants private music lessons, Jena raises her hand. The determined girl takes a permission slip home to her mother.

"Today I signed up for music lessons. It costs fifty cents a week now. Sister wants the slip back tomorrow."

"But we don't have a piano for you to use," her mother protests. "I told you this when you asked last year."

"Sister said pupils without a piano can use the practice rooms in the convent." Jena will not accept another refusal.

Sarah takes the slip from Jena and signs it. "I'll give you the money each week. Don't tell your father."

Wednesday after school, Jena takes her first lesson. Sister George gives her three short beginning pieces to study. The girl practices for a half-hour every day after school. She is home before her father arrives.

Jena writes her brother a letter to share her new happiness with him.

Dear Phil,

I must tell you some good news. Today I started music lessons. I have three little pieces to learn before next week. Sister lets me practice at the convent every day after school for a half-hour.

Mother gives me money for lessons. I can't tell Dad, though. He has changed so much since you went away. It was nicer when he was a bank teller. He's never home any more since he became a manager.

I saw your harmonica in the suitcase when you packed it. Do you still play it? I miss hearing your music.

I can hardly wait two more months for you to come home for Thanksgiving. I hope you learn a lot at college about how to care for animals. They are our friends.

Please write. I MISS YOU.

Your "blood sister,"
Shorty

The following Saturday, Jena finds a letter from Phil in the mail box. She reads it as she walks to church with her mother.

Dear Shorty,
I got your letter today. There's so much to learn, I have to study a lot. I'm not sure I will be home this Thanksgiving. If I can work during the holidays, I'll stay here. I'll try to get home for Christmas, though.
I want you to keep writing to me, even if I don't have much time to answer your letters. I'm happy Mother lets you take piano lessons. Let me know how you progress.
Enjoy your holiday with the family. I'll be thinking about all of you on Thanksgiving day.
Your "blood brother,"
Phil

Jena and Sarah stop outside before entering the church. From her small tan purse, the mother takes out two little white head scarves. She and Jena each put one on their head.

The church is empty when they enter. The light is on in Father Karl's confessional. When Sarah enters, the light goes out. Jena sits in a pew waiting for her mother to come out.

"Have you mentioned anything to your daughter about our talk last week?" Father Karl asks.

"No, Father. But something bothers her. Nothing's changed since then. She still is sullen and stays in her room most of the time."

"Send her in now. Perhaps she will tell me what bothers her. Now put your faith in the Lord. Go with God, dear lady."

Sarah kneels next to her daughter. "It's your turn to go inside. Father will talk with you now."

Once more, the little door slides open. Jena is relieved to hear Father Karl's voice. He is always nice when he talks to her.

"I confessed last week, Father," she tells him. "But I don't think my sin was forgiven. I never heard Father Kelly give me absolution."

"What sin do you feel he didn't absolve?"

Jena repeats the entire confession she made last week. "He told me that if it happens again he wouldn't give me absolution."

"Did you know it was wrong when it happened?"

"No, Father. My sister told me two months later."

"Did you tell your sister what happened?"

"No, Father. She told me how babies are made. That's how I learned it was a sin." She begins to cry.

"My dear child, for something to be a sin, you have to know it is wrong *before* you do it. You learned it was a sin after it happened," Father Karl explains.

"But I never heard Father Kelly give me absolution."

"Perhaps he knew you did not need absolution. You never committed a sin," he emphasizes. "I want you to tell your mother what happened between you and your father. She will be able to help make things better for you. I am absolving you of every sin you ever made. Now go in peace, my child. God loves you."

Jena takes a deep breath. "Thank you, Father."

In the pew, mother and daughter offer silent prayers in the quiet of the empty church.

It is a bright sunny day. As mother and daughter walk two blocks to the grocery store, Sarah expects her daughter to confide what she discussed with Father Karl. But Jena is absorbed in her own thoughts. She has no intention of telling her confession to Sarah. *I can never tell Mother what happened with Dad,* she decides. *Now I know it's wrong. She will hate me because it happened. She and Dad might even fight about it. He had to know it's a bad sin. That's why he told me never to do it again. I can never let her know what he did to me.*

The mother waits for her daughter to talk with her, but to no avail. Her daughter remains silent. They take the groceries to the dairy store and have their usual large size ice cream cones.

Sarah arrives home disappointed there was no conversation about troubles that plague Jena. Whatever the young girl's problem is, Sarah is certain she intends to keep it a secret. *It must be serious for the priest to request that I take her to church with me today*, she silently grieves. Sarah knows no priest can disclose what a person confesses to him. She feels things are more hopeless than ever. *It's all in Your hands now, Lord,* she prays.

CHAPTER 11
REVELATIONS

It has been six weeks since Jena began to study music at the convent. This Wednesday, Sister George phones Sarah after the girl's lesson.

"Your daughter enjoys music and is a good student. She will do much better with more practice time." Sister looks at her pupil. "Jena said I must get your permission for her to spend more time here."

"Jena won't be able to stay more than a half-hour after school. She must be home to have supper with the family."

"Extra practice time would help further her skills. She has the ability to make greater progress. But she needs more time at the piano to accomplish this. Would you allow her to practice Saturday mornings? She could come early and be home for lunch. Would this be satisfactory to you, Mrs. Bordeau?"

Jena knows Sarah grants most everything a nun requests.

"I'm sure you know what is best for her. She has my permission to practice whenever you schedule her. And Sister George," Sarah interjects, "thank you for taking an interest in Jena. Her music seems to be a godsend for her."

"She works hard. She is one of my better pupils."

Sarah notices the thumb problem occurs less often now that her daughter finds enjoyment in her music.

Jena's music is a blessing for her, but it presents

another problem for me. I must let Al know about her music lessons before she goes to the convent Saturday. The thought disturbs her.

This evening, Sarah approaches her husband at his desk. She waits for him to complete the paper in front of him.

He glances up and sees her solemn expression. "What's bothering you, Sarah? What is it you have to say?"

"I didn't tell you this sooner. I waited to see if Jena stayed at her lessons," she states, matter-of-fact. "She began taking piano lessons at the convent in September. She practices a half-hour every day after school."

She hurries to give him all the information at once. "Sister George phoned me today. She said Jena is a good student and would like her to practice Saturday mornings, too. Jena loves her music. But she needs more time at the piano."

"How can you be sure that girl's at practice after school? She could be any damn place for all you know." Al looks down at the pile of papers on his desk. His voice is harsh.

"Sister keeps a record of her practice time. She lets me know how many hours Jena is at the convent each week. You can be sure she wouldn't miss a minute of practice. She loves her music too much. Sister said she is a very good pupil."

"Just remember, you let her get involved in this without my knowledge. It's your job to keep track of her. It will be your responsibility if she gets into any trouble."

Saturday morning, Al is at work in the yard. He watches his daughter skip down the walk. She has a big smile on her face. It has been a long time since he has seen her happy. Jena has been somber ever since the day he struck her.

Monday begins a week vacation for Al. He plans to spend the days at his desk. There is a pile of papers he needs to handle. He examines the morning mail. Among other envelopes, there is a plain brown one addressed to his youngest daughter. He opens it with other pieces of mail. He glances through the booklet Jena sent for several weeks ago. *Why does she need a book like this to teach her about her body? Sarah should have told her these things a long time ago.* He realizes how ignorant Jena must be about her body functions. *It seems as though Sarah will pass her aversion to sex onto her daughters. That may be the result of her not instructing them in the facts of life.* He mulls over these ideas as he flips the pages of the pamphlet. *Hell, she would enjoy the chaste life of a nun more than her marriage to me.*

He dismisses these negative thoughts and directs his mind to his backlog of work. He sits at his cluttered desk and proceeds to use Jena's envelope for a work sheet.

"I'm going to the market, Al. I'll be home soon." Sarah's soft voice rings out from the living room.

When the main road was closed to remove trolley tracks, Sarah began to shop at Abe's store, a half-block from the house. The store is neat and clean. She likes the convenience of shopping close to home. Sarah has shopped at the small store over a year. She always buys the best meat and produce. Abe appreciates her patronage.

A tiny bell jingles as Sarah enters the door. She sees two salesclerks stack groceries on shelves at a side wall.

Holly has worked here several years. She is an attractive woman in her mid-twenties with dark brown eyes and flaming red hair. Sarah can hear her loud, coarse voice as she instructs the new girl.

"Put the large, heavy cans on the bottom shelf. The small ones go up on the top shelves."

This is the first time Sarah has seen Mary. The young girl started working here after her graduation in May. She is a petite, eighteen-year-old blonde. Her blue eyes twinkle when she laughs. Sarah walks to the rear of the store. She sees Abe, a tall man with deep brown eyes, standing behind the meat case. His white smock is a sharp contrast to his smooth black hair.

"Good morning, Mrs. Bordeau. What can I help you with this morning?" His face lights up with his usual friendly smile.

"I want you to grind two pounds of lean beef, one-half pound of both pork and veal together, please."

"Is there anything else today?" Abe asks as he wraps the meat.

"A pound of baked ham, please."

He hands her the packages. "Thank you. Have a nice day," he says, in his deep masculine voice.

Sarah likes the fact Abe is such a polite man. She enjoys the attention he gives her. At the front counter Mary puts bread and milk in a heavy brown bag. Vegetables and the two meat bundles are placed in another one.

"Will this be on the tab until pay day, Ma'am?" she asks in her sweet Irish brogue. She reaches toward a stack of small yellow tablets beside the register.

"No, Dear. This will be cash."

After Sarah leaves the store, Holly informs Mary, "Mrs. Bordeau never buys ready-made meat loaf from the case. She always gets it ground fresh. And she always pays cash. Her husband is the new manager at Sage Bank."

On Saturday, Sarah sends Jena and Laura to Abe's with a list of groceries to buy. After Jena comes home she writes a letter to her brother.

Dear Phil,

I wish you didn't have to work so much. You weren't home for Thanksgiving or Christmas. When are we going to see you again?

Last Sunday, Mother, Laura and I went to visit Sister Rita. She looks strange in her black habit. Soon she'll study to be a nurse. Then she'll wear a white habit. She looks happy now.

I practice the piano at the convent thirty minutes every day after school and sometimes two hours on Saturdays. I know five pieces. I'm on a new one now. It's Beethoven's SONATINA IN F.

I forgot to tell you this before. Dad took me into your shed once, the week after you left. He was surprised to see the drawings of Barry and Rusty. I told him about the poem I wrote, too.

I miss you a lot. Write me when you get time.

Your "blood sister,"
Shorty

Jena takes the letter to her father's desk to get a stamp. She sees the envelope addressed to her among his papers. There are numbers written all over it. She puts a stamp on Phil's letter and grabs the envelope. Tears run down her cheeks as she walks down the sidewalk. She drops Phil's letter in the mail box and runs home.

In her room, she looks at the drawings of female organs in the pamphlet. She reads it takes nine months for a baby to grow and be born. *There's no reason now to keep tilting the mirror and waiting for my tummy to get big. Why didn't mother or Aunt Marge tell me how long it takes for a baby to grow? I worried for a year. I thought my tummy would get big. I was afraid everybody would know what happened to me,* she agonizes. *How could Mother and Dad be so cruel? I wish they weren't my parents.*

After dinner, Laura and Jena play a game of checkers on the dining room table. Their parents are standing in the doorway between them and the kitchen.

"Why don't you talk to these girls? They should be told how their bodies develop and grow. You can't keep them ignorant forever, Sarah," he bellows.

"They know more than you think they do," she murmurs.

"How do you know what they think about? Do you ever talk to them about these things? One of your duties is to instruct your daughters about becoming a woman. The other is to fulfill your responsibility as a wife." His face turns crimson. They stand face to face. "Just remember this. What you don't give me, I'll get from the girls."

Sarah glances at her daughter. A sudden thought strikes her with fear. *This may be part of Jena's problem. Maybe something has already happened to her. Why else would Al ask those questions?* Tears run down the woman's pale cheeks. She turns away from her husband. She goes to the basement. With her face buried in her hands she paces back and forth on the cement floor. *No! No! That could never happen. Nothing like that could ever, ever happen. I refuse to believe it could happen. I'll never think about it again.* She sighs and dismisses the idea from her mind. She sits at the small table with black wooden beads in her hands and prays the rosary.

At bedtime, Jena tells Laura, "I didn't see Mother all evening. I wonder where she went."

"I saw her go down the cellar after Dad hollered at her. She's probably still down there."

Tears fill Jena's eyes as she kneels by her bed and prays. *"God, help me get out of this place. Don't let anything bad happen to me again. Please, let someone who can love me and want me come and take me away."*

Fear deepens within the girl. She avoids her father when he is home. The more she begins to understand what happened between her father and herself, the stronger her fear, guilt, and anger grow. She and her sister keep too involved with their own concerns to pay much attention to the hostility and problems that surround their parents.

After Jena comes home from the convent, she roller-skates on the sidewalk with Laura or reads a book. She and her sister go to a movie one Saturday. Shortly after they leave the house Sarah goes to Abe's store. The door is open. The clerks are in the corner, out of sight. They are busy and don't see the customer enter. Sarah hears Holly's loud, coarse voice tell Mary about a man who visited her apartment last Saturday.

"I saw him at the bar. Later, he slipped out the back door. No one saw him come upstairs to see me," Holly laughs. "It was his first visit. But I'm sure it won't be his last."

"Who is he?" Mary asks in her soft lilting voice.

"If I tell, you must promise not to reveal it to another person. This must be our secret."

"I promise not to tell a soul." Mary crosses her heart with her finger.

"I like the guy. I want to see him again. You must vow not to let anyone know what I tell you," Holly repeats.

"I promise. I promise. Now tell me who it is."

"I'll give you a clue," she teases. "His wife is a prude who doesn't like to sleep with him. And he has a daughter who's in the convent."

Sarah is stunned. She stands at the counter unable to move.

"You mean to tell me you went to bed with a Catholic man? A Catholic man who's married?" Mary is not laughing any more. Her expression is serious. "Oh, Holly, that's a mortal sin."

"It may be for you, but it's not for me. I don't worry about that kind of thing. He should be the one to care about it being a sin. Just because he has a daughter in the convent doesn't make him a saint," Holly grins.

Sarah rushes from the store. She boards a bus. The driver lets her off in front of the large grocery store downtown. She decides never to step foot in Abe's store again. If she runs out of bread or milk she will send the girls to get it.

One hot summer afternoon, Jena walks alone in the back door. She is surprised to look in the hallway and see Abe at the front door. With her back to the kitchen, Sarah does not see her daughter.

"Mrs. Bordeau, I would like to talk with you." His voice is so low, Jena strains her ears to hear. "May I step inside?"

Sarah opens the door for him to enter.

"It's been several weeks since you shopped in my store. Have I done something to offend you?"

"No. You have always treated me with respect."

"Are you dissatisfied with the food in the store?"

"No. You have the best meats and produce in town."

"Then why are you staying away? Whatever the problem is I'll do my best to correct it. You're one of my best customers. I don't want to lose your patronage. What have I done wrong?"

"This has nothing to do with you, Abe. It is one of your clerks. And there is no way you can remedy the situation." She lowers her head. A blush creeps into her cheeks.

"Tell me what the problem is. It may not be as hopeless as you think. If she's made some kind of mistake I'll have her correct it for you."

"It's a personal matter. This problem can not be fixed."

"If one of them was rude to you, I'll have her apologize." He smiles in relief. "That won't be difficult to fix."

"It's nothing so innocent, I'm ashamed to admit. The last time I was in your store I overheard Holly brag about having an affair with a married man." Sarah's face turns red. "I'll not support any business where I must deal with this type of woman. I'll not be back to your store as long as she's there."

"Please try to understand, Mrs. Bordeau. I can't control the actions of the girls after they leave work each day."

"She is blatant about her immoral behavior. I won't associate with a wench like her."

"I'll discuss this with Holly. Please Mrs. Bordeau, give us another chance. Mary is a good Catholic. I know you'll have no objections to her behavior. I will have her take care of you when you come back to my shop."

Jena moves across the kitchen to listen better.

"I hear my daughter. I can't talk about this any longer."

"Please think about what I told you," he reminds her.

After the store closes this evening, Abe talks with Holly. "I've lost a good customer because of your conduct in the store. You should know better than to discuss your private affairs in here where customers can hear. I'll not lose any more business because of your loose tongue. You are to keep your personal life separate from your work here at the store."

"You must mean the Bordeau woman," she grins. "She must have heard me tell Mary about her husband. We never saw her in the store that day."

"You need to have more regard for our customers. Mrs. Bordeau is a decent woman. She was shocked to hear you discuss her husband. You've brought trouble to that woman. You could even jeopardize his job. This is nothing to laugh about. It's a serious matter."

"Women get over this kind of thing. Most men cheat in their marriage."

"My livelihood depends on this business. I can't have my own clerk ruin it for me. I'll not lose any more customers because of you."

He goes to the register and takes money from the drawer. "This is your final pay. I don't want you here tomorrow."

Several days later, Laura goes to the store for a quart of milk. When she returns home she tells her mother, "A new girl works at Abe's. She's pretty. Her name is Faye. Abe hired another nice Catholic girl like Mary."

Lord, let Holly find another job out of town, she prays.

Al no longer approaches Sarah in bed. Some Saturday nights he comes home with the smell of liquor on his breath. These are the nights she suspects he has been with Holly in her apartment. But unbeknown to Sarah, Al has not seen Holly since Abe fired her.

Sarah seldom leaves the house now. She fears the neighbors may be aware of her husband's unfaithfulness. She worries his affair may jeopardize his job. Her body gets thinner. Her face becomes drawn and pale. The only time she ventures out is to attend Mass and shop for groceries downtown.

Jena increases her time at piano practice. Laura spends long hours at Megan's house. Sarah spends most of her time alone in the house.

"Megan and some of her friends belong to the Girl Scouts. They have fun at troop meetings. They go on picnics and do lots of other good things. Can I join their scout troop?" Jena asks.

Her mother answers immediately. "No. You can't."

"Why can't I? What if Laura joins with me?"

"Your father would never allow it."

"Please ask him, Mother. He might let me if Laura would go with me," she begs.

"Laura already asked him. He told her no. He'll say the same to you. Don't ask again." Her voice is firm.

Jena's absorption in her music provides a refuge from fear and anger. She finds tranquility and safety at the convent. She is engrossed in her practice one Saturday. It is past lunch time when Sister George enters the room.

"You have been here two hours, Jena. Did you bring a lunch with you today?"

"No Sister. I'm not hungry. Do I have to leave now?"

"You can practice a while longer. But stay here until I come back. I have something to give you."

Several minutes later, Sister returns with a small tray in her hands. Beneath a white cotton napkin is a ham sandwich and a glass of cold milk. She sets the tray on a table. "The cook is away from the kitchen. I was able to make a light lunch for you."

Sister George sits at the table beside her pupil.

"When I was a young woman I was a concert pianist. When I decided to enter the convent, the maestro became very angry. He told me I was ruining my life. He said I was destroying a good career. But I feel God gave me a vocation to teach music. It makes me happy that you love music, also."

This is the first time the nun talks about her personal life with Jena. "I'm glad you are here to teach me."

"I'm happy you feel this way." Sister stands and walks to the door. "You can leave the tray in the room when you finish your food. And continue to practice as long as you like."

Sarah has lunch dishes washed and put in the cupboard when Jena comes home. The young girl has a big smile on her face.

"Where have you been all this time?" Sarah stands on the back porch with her hands on her hips. She has a worried look on her face. She glares at her daughter.

"I was at the convent. You told me this morning that I could go," she reminds her mother.

"But you didn't come home for lunch. Aren't you hungry?"

"No. Sister George gave me a sandwich and milk."

"You don't go to the convent to eat. We send you

there to practice. You are not to stay there three hours. I want you home for lunch. Do you understand me?"

"Sister said I could practice that long."

"I'm telling you to practice only the hours that you're scheduled. It's a good thing your father isn't home. If he knew how long you were away, he wouldn't allow you to go back."

Sarah broods over her family. She frets about the shift in Jena's personality. She worries about the girl's isolation from her classmates. The drastic change in Al's life style causes her great pain. She fears there will never be a solution to her problems.

Overcome by depression, she speaks with Father Karl again. In the privacy of the confessional she finds courage to divulge her most personal secrets. She receives absolution for her brief confession.

"Before I go Father, I need to talk with you again. I am desperate for your advice." Sarah breaks down in tears.

"What is the situation between you and your husband?"

"His work keeps him occupied much of the time. We knew this would happen when he was told of his promotion."

Sarah pauses to regain her composure. "Saturday evenings he goes to a bar to be with men friends. I know for certain he's been with another woman." Her tears flow down again.

"Do you continue to share the same bed?"

"Yes, Father. But he hasn't approached me for quite some time. I won't complain about that, though." She pauses. "Our children are grown. I'm forty. I don't want another baby now."

She pauses long enough to gather her thoughts.

"You know the Church forbids the practice of birth control."

"My dear woman," Father Karl cautions her, "you

can not deny your husband marital relations to avoid pregnancy."

Sarah offers her ultimate excuse. "But he's been with another woman," she sobs.

"Place that issue in God's hands. You must resume your conjugal relationship. Remember the vows you made when you married. You are to love one another. Now pray for God's help."

Sarah follows the priest's advice. Tonight in bed she remains close to her husband. She does not refuse his intimate overtures. For the first time in several weeks, Al finds physical satisfaction with his wife. Tonight in his own bed, Al enjoys intimacy at home.

CHAPTER 12
SELF-CONDEMNATION

Sarah pours hot oatmeal into cereal bowls. Jena's eyes are fixed on her mother. She follows her every move. *I wonder if Dad and Mother get together when they're in bed. Maybe they never do any more. That may be why they didn't have more babies after I was born.* The booklet Jena received in the mail helped ease her mind. It was a relief to read she will not have a baby now. She no longer has the desire to play with dolls. They rest in the corner of her closet. Music becomes an obsession. It is the sole activity that interests her.

Jena stands in line at the school yard this morning. The seventh grade gathers together. She overhears two of her classmates talk about her and Laura.

"Look how big Jena is now," Ruth says. "She must stuff rolled-up tissue or nylon stockings in her bar. Laura is older but her chest isn't big at all."

"Laura's taller and thinner than her sister. Maybe that's why her bust looks smaller. You're just jealous because you don't have anything." Carrie chuckles. "You can't even wear a bra yet."

"Why would I be jealous of her? She used to be lots of fun. Last year she changed. Sometimes I see her put her thumb in her mouth. How could I be jealous of somebody that weird?"

Jena walks behind Carrie and Ruth as they enter the classroom. She listens to them continue their conversation.

"You're wrong, Ruth. I don't think Jena stuffs her bra. Only you would think of that. I guess that's what you'll do if you don't get anything." Carrie laughs out loud.

On this first day of school, Jena sits in the last row at the back of the room. Unconsciously, she puts her thumb in her mouth. Sister Donna sits at her desk in front of the class. The short, pudgy nun glares at her young pupil. Jena gazes back at Sister's stern, red face. The nun ignores the girl all day.

After school, Jena finds solace at the piano. She walks in the back door near dinner time. The house is quiet. The house is too quiet. She stands rigid inside the door. There is not a sound from Laura or Sarah. *What will I do if Dad's in his room? What will happen if we're in the house alone?* She panics. She recalls his words to her mother: *"What you don't give me, I'll get from the girls."* She stands immobile. Her body trembles.

"Mother," she calls. There is no answer.

"Mother." She calls louder. Still no answer.

Jena's face turns white. She stands frozen to the spot. "Sarah!" she screams. "Sarah!"

Her mother rushes up the basement stairs. "Jena. what are you shouting about?"

"I couldn't hear you down there. I was worried I was alone in the house." She sighs. Her body becomes limp.

"I've been home all day. You know you never come home to an empty house."

Jena turns and walks toward the hallway. Laura comes from the porch into the kitchen. She follows her sister upstairs and into her room. She closes the bedroom door.

"Why did you shut the door?" Jena asks.

"I don't want mother to hear what I say to you. I was in the yard when you hollered, 'Sarah.' She's our mother. You're never to call her Sarah."

Laura stands in front of her sister. She stares into

her eyes. "Call her Mother," she orders. "You call her Mother."

"Well, what if she's not my mother? What if somebody else is? Not her. What if neither she nor Al are my parents?" Jena glares at her sister. She clenches her fists by her side.

"What do you mean? You know they're our parents."

"They may be your parents. They may not be mine. Maybe they got me from some other people."

"How can you say such a crazy thing? You know they're your parents." Laura has a perplexed look on her face.

"Sarah may be my mother. But Al can't be my father," Jena vigorously insists.

Laura's face turns fiery red. "Don't you say that. Don't you ever say that about our mother. How could you even think such an evil thing? Mother would never commit a sin with some other man," Laura hollers. "Dad is your real father. Don't you ever question that again." She turns and stomps out of the room.

Jena does not tell her sister why she doubts Al is her father. *No real father would do to his daughter what he did to me. I don't know how I got born. But he just couldn't be my real father.* She tries not to think about it any more.

After Laura leaves the room, Jena closes the door again. She takes off her school dress. The young girl abhors the reflection of the mature figure she sees in the mirror. *No wonder Ruth talks about me. I'm too big. I'll never be like Laura. She's slim and pretty. No wonder the boys stare at her.*

She thinks about how boys look at Laura when she is with her.

Downstairs, Laura talks to her mother. "I think something is wrong with Jena. She said crazy things to me. She doesn't make sense when she talks."

Lord, let me know what bothers Jena, she prays.

"What did she say to you?" She tries to speak calmly.

"Just dumb things. Nothing she says makes sense. She acts like a stranger, not my sister. What she said is so dumb. I won't even repeat it. She acts so strange. She doesn't even talk with any one at school any more."

This evening, Sarah tries to figure a way to get Jena to mix with her classmates. She decides to have a surprise birthday party for her.

The week before Jena's birthday, Laura takes six party invitations to school. "It's a surprise," she tells the girls. "Don't let Jena find out about it."

After dinner, Jena approaches her mother. "Laura was talking to some girls in my class today. Later I overheard some of them talking about going to a party next Saturday. I don't want you to have anything for me." She frowns. "If you do, no one will come to it anyway."

"You know the family always celebrates birthdays alone. Those girls must have been talking about someone else."

A half-hour before the party is to start Saturday, Sarah sees Jena huddled on the sofa with a book in her hand.

"Why don't you go for a walk? It will be good for you. Strong winds made the air cold. Don't stay out any longer than a half-hour."

Jena feels certain there is to be a party for her. Forlorn, she walks several blocks. She goes past the yard where she and her brother built Frosty six winters ago. *I wish Phil were home now so things would be happy around here,* she frets.

It has been an hour since Jena started her walk. Her six classmates have been waiting at the house thirty minutes.

A somber girl enters the front door. She hangs her coat on the clothes tree in the hall. Laura and the girls rush out from the dining room. "Happy Birthday, Jena!" they shout.

It shocks her to see both Ruth and Carrie in her house. She is speechless. She follows the girls into the living room. Laura leads games of Pin The Tail On The Donkey and passes out prizes to the winners. After games of bingo, Sarah serves cake and ice cream.

"Thanks," Jena says glumly, as she opens each present. She recalls the conversation she heard in the school yard between Ruth and Carrie. There's nothing she can think of to say to them.

The girls stare at her as they put on their coats.

"Thanks for your presents," Jena tells them.

When the door closes she turns to her mother.

"You lied to me. I knew you would have a party. I told you not to have one for me." She puts her face in her hands and cries. "I can't trust anyone. Not even you."

"I just tried to make a happy birthday for you."

"It would have been better if you didn't have some of those stupid girls here. They talk about me behind my back."

After dinner, Al inquires, "How did the party go?"

"I should have told her about it. She wasn't surprised." Sarah breathes deep. "I never thought she would be so upset."

"What happened?"

Al's lips are taut, his brow furrowed.

"Before the girls came, I told her to take a short walk. We waited a half-hour for her. She was not happy to play the donkey games or bingo. She thanked each girl for her gift. But no one had a good time."

Al goes to the living room. Jena is on the couch reading a book. He looks at the games on the lamp table.

"Your face looks like that donkey on the box. Look at yourself in the mirror. Maybe then you'll keep that damn thumb out of your mouth. You should thank your mother the girls came here today." He throws up his hands and turns away.

Jena closes her book and carries it up to her room.

Each day the troubled woman watches her daughter drift deeper into isolation. After dinner the girl does homework. Then she reads a library book, either on the sofa or in her bedroom. Her routine seldom varies.

Sarah constantly complains, "Jena, go outside and get some fresh air. You'll ruin your eyes when you read so much."

It is as if the woman talks to a deaf person. Jena ignores her mother's command. She remains absorbed in the world of make-believe printed on the pages of her book.

Thanksgiving Day arrives. With Phil absent from home it is just another ordinary day for Jena. It has been eighteen months since he left home. She writes to him hoping he will listen to her request.

Dear Phil,

Thanksgiving Day was not a happy time with you away. I hope you come home for Christmas. Please try to get away from work and spend this holiday with us.

Mother had a surprise birthday party for me. It wasn't any fun. I would have been happy if you were here.

I miss hearing you play the harmonica. I like my music. Sister George is nice to me. I can play Schubert's SERENADE, Tchaikovsky's SWEET DREAMS, and Beethoven's FUR ELISE. I'll play them for you at Christmas time.

I miss you and hope you'll be home soon.

Write to me when you find time.

Your "blood sister,"
    Shorty

By Christmas Eve, Jena has not heard from Phil. As

Sarah and the girls prepare for Midnight Mass, the front door opens.

"Surprise!" Phil shouts from the hall.

Jena runs downstairs. He looks much taller than when he went away. She throws her arms around him. "You didn't write me you'd be here."

"Your letter came too late for me to answer."

Tonight, Al walks to church with his family. It is the first time they all go to Mass together since he returned from his meeting out of town. Sarah smiles at her husband as they walk together in the new-fallen snow.

Jena sits next to her brother in church. The special music and decorations give a festive atmosphere to the Mass. Snow continues to fall. They saunter along the sidewalk admiring the homes decorated in holiday splendor. They arrive home in the early morning hour. After rolls, coffee and cocoa, they gather near the tree.

"I don't care what is in my package," Jena tells Phil. "I want you here for Christmas. My best friend is beside me."

Sarah has placed Phil's gifts under the tree hoping he would be home for the holiday this year. He finds the usual trousers, shirts and socks in his package. In a slender box is a silver pen from Jena. "This is for you to use when you write to me," she smiles.

Phil, Laura and Jena waken late the next morning. The aroma of cloves and cinnamon drifts to their rooms.

"Mother's cooking is one thing I miss at school. I could sit and enjoy the smell of ham and pumpkin pie forever."

Phil devours his dinner as though it is his last one.

This week is the first time Jena has been happy at home since her brother went away. One afternoon Phil goes to the convent with her. He meets Sister George.

"She plays very good, Sister. In her letters she writes a lot about you and the music she plays."

"She's a good student. We've had some nice talks together. She loves music. I pray she continues lessons for many years."

"I'll mention it to Mother. That may help."

The duo walks on a soft fluffy blanket of snow as they travel home. After a short snowball battle they go in the house.

On the kitchen table are mugs of hot chocolate, with tiny marshmallows floating on top.

"This is just like old times. It's good to be home. It's great to taste Mother's home cooking and her hot chocolate. Food is not this good at college."

He wraps his fingers around the hot mug. Sarah joins them at the table. Phil tells her about his conversation with Sister George. Sarah listens, but makes no comment.

In the evening, Phil plays lively tunes on his harmonica.

"I remember when you got that for Christmas," Jena says.

Phil is home for nine days. On Sunday, and New Years Day, Al again accompanies his family to Mass.

Two days later, Al is at work. Laura helps her mother do dishes. Jena walks with Phil to the bus stop. She stands in the melting snow and looks at Phil on the bus. She watches as her only true friend rides away.

Jena walks up the sidewalk to the house alone. Tears run down her face as she drags her boots through the snow. She enters the front door. Once more, fear becomes her unwelcome companion.

The winter snow slowly disappears. School resumes. The seventh grade begins preparation for the sacrament of Confirmation. The entire parish looks forward to this blessed event. The Bishop visits his flock and administers the sacrament to students who have reached their twelfth birthday. Jena rues thinking about that day. The white dress and veil she will be forced to wear intensifies the guilt and anger she feels. She needs no such symbols to remind her of lost innocence. Now she must listen to Sister Donna stress the two commandments that pertain to purity.

"Confirmation is a sacrament by which you become full members of the Church. With it you receive the Gifts of the Holy Spirit. You are now at an age when you approach adulthood. As your body matures, you will be tempted by sins of pride and lust. You must be alert to avoid persons, places and things that tempt you to commit sins of the flesh. At times it will be a struggle to overcome impure thoughts, words, desires and actions. You must remember that the Holy Spirit dwells within you. Your body must remain a venerable sanctuary."

The red-faced nun keeps her eyes fixed on the pages of her book as she instructs the class.

The subject distresses Jena. She wishes there was a way she could avoid this important event in her life. She lies huddled in bed at night riddled with guilt. In a fetal position, she lies with a thumb locked securely in her mouth. She suffers restless nights.

Jena dreads the ordeal as the day approaches. After the final day of instructions, one at a time, the class is led to that dark closet. She confesses foolish deeds. "I fought with my sister. I was disobedient to my mother."

She feels no relief from the priest's absolution as she says her penance. *No words from the priest can make me a worthy child of God,* she reflects. *Only God understands my sin. Only God can forgive it.*

Bishop Burne arrives the next day. It is a cool Sunday in mid-April. The girls wear white dresses and short, sheer veils. The boys have on dress suits and ties. The class walks in pairs from the classroom, around the block, into the church. The Bishop celebrates a Solemn High Mass. Fathers Kelly and Karl assist him. After reception of the Holy Eucharist, members of the class kneel at the altar rail. One by one, the Bishop extends his hand over each of them. On each forehead he forms a cross with holy oil. He confirms them with the chrism of salvation. As he anoints them he prays: "Accipe signaculum doni Spiritus Sancti." ("Be sealed with the Gift of the Holy Spirit.") Then he strikes a light blow on the cheek of the child.

Jena recalls the painful blow of her father's hand on her jaw two summers ago. To her, that of the Bishop symbolizes her unworthiness to receive this sacrament. *He must know the soiled state of my soul.* Today she feels anger and guilt. *I hate you Dad. You stole my innocence and brought me sin and shame.*

The class walks out into the bright mid-day sun. Marie Reinor is Jena's sponsor. She and her husband Bill, Uncle Ray and Aunt Peg, join the Bordeau family for dinner.

"This will be our final celebration until Laura graduates in four years," Sarah mentions, as she serves dessert. Jena is nervous. She wants to go to her room and get out of the white dress and veil. She wants to put on her Sunday dress.

Monday at school, Sister Donna informs the class of one more event about to occur. "Our girls have been chosen for the May crowning this year. It is an honor. You will wear your Confirmation dress and veil."

For this annual event, one girl is selected to place a wreath of flowers on the statue of the Virgin Mary. As the nun speaks, Jena makes a silent vow. *I'll never wear that white dress and veil again. It's an insult to God. This is one humiliation I'll not take part in.*

The first Sunday in May, Sister Donna leads the girls to church. All of them, except Jena. She sits in the back pew with her mother.

"Why do you refuse to be part of this ceremony to

honor the Mother of God?" Sarah is appalled by her actions.

"I won't walk down the aisle again and have everybody watch me in that dumb dress and veil."

"Once you make up your mind there's not a thing anyone can do to change it. You're as stubborn about this as you were about your birthday party."

Her classmates fill the front pews. The organist plays "Salve Regina," as the girls walk to the side altar. Megan climbs a tall ladder. She reaches up to place the crown of flowers on the statue. Her arms are extended toward the Virgin's head. Her flimsy veil brushes against a candle and burst into flames.

An usher runs down the aisle and pulls the burning veil from Megan's head. He throws it on the floor and smothers the flames with his shoe. Loud gasps echo through the church.

Jena sits immobile, terror stricken, as she watches the calamity. *It's all my fault this happened. I was unworthy to receive Confirmation. Now God punishes me because I refused to honor His Mother today.* Jena sits next to Sarah, silently condemning herself.

Jena's mental wounds continue to fester. There is no solace within the family. She has no friend, no one she can trust. *My life is in Your hands Lord. Only You can free me from this shame. Only You can cleanse my soul from sin.* She talks to the only One who understands what she is going through. Then she sinks into fitful sleep.

CHAPTER 13
A HAPPY SURPRISE

Sister George gives Jena the bad news after her weekly lesson today. "When summer vacation begins in two weeks the convent will close for renovations. All the sisters will be away. The practice rooms will be closed for three months. We will resume your lessons in September."

Jena comes home heartbroken. She goes from the kitchen to the basement in search of her mother. As she walks to the dining room she finds Sarah seated on the living room sofa.

The woman sees the tragic look on her daughter's face. "What's happened at school today?" she asks.

Jena stands near the doorway. "Today Sister George told me the convent will be closed all summer. No one will be able to use the practice rooms until next September. I don't know what I'll do for three months without my music," she cries.

Sarah pats her hand on the seat next to her. "Come here and we can talk about it."

Jena walks in the room. Her mouth drops open. She is stunned by what she sees. In the corner of the room stands a mahogany upright piano. Above the keyboard, inside narrow sliding doors, a set of rollers holds a thin, perforated piece of sheet music.

"Where did this come from?" she squeals.

"When Phil was home he told me about his conversation with Sister at the convent. She said you will do better with more practice. When she called later to tell me about the convent closing, I had a talk with your father." Sarah smiles, pleased to see the glow on Jena's face. "He told me to look for a piano of our own."

"Did Sister tell you where to buy it?" Jena gets up, goes to the piano and runs her fingers over the ivory keys.

"No, she didn't. I saw an advertisement in the newspaper for a used one. Your father decided we should buy it."

"I'll bring my music home tomorrow. I won't need to practice at the convent the last weeks of school."

"It will be nice to finally hear you play," Sarah tells her. "Tonight you can use the sheet music from the piano bench. It winds on the rollers and plays as you pump the pedals. After supper we can listen to some popular tunes. You can try some of them now for us to hear."

"Laura can do that. I'll wait until I have my own music. I don't want to sit and let the piano play without me touching the keys."

This evening Jena does supper dishes. She has a difficult time believing her parents would do such a wonderful thing. She whispers thanks to God for this miracle as Laura sits and pumps the pedals. Her mother and sister sing songs to melodies that seem to flow in the air. Jena can't remember when she last heard her mother laugh and be as happy as she is this evening.

It was two years ago that Sarah first saw her daughter huddled on the sofa with a thumb in her mouth. The more Jena plays her music the less she engages in that offensive habit.

An ecstatic girl kneels beside her bed tonight and prays. *Thank You, Lord, for this wonderful gift. The piano could only have been sent by You. I probably shouldn't ask for anything else, but maybe You can find a way to send a solution for some other problems I have here at home. Thank You again, Lord. Amen.*

When Jena goes to collect her music at the convent

Thursday, Sister welcomes the good news. "I'm very happy for you. When I return next fall, if there's ever a problem when you practice at home, you may come back here any time."

This summer Jena spends many hours at the piano. One day Sarah tells her daughter, "Play that nice piece Sister gave you before she went away."

"The name of it is ARAGONAISE, Mother. I'm glad you like it. It's one of my favorite pieces, too."

Every time Jena practices she remembers to play Sarah's special request. The piano is a godsend for both mother and daughter. It brightens Sarah's life and finally puts an end to Jena's bad habit. In the daytime music drives frightful ogres from the young girl's mind. During hot summer nights dreadful demons appear to prevent peaceful slumber.

Tonight Jena drifts off to sleep thinking about Phil, wishing she didn't have to wait five months until he comes home for the holidays. In the still of the night she is terrified by a recurrent nightmare.

She is walking along railroad tracks. In the distance she sees a train speeding toward her. She hears a shrill whistle blowing. Soon a huge black engine speeds toward her. She begins to run from the tracks. Her shoe string gets caught beneath a rail. Jena struggles to get free. She cannot untie her shoestring to free her foot. She watches the train rush toward her. The whistle shrieks on and on as the train speeds closer. The small girl stares at the monster about to overtake her. "Help me! Help me!" she yells.

Jena wakens to the sound of her voice crying out in the dark room. Her body trembles, drenched with perspiration. She lies awake. The blare of the train whistle echoes in her mind.

She does not remember her dream the next day. She goes about the chores her mother assigns her. This Saturday Jena scrubs the bathroom floor and vacuums the living room carpet. Laura washes and waxes the kitchen floor. Al tends to his yard work in the morning. In the afternoon he retreats to his room. From his desk radio he listens to a baseball game. The announcer's loud voice calls the plays. Shouts from excited fans blast through the house. Jena is unable to concentrate on her music with this incessant commotion.

It is a blessing for Jena when Sister George returns in August. At her first music lesson Sister inquires, "How have you managed practice at home the past months? Did you have any problems?"

"I learned most of the pieces fairly well. I find it easy to practice weekdays, but Saturdays are a problem."

"Is it too much work for you? Are you tired of playing by the end of the week?"

"Oh, no Sister," Jena replies. "The problem is too much noise. Weekends Dad listens to baseball games. The radio is so loud I can't concentrate on my music. It was a lot better when I came here on Saturdays."

"Remember what I said when you got the piano at home. You may practice here any time you want. I'm giving you extra work to prepare for our recital this year. You can start to study here again on Saturdays."

"What if my mother won't let me?" Jena frowns.

"You have progressed beyond your required program outline. I will phone her and explain that the recital requires extra work. You need help with the more advanced piece you must learn. Your mother won't question my word," Sister insists. "This new work will be difficult, but I know you will be able to master it in time."

"My mother likes to hear ARAGONAISE. I play it for her every time I practice."

"I believe she'll like these new pieces." Sister hands

Jena two new compositions to study.

Jena has lost interest in going to the movies. Saturday is the day she has the most time to practice. This becomes her first priority. Now Laura and her friend Megan go to the theater together. They take short bike rides around the back roads near home. Once in a while Jena joins them when they roller skate on the sidewalk in front of the Bordeau house.

Music occupies the greatest part of Jena's life. It calms her days. At night, bad dreams continue to invade her sleep. The same nightmare appears and frightens her.

Her foot gets stuck on the railroad track as the train speeds toward her. There is no escape. The train is about to run over her. "Help me! Help me"! she screams.

The nightmare comes to an end as a sudden jolt wakens the girl, soaked with perspiration. She trembles, terrified by the sound of her voice crying out in the dark room.

Seated at the breakfast table with the family, Sarah continues to interrogate her daughter. The woman repeats her question once more.

"What is the matter with you? Laura tells me your screaming wakens her at night. What frightens you? Tell me," her mother demands.

"There's nothing to tell you. I don't remember what happens in my stupid dreams. And I don't want to talk about it," she cries, and stomps from the room.

After Jena leaves the kitchen, Sarah turns to her husband.

"Al, this attitude of Jena's frightens me. Will you phone Ray while I'm at Mass with the girls? I think it will do all of us good to take a walk in the country. If it's okay with Ray and Peg, I'd like our family to visit them this afternoon. It might help Jena if she gets away from the house awhile."

"I'll tell you what Ray has to say when you get home."

Al relaxes in the upholstered chair in the master bedroom. Bright sun shines through the window. The radio blares as today's game is about to begin. After Sarah returns home, he turns down the volume when he talks to her.

"My brother will expect you this afternoon. Peg has a beef roast in the oven. The meal should be ready when you and the girls get there. Ray will drive you home in the evening."

"It's such a beautiful day. I thought you might want to come with us. There won't be many more days like this. Now that the leaves are off the trees, cold weather will soon be here. Then we won't take long walks. Come with us," she urges.

"There's a double-header today. I don't want to miss it."

"Jena never spends any time with you any more. That could be part of her problem. I'm sure it will make her happy if you come with us. It will make all of us happy."

"Don't worry about her so much. She's just in one of those girl stages. She knows ball games are an important part of my weekends. You go and enjoy your visit," he insists.

Sarah finally accepts defeat. She and the girls depart without Al. About half-way to Ray's house, they stop on a narrow wooden bridge. They lean on the thin rail to watch small fish and minnows swim in clear, cool water. Bright red and brown leaves float among tiny bubbles that ripple down the narrow stream. Farther into the country, Sarah and the girls walk along a long, dirt road that leads to Ray's house. In the distance, Peg and her daughters sit on the front porch.

"You made it in good time," Peg smiles as she greets them.

"We took time to enjoy the scenery. It feels so good to be in the fresh air and smell the flowers. We stopped on the little bridge to watch the fish in the creek and take a rest."

Sarah talks between sips of cold lemonade. "The water is so clear. We could see colored stones at the bottom of the stream. But I'm sure you must have seen all this many times."

"We rarely walk across the bridge. Ray drives us into town so we miss the things you enjoy so much."

Kim, 12, and Lily, 15, near the same ages as Jena, 12, and Laura 14, take their cousins to an upstairs bedroom. Jena takes a jig-saw puzzle from a shelf and spreads the pieces over the desk. Laura takes a box of Chinese checkers from a shelf. She, Kim and Lily return downstairs and play on the porch until dinner time.

After the meal is finished, the four girls sit outside. They watch the older sisters, Dana and Kory drive away in a car on a date with their boy friends. Peg, Ray and Sarah sit and talk in the living room.

"Jena is so quiet and stays by herself most of the time," Peg tells Sarah. A concerned look appears on her thin face. The short, slim woman brushes thick, curly brunette hair from her forehead. She has deep brown eyes. "Doesn't she feel well? She's always been so active. I've never seen her so still."

"I'm worried about her Peg. That's actually the reason for this unplanned visit," Sarah admits. "She screams out loud in her sleep. Either she can't remember what she dreams or she refuses to tell me about it. I thought a long walk in the country would do her some good. But she remains as isolated as ever."

Sarah dabs tears from her eyes with a dainty, white linen handkerchief.

"Maybe all she needs is a vacation," Peg suggests. "Why don't you let her stay with us this week? You can pack some clothes for her when Ray takes you and Laura home. He can bring them back here and give them to Jena."

"I'm sure Al won't object. He doesn't see much of her any more. They always spent so much time together with yard work. But since his promotion, he seldom spends time with any of us. Perhaps that's part of her problem. She could be angry that she and her dad no longer work together. I wish she would tell me what bothers her."

Sarah brushes tears from her cheeks. She lowers her eyes as she rubs the tiny cloth between her fingers.

"You need something to calm you down." Peg goes out of the room. She returns with two aspirins and hands them to Sarah. "These may help you to feel a little bit better."

Sarah takes them with a drink of cold lemonade.

Ray goes out to the porch. "It's time for us to leave," he tells Laura. "I want to get back home before it gets late."

Jena comes inside when her mother calls her.

"Your Aunt Peg offered to let you stay here for a few days. We think you will enjoy spending some time in the country. Your Uncle Ray will bring you clothes. You can have fun with Kim and Lily." Her mother smiles. "I'll see you next Saturday when you come back home." Sarah gives her daughter a hug, then she and Laura drive away with Ray.

Jena shares a room with her two younger cousins. On a bed in the corner of the room, Jena has her first peaceful sleep since her brother was home for Christmas. In the mornings, Jena goes with Kim and Lily to the hen house. They fill a small basket with fresh eggs. Aunt Peg cooks them for breakfast.

The three girls roam the countryside in the afternoons. One day Jena sees a tractor in the barn. "Who uses this?" she asks Kim.

"My dad does. He plows the field before he plants our garden every spring."

The next day Jena overhears Lily and Aunt Peg talking in the kitchen. "Jena doesn't say much any more," Lily tells her mother. "When she walks with Kim and me, she's always quiet. I don't think she likes it here."

"Aunt Sarah said she is worried about her. She doesn't know what's wrong. She hopes Jena will be happy here in the country, but it doesn't seem to be helping her. Your father's taking her home this evening. Aunt Sarah wants to be sure Jena goes to Mass tomorrow."

"Why would it be so awful if she missed church one Sunday?" Lily scoffs.

"Sarah is very strict about their religion. Sometimes I feel she may be too rigid. Perhaps this is why your father never goes to church. He may feel the rules are too severe." Peg takes a deep breath. "It certainly was a shock when Rita broke off with Bob and entered the convent. For so many years she claimed she was going to become a nurse."

"She still can be one. Aunt Sarah told me that's what she will study after she finishes being a postulant."

"Sarah said Bob took it real hard when Rita decided to break up the day before he left for college. It seems as though she couldn't make up her mind what she wanted to do with her life. I'm surprised that with all the praying that family does, they have trouble with Jena. She was always carefree. She's the last child I thought would have problems."

"You know what Aunt Sarah says, 'God will take care of us. He knows what's best.' I wonder what she thinks God is doing for her family now," Lily quips.

"I'm sure it's nothing serious," Peg states. "Time seems to heal most problems."

Jena has tears streaming down her cheeks as she

goes upstairs to pack. She avoids eye contact with Aunt Peg as she thanks her for the visit. She is silent as Uncle Ray drives her home.

When she sees her mother, Jena doesn't mention the long conversation she overheard between Lily and Aunt Peg.

"How did you like your visit?" Sarah asks.

There is a sad expression on her daughter's face. "They live different than we do. I like the country but I don't think Kim or Lily wanted me to stay there." Jena looks into Sarah's eyes. "Don't ever send me there again."

Sarah knows it is useless to ask why she feels this way. Jena sits down at the piano and murmurs, "I'm glad we have the piano now. I missed my music all week."

CHAPTER 14
DECEMBER 1941

Jena returns home from Sunday Mass anxious to tell her brother about the piano at home and her week in the country. *I'll not tell him about my bad dreams*, she decides. *I just want him to read about good things that happen here while he is away.* She sits at the kitchen table. Her pen moves rapidly across white stationery. Sarah busies herself at the counter preparing dinner.

"Mother, do you think I should tell Phil we are having roast turkey with stuffing today? He told me that's the meal he misses most at college. Would that make him homesick?"

"I think there are better things you could write about than what I cook for dinner."

"My letter is almost finished. I just wanted to know if I should tell him about his favorite meal."

Jena scans the letter before she puts it in the envelope.

Dear Phil,
It was a warm day last Sunday. Mother, Laura and I walked to Uncle Ray's house. He drove Mother and Laura home in the evening. Aunt Peg asked Mother to let me stay and visit for a week. It was such a long time since we went there. I forgot the country is so beautiful where they live. It was like the times we would roam the woods when we lived on the hill.

They have three cats. I liked Rusty more than the cats. In the mornings I would go with Kim and Lily to the barn to collect fresh eggs. We had them for breakfast every day.

We have a piano at home now. You told Mother what Sister said about my music. There was a piano in the living room one day when I got home from the convent. It is a roller piano. Laura pushes her feet on the pedals and plays it. We sing some popular songs from the sheet music that came with it.

Sister gave me some advanced pieces to practice this summer. I now play DANCE OF THE DOLLS, FUR ELISE, and WALTZ IN A MINOR.

Laura told me she lays on her bed and listens to me play. Mother said she likes my music, too. You can hear me play the next time you're home. Uncle Ray doesn't have a piano so I was happy to get back to my music.

Monday, Laura and I begin eighth grade. Next year we'll be in high school. It's scary to think about that.

I'll soon be thirteen. Before long, I can go away to school, like you did.

I hope you will come home for the holidays this year. We had a great time together last Christmas.

There's not much else to tell you. I miss you.
Your "blood sister,"
Shorty

Two months pass before Jena hears from her brother. One Saturday morning she finds a letter in the mail box addressed to her. She rushes in the house, away from the cold wind this crisp autumn day. She stands in the hallway and rips open the envelope. It is a short message written on notebook paper.

Dear Shorty,
This will be brief. Things are hectic here at school.

I'm studying hard for semester exams. I just want to let you know I won't be home for Thanksgiving. I plan to be with the family for the Christmas holidays.

Take care of yourself. And enjoy your birthday. I'll be thinking about you then.

Your "blood brother,"
Phil

Jena runs to the living room. "Mother," she shouts, "I just got a letter from Phil. He said he'll be home for Christmas."

"You've got six weeks to wait. Just calm yourself child."

Time creeps by for Jena. She grows impatient. There are still two weeks before her brother comes home.

It is a Sunday morning. Sarah and the girls are together at the breakfast table. Al is at early Mass, as usual. Soft music from the radio in the living room drifts to the kitchen. The music stops abruptly. There is a brief moment of silence.

A man's voice strains as he interrupts the program. His voice quivers. He clears his throat. He is frantic as he shouts into the microphone: "Japanese planes have attacked Pearl Harbor. About 75 planes were spotted over the island of Oahu. The first attack came at 7:55 a.m. Hawaiian time...."

Sarah's face turns white. She is stunned, unable to utter a sound. Al walks in the door as the news release ends.

Jena does not understand the horror the news reveals. In the first display of emotion Al sees from her in months, he listens to her exclaim, "A war. This is exciting."

"Sarah, what the hell is she raving about?" Al demands.

"We just heard an announcement on the radio. The

Japanese bombed Pearl Harbor this morning. We're at war with Japan."

Al's face turns red. He roars at Jena. "You think war's exciting? War is hell. There's nothing good about it. Countries battle one another. Our boys leave home and many of them will be killed. Your brother may be called to fight overseas. We may lose him."

Jena's face is white. Tears erupt. They run down her cheeks.

"Oh, no! Not Phil!" she yells. "Not my brother. He can't go to war and get killed. God won't let that happen to him."

"Jena got a letter from him yesterday. He plans to come home for Christmas. Do you think he could be called to the army before that?" Sarah wrings her hands as she paces the floor.

"We have to listen to the radio. The President will make an announcement. We'll know something soon. Some men will enlist right away. Others will be drafted." He considers another possibility. "Phil might be allowed to finish college before he is drafted."

"That would keep him here for eighteen months. The war might be over by then." A glimmer of hope appears in her eyes.

The nation erupts into chaos this cold winter day. A sense of tranquillity no longer exists. At Mass, Father Karl offers prayers for the victims of the sneak attack on our military base at Pearl Harbor. Sarah and the girls pray aloud with the congregation. They silently pray that Phil, safely in college, will be spared from active duty in the war.

Two weeks later, Phil arrives home with his books and two large suitcases. It is a sad Christmas, not only for the Bordeaus, but for all families throughout the nation.

Al joins Sarah, Phil and the girls for midnight Mass. Jena and her brother walk side by side in new-fallen snow. Opening presents after church is more ritual than pleasure. The turkey dinner is clouded by a pall of fear and apprehension. At age 20, the war strikes a sharp blow to Phil. He is drafted along with millions of other young men who will face injury or death in a foreign country. Phil dreads the prospect of going to some far-off land. He finds little consolation in the fact he and Barry will travel together. Fear cuts through his soul like the thrust of a bayonet. He shares this terror with no one.

On this cold, snowy evening, the family shares a sad farewell meal with Phil. This first Friday of the New Year, in gloomy silence, the Bordeau family walks to the train station. The platform is crowded with people who wait with sons and brothers about to depart. Many will disappear from their lives, never to return home again.

Jena squeezes her brother's hand as they push their way through the dense crowd. In the distance, a train approaches. A white trail of smoke draws an ominous streak through the twilight sky. A shrill whistle blows, stabbing the crisp air. To Jena, it feels like a dagger piercing her heart. The train pulls to a stop. The family huddles close to Phil as a tall, slim Army sergeant reads names alphabetically from a sheet of paper attached to a clipboard.

Jena snuggles close to Phil. Young men queue up as the soldier calls out names in a loud, brusque tone. Puffs of frost pour forth from mouths of people crammed together.

"Philip Bordeau," the sergeant shouts.

Jena's tears begin to flow. She pulls a new deck of cards from her pocket. "These are for you to use at camp."

She sees tears roll down her brother's cheeks. The sergeant motions him toward the steps of the train.

"Good-bye, Phil," the family shouts. "God bless you!"

"So long, Phil. Write to me," Jena cries.

He passes through a lighted car. The family watches

as he takes an aisle seat. He keeps the window seat empty.

When the sergeant calls, "Barry Kale," the young man waves his hand. His parents and the Bordeaus shout farewells.

Inside the train he takes the seat Phil has saved for him. The sergeant follows the last man into the train. Tears freeze on cheeks red from the bitter cold.

Steam vapors escape from a vent on top of the engine. They hiss and float up toward the sky. The shrill whistle echoes once more. Giant wheels turn around and around on shiny, silver tracks. The crowd stands immobile until the train becomes a tiny dot of light that disappears into the dark, lonely night.

The Bordeaus join other towns people on their somber walk home. Icy snow crunches under heavy boots. The sound crackles through the rigid silence that dominates the town.

At home, Jena rushes to her room. Downstairs, Mrs. Bordeau hears the mournful sobs of her youngest child. A short time later, she hears Jena cry in her sleep, "Help me! Help me!"

Sarah paces the floor. Her black rosary slips between her quivering fingers. Silently she prays, *Dear Lord, heal our family's wounds. Put an end to this terrible war. Bring peace to the world.* The woeful woman roams through the house unable to rest. Her body trembles while her family lies asleep in soft, warm beds.

CHAPTER 15
A TIME TO WEEP

Sarah grows weary of Jena's eagerness to don a uniform for school next fall. She has five months before eighth grade is completed and already she grows impatient for a change in dress style. The woman worries the young girl cannot accept the physical changes in her body. It may be possible Jena hopes loose jumpers will conceal her mature figure. It's as if she is embarrassed, even fearful, of becoming a woman. *Could this be why she evades her father?* The problem continues to mystify Sarah. *Thank God I'm done with the monthly curse. I thank the Lord I won't have to face this ordeal with another daughter, after the trauma Jena experienced. Now that Al and I have resumed conjugal relations, I need not worry he will spend time with another woman,* she silently rejoices. It is close to a year since she has followed Father Karl's advice and now her fear of pregnancy has passed.

With the holidays over and Phil away at camp, she attends to the matter of her annual checkup. "It's been a long time since you've been to see me," Doctor Mueller scolds. "You know that it's important to take care of your health. I notice in your file it has been eighteen months since your last visit."

He looks through her folder and asks, "How have you been? Are there any problems since your last visit?"

"I've not been ill. I'm happy to tell you I've reached my menopause. It's been eight months since my last regular period and four months since I've had the last light one."

Doctor Mueller completes every test necessary for her physical. He leads Sarah into his office and instructs her to be seated near his desk. He is always stern, but today his usual gruff manner disappears. His demeanor is serious.

"Did you find something wrong with me?" She searches his face for some positive sign from him.

"You're not ill, Sarah. And you're not going through change of life." An unusual softness enters his voice. "What I do find," he says gently, "is a pregnancy."

"That can't be true, Doctor," she gasps. "There must be some mistake. I'm forty-one. I can't have another baby now."

"I've been very thorough in my exam. I assure you Sarah, you are pregnant."

"But I thought I was going through menopause." Tears fill her eyes. "What will I tell Al and my family?" she sobs.

There is no harsh lecture, no criticism, just a doctor being gentle as he reveals a diagnosis his patient refuses to accept. He answers softly. "Tell them you will have a baby in June. I must caution you to have regular monthly examinations. Sometimes there can be complications with a pregnancy at this stage of a woman's life."

Sarah is oblivious to what Miss Winters says. She reads the small card the nurse hands her: "Next appointment February 20 - 10 a.m." *How can I tell Al I'm pregnant? I'm afraid of his reaction. How can I explain this to the girls and Phil? The news will shock them as much as it does me. Lord, why did this happen to me?* she agonizes.

The glow from Sarah's soft, brown eye vanished long ago. Not even a look of contentment graces her still-attractive face. This evening Jena stands beside her at the kitchen sink. Tears roll down the woman's cheeks as she rinses dinner dishes. Her daughter wipes the blue and white stoneware in silence. *Mother must be sad because Phil is going to war,* the girl surmises.

Jena is the image of Sarah, as a child. Her oval face, fair complexion and brown eyes have the same doleful expression as this devastated woman. Finally, the girl breaks her silence.

"Are you sick, Mother? Are you sad because of Phil? Do you think he will go overseas and get hurt?"

"I feel fine, Jena. Don't ask so many questions. Go and practice your music," Sarah orders.

At bedtime, Jena goes to Laura's room. "I saw Mother cry after dinner tonight," she whispers. "Do you think she's sick?"

"She must be worried about Phil. After basic training, almost all soldiers go overseas. That's probably what's wrong."

"But I never saw her cry before," Jena goes on.

"Phil's never gone to war before, either."

"I pray every night that God will keep him safe. Maybe the war will end before he goes overseas." Jena wipes tears from her eyes.

"You two were pals. Mother and you get real sad and worry about him. He's also my brother. I pray he'll be safe, too."

In the privacy of their bedroom, Sarah approaches the father of her unborn child. "I saw Doctor Mueller today." She hesitates, then turns her face away from him.

"I know. It was for your regular checkup."

"He was upset that it was eighteen months since my last visit. He had some bad news for us."

"Well, what's the matter this time?" he groans.

"I don't know how to tell you." Her body trembles.

"Whatever it is, say it and get it over with."

"He told me we're to have a baby." Her words rush out.

Al grins. "Doc must be too old to know what he's doing."

"I told him it must be a mistake, that I was sure I'm going through menopause. But he assured me I'm pregnant." She turns her back to him. Her eyes fill with tears.

This message gets to him. "You're pregnant. He said you're pregnant," Al roars.

"I was so sure it was change of life. But he was very careful with the examination. When he said I am pregnant, I was as shocked as you are. He told me the baby is due in June." Once again she repeats the doctor's diagnosis, trying to accept the fact.

"Hell, you avoid me so much. How often do we ever get together? The few times anything does happen between us, you get pregnant," he growls.

"I didn't make this baby by myself. You want me to please you. I try to be a good wife. And this is what happens."

"Rita and Bob should be married and have a baby. I thought when I reached forty-six, the next baby in the family would be a grand-child. But what does that girl do? She locks herself in a convent. Now we're the ones to bring a new addition to the family. Well, it's too late to change things now."

"There must be a reason God sent us this child."

"You can believe God sent it, if that makes you feel better. I just want it all to be over," he fumes.

Al turns from the room, exits the front door and enters the cold winter night. His footprints in the snow lead to the corner bar.

Alone in her sorrow, Sarah remains despondent as she lies awake in a half-filled bed. Her husband returns after midnight. The strong odor of liquor fills the room. He slumps into bed. Within seconds, he is asleep.

Sarah gains little weight the next two months. The

loose dresses at home and the coat she wears outdoors conceal the slight change in her figure. Until now. She begins to gain weight the following two weeks.

It is the second Sunday in April when she decides to tell her youngest daughters the news. Seated with the girls at the breakfast table she clings to her coffee mug as though it will furnish her support for this fateful task.

"After Phil left in January," she begins, "I went to see Doctor Mueller for a checkup."

"Are you sick Mother?" Jena interrupts.

"No. It was my annual visit. There's nothing the matter with my health." Then she quickly states, "Doctor Mueller said I'm to have a baby."

Unprepared for the shock, Laura blurts out, "You can't mean that. You're too old to have a baby. Rita is twenty-two. How can you have a baby now?"

"Women my age are still able to bear children. It may not happen very often, but I assure you, I am pregnant."

"When will you have this baby?" Laura asks curtly.

"Doctor Mueller said it's due in mid-June."

Jena is dubious. "Why don't you have a big stomach? A baby is supposed to make you get bigger." Her question is made as a challenge. She seeks an explanation.

"I haven't put on much weight so far. I'm gaining more now. It will soon be obvious to everyone that I'm pregnant."

"Why didn't you tell us in January, when you learned about it?" This is more of a confrontation than a question from Laura.

The mother tries to ignore the hostility in Laura's voice. "I wanted to wait until it shows." Her tone is devoid of emotion. She merely presents a factual statement.

"Where will the baby sleep?" Jena presents a more pleasant aspect of this sudden surprise.

"We'll use Phil's room for now. I'm going to Bridgeport with Aunt Peg to buy a crib, dresser and layette. Everything will be ready when I bring the baby home."

"I can't wait," Jena exclaims. Her face lights up as she rubs her hands together. "It will be like a doll to play with. I'll write to Phil today and tell him the good news."

"No Jena. I will tell Phil and Rita."

The next day Peg drives Sarah to Bridgeport. The baby furniture arrives by truck Friday, when Laura and Jena are in school. By the time they arrive home, their brother's room has been converted to a nursery.

This evening Sarah writes to her son.

Dear Phil,

I am happy you will be home with us soon. Before you get here, I have some important news for you. I am to have a baby in June. I've made your room into a nursery until you are discharged from the army. Then Jena and Laura will share a room again. Jena is anxious for you to use her room while you are on furlough. We pray God will keep you safe and well. We all look forward to having you home soon.

Love as always,
Mother

She mails Phil's letter, then makes a phone call to Sister Rita. This is the first call to her daughter since she entered the convent.

"Is something wrong at home?" Sister asks. "Has anything happened to Phil?"

"There's no problem. I want you to know Phil will be here next Friday for a two-week furlough. All of us will visit you his first Sunday home. But there is some important news I must tell you before we see you." She pauses briefly. "In January, Doctor Mueller told me about my pregnancy. I am to have a baby in June."

Sarah thinks about Laura's outburst when she heard

the news. She is relieved to hear Sister's response. Her voice is calm and compassionate.

"This must be God's way to fill the void in your life now that Phil's in the army. I'll pray all goes well for you and the baby. Take care of yourself," she urges. "Tell Phil I'm anxious to see him and I pray for his safe journey home."

With this burden off her mind, Sarah awaits the arrival of the baby. She confines herself to the house the final weeks.

Phil arrives home six weeks before Sarah is due to give birth. He goes upstairs, sees the nursery in his old room and plops his duffel bag in Jena's bedroom.

"You'll not get much sleep at night once the baby's here," he warns Jena. "You're old enough to be a great help to Mother. Take good care of the little one for her, Shorty."

"It will be nice. I'll have over two months to be with it before school starts in the fall. I told Mother it will be like taking care of a real live baby doll." She laughs at the idea.

The family visits Sister Rita after Sunday Mass. She embraces Phil. This tall slim soldier is about to be swept into battle in some distant foreign land. She is exuberant to be with her young brother before he departs.

"You look good in your white habit," he comments. "Jena keeps me informed of all the news about you. I see she's been truthful. You look as happy as she tells me you are."

"And look at you," she smiles. "You're quite a handsome man in your crisp new uniform. You must have women trail you every place you go," she teases.

"There's no time for any of that. We're too busy preparing to battle the enemy."

"When do you expect to go overseas?"

"That's all secret information. We soldiers don't even

know the destination until we're on our way. We have two weeks of furlough. After that, what happens to us remains in God's hands."

Sarah is relieved there is no mention of the baby. Her concern now is for Phil to enjoy the short time he has with his family. There are profuse farewells as they leave Rita standing outside the convent door.

Several times during his stay at home Phil journeys up the hill to visit with Barry and his parents. In the evenings, he plays games in the dining room with the family.

He listens to Jena practice. Later, Laura pumps the piano pedals as they sing to the melodies of piano-roll music.

"Play us some tunes on your harmonica."

"Okay, Jena. But I'm out of practice. It's been a long time since I've had this in my hands."

The family listens to his lively renditions. "You were just kidding," Jena laughs. "You still play real good."

Once again the family walks to Sunday Mass together. Sister Rita joins them at church to share prayers on this special occasion. Father Karl offers Mass for every man and woman serving in the armed forces.

After church, he greets the young soldier. "We all wish you God's blessings. You are in our hearts and in our prayers. God bless you, my son," Father prays.

The family sits at the dinner table as strains of soft music drift from the living room radio to the dining room.

"I sure enjoy your turkey dinners, Mother. I wish it were possible to bottle the smell of it cooking so I could savor the aroma when I'm far from home. Nobody else can make apple pie taste good as yours." Phil validates this praise as he slowly consumes a second large serving of pie a la mode.

The Bordeau family stands on the Sage train platform this cool spring evening. There are no dry eyes among them. As Jena huddles close to Phil, she traces her finger along a single chevron on the sleeve of his khaki uniform. He takes his hand from his pant pocket and shows her a deck of worn cards.

"Barry and I played with these many nights at camp," he whispers. "I think of you Shorty, every time we use them."

He puts his arms around Sarah as he is about to board the train. "You take good care of yourself and that new baby," he tells her.

The loved ones shout their goodbyes. Phil flings his duffel bag over his left shoulder. He boards the train and takes a seat by the window. The family waves as the train pulls out from the station. They stand motionless as it disappears from sight.

They plod their way home. Not one of the family notices the beauty of the night as brilliant stars twinkle in the sky above.

"Why didn't Barry get on the train with Phil?" Jena asks.

"He left earlier. They won't be together now. Barry's in the infantry. Phil's in the medical corps," Sarah answers.

Weeks later, when Sarah goes into labor on the second Wednesday in June, she phones Peg. Jena and Laura watch their aunt carry a small suitcase as she walks their mother to the car. The girls return to the table and continue their breakfast in silence.

Twenty minutes later, Peg stands at the hospital admittance desk as Sarah is signed in. Peg phones Al at work.

"Sarah's in the delivery room."

"Let me know when the baby gets here. I'll be at the bank until we close. Then I'll take a cab to the hospital."

It is three-thirty. Peg phones Al again.

"Sarah had the baby. She's in her room now," she

informs him.

"Is it a boy or a girl?" he asks.

His reaction neither surprises nor shocks her.

"Sarah had a six-pound five-ounce girl."

Now he asks, "How's Sarah?"

"She's just fine. She said it was the least difficult birth she'd had. She feels Doctor Mueller was right when he insisted she have this baby at the hospital."

"But it will cost a lot more than the other four who were born at home. Tell Sarah I'll have dinner with the girls then go to the hospital."

Peg phones Laura at home. "Your mother had a baby girl an hour ago," she tells her.

"How's mother? Is the baby all right?" she ask.

"They're both fine. You're to have dinner ready for your father when he gets home. He'll visit your mother after the evening meal."

Laura has fried ham, boiled potatoes and green beans prepared at dinner time. The girls sit opposite Al at the table. There are few words spoken during the meal. Laura initiates the conversation.

"Dad, tell Mother I said hello and hope she feels good. When will you be home tonight?"

"I'll be with your mother until visiting hours are over. I should be home about nine o'clock. I want you girls in bed by the time I get back."

Jena does not say a word. After Al goes out the door, she tells Laura, "We're more excited than he is."

"He's had four kids. Men don't get excited about babies like women do."

"It's been a long time since I was born. He should be happy that mother and the baby both are okay."

"Well, I never want a baby when I'm over forty," Laura declares. "I'll get married and have my kids when I'm young. This baby is like a second family."

"That's one thing you're right about. This baby will

be four years old when I graduate. If I go away to college she won't even get to know me."

At bedtime, Jena approaches her sister. "Laura, I'm afraid to be alone in my room while mother's in the hospital. Can I sleep with you until she comes home?"

"There's nothing to be afraid of here."

"But I'll have bad dreams if I'm alone in my room."

"Okay. But only while mother's away. I don't want to hear you scream in your sleep. You'll have to go back to your own room when Mother gets home."

Jena feels slightly safer now that Laura agrees to share her room. Her sister will be close to protect her from anything bad happening to her while their mother is away.

The girls are impatient to see their new sister. Al goes to the hospital every evening to visit his wife. The first three nights he returns and tells the girls their mother and baby sister are fine.

"When will they be home?" Laura asks him.

"Your mother will be home Wednesday. The baby has fluid in her lungs. It has to clear up before she can come home."

Before Sarah is released Wednesday morning, Father Karl goes to the hospital to baptize the baby. Peg takes Sarah to visit Angelica every afternoon. Each day she tells her daughters their sister is still ill.

The baby is two weeks old when she dies. Following an Angel Mass, Al, Sarah and their three daughters attend a private burial ceremony. The body is laid to rest in a tiny casket in Al's mother's grave on top of the grandmother's casket in Sage Cemetery.

The day after the funeral service a Gimbel's truck stops at the Bordeau house. Two men remove the unused baby furniture and return it to the store in Bridgeport. In the evening, Al and Ray bring Phil's bed and dresser from the cellar and place it in the empty room.

Jena never saw her baby sister before she died. She watches her mother shed tears as she goes about her household routine day after day.

"Why does God let a baby die, Mother?" she asks.

"He must want another angel in heaven," Sarah sighs.

It is the first experience Jena has with the death of anyone close to her. It intensifies her worry for the safety of her brother fighting in a war, far away from home. It is another sorrow for the young girl as she struggles with nightmares that continue to cause endless nights of restless slumber.

CHAPTER 16
FLIGHTS OF FANCY

On the way to Sunday Mass, Sarah, Laura and Jena are joined by a neighbor, Myra Adams. This is the first time Sarah has left the house since the death of her baby, four weeks ago.

"It's good to see you out with your daughters again," the short, plump woman smiles. "When none of the neighbors saw you in the spring, we were concerned for you. I was relieved to learn you weren't ill." Myra clutches Sarah's hand and looks into her dark, sad eyes. "With a new baby you wouldn't have had much time to fret about Phil being away at war. I'm sorry for your loss," she murmurs softly.

"Mother said baby Angelica's in heaven now," Jena says. "She may be Phil's guardian angel. She can watch over him and keep him safe while he's away."

"You're a good Christian family," the woman remarks. "I'm a Christian, too. But I would be angry if a child of mine died. With you having a daughter in the convent, I can understand your thoughts about angels. You have been blessed with a decent husband. The loss of a baby must be a burden for him, also."

"Early in my pregnancy, the doctor cautioned that my age could put both the baby and me at risk. It saddens our family to lose her, but I lived with that possibility for months."

Sarah becomes weepy and wipes tears from her eyes. "Your husband must give you the strength to get through this sad time. With his support, it's just a matter of time before God heals your sorrow."

So this woman believes Dad's a good man. It would shock her to know the truth about him, Jena seethes in silence.

"God has blessed us in many ways," Sarah admits. "Rita chose the religious life and Al's job provides for our every need. Last week he received a commendation at work from the district manager. Sage Bank leads all others in the sale of War Bonds. Now that our shipyard builds boats for the navy, and Sage Bank has a contract with them, our bank is number one in the district."

Her eyes begin to glow. A look of pride spreads over her face.

Laura is silent as she walks beside her mother. She offers nothing about the baby, or angels, or anything to do with the war.

That must be why mother never complains any more about money for my piano lessons, Jena reasons. *Dad makes a lot of money. And he doesn't have to pay for Phil's college now.*

Jena continues to worry about her brother. In the few letters he sends, there is no mention of where he is. Black marks blot out many words he has written. Each time a letter arrives, Jena remarks to her mother, "I pray each day Phil's not in the battles we read about in the newspaper."

Every time, Sarah responds the same way to her daughter's comment. "Men in the medical corps must be with soldiers in the midst of battle. They care for the wounded. Phil may be in a danger zone. That could be why his letters are censored so much."

Sarah is very thin since the birth of the baby. Jena looks at dark circles under her mother's sunken eyes and wonders if the woman is still sad because the baby died or because she worries about Phil and his safety.

A letter addressed to Sarah arrives today. "It's a short note from your brother," she says in a mournful tone. She reads it then hands it to Jena.

Dear Mother,
I'm too busy to write more often. Our work keeps us busy. Tell Shorty I still have the cards she gave me. There's nothing going on over here I'm allowed to write about. All of us want to get this war over with and come back home. Keep your letters coming. I look forward to mail. Keep us in your prayers. We all need them. Tell Barry's parents I said hello.
Love to all,
    Phil

"Phil must be in a safe place now. This is the first letter with no black marks on it," Jena sighs. "I miss him so much." Her eyes fill with tears. "I miss the times we tossed barbells back and forth and how we would sit in the shed and talk. We sat at the table and he drank sassafras tea the night before he left for college. God can't let anything bad happen to him," she cries. "He wouldn't. We need my brother home to keep us safe."

In the afternoon, Jena goes to Abe's store with a list of groceries to buy. Today she carries two full bags up the walk. In her hand is loose change Sarah lets her keep.

"Mother, the bags are so heavy I came straight home." She puffs as she sets them on the table. "I'm going to take my dimes and go down to the candy store. Maybe Jeff will give me some of those tiny gumdrops today."

"Jena, Jeff is ill. He went to a sanitarium a few days ago. He isn't there to give you kids free candy anymore."

The young girl's eyes open wide. Her face turns ashen.

"How could he get sick so fast? Why would he be in a hospital?" Jena raises her voice in disbelief. "It must only be a rumor. I saw him in the store last week. He didn't look sick to me."

"He has tuberculosis. That must be why a man in his mid-thirties was always so thin. He isn't allowed to handle food in the store any more. He sold the business before he went away."

"He's such a nice man. He was good to all of us kids. And I didn't even tell him good-bye," she whimpers.

Jena is anxious to meet the new owner. She runs down the walk and stops at the little store next to Abe's. She looks through the glass door. There's no one at the counter.

A small brass bell above the door jangles as she enters. She listens to it echo, "Jingle. Jingle. Jingle."

As she stands in front of the display case, Jena's eyes dart around the room. Magazines and newspapers are scattered on back shelves. She turns her head and stares at penny and nickel candies inside the glass case. No one is here to wait on her. Jeff had soft music flow from his radio all day long. It is quiet in here today. Suddenly she misses the tall man with deep blue eyes and big smile. *I bet there won't be any free gumdrops and licorice sticks like Jeff gave me,* she reflects. Just gazing around the messy store she finds things are different from when her friend handled the business. She misses Jeff's cheerful, "hello."

Jena wishes somebody would come so she could buy something.

She hears a sound come from the back room. The drapery on the doorway opens. A heavy man seated in a wheelchair appears. Perspiration covers his red face. His T-shirt is wet under the arms and around the neckline. He struggles to guide two large silver wheels through the narrow aisle. He manages to get the chair behind the counter.

"What do you want to buy?" he asks, with a wheezy

voice.

"Give me five sticks of black licorice."

"What's your name?" His deep voice is hoarse.

"Jena. What's yours?"

"Sam. It's so hot today. Do you like summertime?"

"Yes, I do." She looks at more candy in the case. It is difficult for her to choose what she wants.

"Is there anything else for you?" He sounds impatient.

"A banana popsicle. It'll keep me cool."

"Go to the freezer and take one out."

As Sam puts the candy in a bag, Jena bends over the freezer, lifts out the twin popsicle and returns to the counter.

"Here's your candy."

He stretches his arm toward her. She hands him a dime. He takes the coin and holds her hand.

"Come back again soon," he puffs.

Jena pulls her hand away. She is relieved to hear the rattle of the metal bell as another customer enters. She rushes past a tall, dark-haired man and out the open door. She runs up the sidewalk onto the front porch. Her heart beats fast as she sits on the glider and licks the frozen treat.

Sarah steps outside and stands in front of the door. She seldom goes to the candy store and hasn't seen this owner.

"How do you like the new man?" she asks Jena.

"Sam sits in a wheelchair. He's old, heavy and his clothes are all sweaty. I bought five pieces of licorice and he didn't give me a free strip. I wish Jeff would come back. I like him."

"He has to stay at the sanitarium in the mountains for several months. He'll never come back here. You'll have to get used to it. Jeff is too ill to work."

"I don't want to go in that store any more. There are

new back shelves with magazines tossed around on them. Jeff had the place neat and clean, not messy like it is now. Laura can go there if she wants to. I'll give her the money to buy something for me."

When she shops at Abe's, Jena saves most of the change her mother lets her keep. She never ventures into the candy store alone. She only goes there when Laura is with her.

It is another hot, lazy summer day. After lunch, Jena approaches her mother. "There's a new movie at the Strand. It's a good war story with Humphrey Bogart and Ingrid Bergman. Can Laura and I go to see it this afternoon?"

Sarah gives her usual reply, "Ask your father."

"I'll just have to come back to you. He'll tell me to ask you again. I really want to see this movie. It's about the war. And my favorite movie stars are in it. Can we go?"

"I told you to ask your father," her mother insists.

Jena goes to her parents' bedroom. She sees Al reading in his upholstered chair. His right leg is bent over the arm.

"Dad," Jena calls out.

He raises his eyes from the book. "What's the matter?" He does not seem angry. She walks toward him.

"Mother wants to know if Laura and I can go to a movie."

"What's the name of it?" He turns his eyes away from her.

"It's "Casablanca," a war movie. Can I go?"

"I don't have any spare change now." She notices he does not check his pockets or wallet before he answers.

"Can I go if I have enough money of my own?"

"If your mother allows you, then you can go."

He begins to read again.

Jena walks from the room. She passes Laura in the dining room. "See if Dad will give you money for a movie this afternoon." She whispers so their father won't hear. "Mother said we can go if Dad says it's all right."

Laura stops by the bedroom door.

"Do you want money for the movie?" he asks.

"Yes. Jena said we could go if I get some money."

"Here's some change. Now you can go."

Jena overhears the conversation and goes back to her mother.

"Dad said he doesn't have change for me. If I have my own money he'll let me go." She stands and stares at her mother. "When he saw Laura, he called her in the room and asked her if she wanted money for the movie. He has enough for her but none for me." Her face is flushed. She looks at her mother with a cold, angry stare.

"If he gives Laura money, I'll pay for your ticket to the movie."

Sarah dries her hands on the blue apron that covers the front of her floral cotton dress.

Laura bounces into the kitchen. "Dad gave me some money. This will buy tickets and popcorn for both of us."

"Leave now and be home in time for dinner," Sarah says.

When they leave the house Sarah breathes a sigh of relief.

Once inside the theater, Jena forgets about her father's rejection. The story holds the imaginative girl spellbound. Jena sits captivated as the plot unfolds.

Rick is a saloon owner who falls in love with Ilsa in Paris. Her husband is Victor Lazlo, a resistance leader and national hero. At the time she meets Rick, Ilsa believes her husband has been captured and killed by the Nazi. When she learns her husband escaped and is alive, she disappears from Rick's life.

Once more their lives and destinies come together in

Rick's cafe in Casablanca, to the sound of their love song, "As Time Goes By."

The bittersweet story ends as Rick arranges for Ilsa and Victor to escape together on a plane to freedom. As they part at the airport, Rick assures Ilsa, "We'll always have Paris."

Jena flees from reality as she is drawn into romantic suspense. Outside the theater she questions Laura. "Do you believe love like that can ever exist between a man and woman?"

"Oh Jena," she huffs, "it's only a movie. The bad guys lose, the good guys win, and the hero always gets the girl."

At the dinner table, Sarah asks the girls, "Did you like the movie?"

"Oh, Jena believes some of these stories could be true. She thinks people can fall in love and be happy ever after," Laura laughs. "She doesn't believe people just make up these stories so there's movies for us to see."

"That stuff about the war is true. Look how we have to sacrifice with food coupons and rationing. And we aren't even where the bombs fall," Jena contends.

"You know that your father sells War Bonds at the bank. And we do have food stamps and gas rations," Sarah concurs. "Almost every family in the country has at least one person in the armed service. We don't need bombs to fall here to let us know we're at war."

"There are men who make a lot of money because of the war. They steal visas from travelers and sell them to people who want to get to a country that's safe," Jena goes on. "That's how the couple in the movie escaped from Casablanca."

"She really thinks that's true." Laura laughs at her sister again. "The more exciting a movie is, the more Jena likes it."

"Some of these things really do happen. It's dangerous for people caught in the middle of a war," Sarah maintains.

"It's true some men and businesses make money in war-time," Al admits. "Sage Bank makes more money than any other branch office now. The metal works has a government contract to build boats for the navy. And our bank handles their accounts. It is sad but true that the only time some people can get rich is during a war."

Dad makes a lot of money now. And he won't give me a few cents to see a movie. The only time he lets me have money is when Laura wants to go. She can't go alone, so he'll give her enough for us both, Jena fumes. *He doesn't know Mother lets me keep change from the store, or that I save most of it. He must think if he doesn't let me have any money, he will keep me trapped in this house.*

Al is at the bank, Sarah is doing laundry and Laura is busy cleaning upstairs. Jena polishes the mahogany table and chairs, buffet cabinet and china closet in the dining room, then vacuums the carpet.

Now is a good time to clean inside the china closet while no one is around to bother me, she decides. She washes the crystal glassware and delicate tableware and returns them to clean glass shelves. She stands on a chair to dust on top of the cabinet. Behind the ornate facade she feels some paper. She lifts up a magazine. On the pink cover is a picture of near-naked women. On inside pages are women in obscene poses. They wear black garter belts with net stockings and tiny, black lace panties on their near-nude bodies. She tosses the tabloid back to its hiding place.

Jena recalls the first time she was in Sam's candy store. There were rows of magazines tossed about on back shelves. Jeff had family magazines and newspapers up front, where everybody could see them. *The magazine probably comes from Sam's place. He's just a dirty old* man. He grabs my hand and won't let go of it. This trash must come from his place. It's not safe outside the house and I'm afraid to be inside it. What happened to the safe, happy world Phil and I enjoyed when we lived on the hill and here, before he went away?* Now, it seems like an illusion.

When Jena goes to bed tonight, thoughts of the magazine bring newfound fears. She tosses and turns in fitful sleep.

Laura grabs her sister's arm and shakes it.

"Wake up, Jena. Wake up," she hollers.

The bewildered girl jumps up. She sits and looks at her sister. "What are you doing in here?"

"You were screaming in your sleep."

"I had a bad dream," Jena sobs. She clings to the sheet.

"What did you dream?"

The nightmare flashes before Jena.

She is in a place that looks like the upstairs hall. There is a row of doors on each side. She opens each door, one after the other. The rooms are pitch black, too dark to see anything inside. At each door she hopes for a way to escape. She leans on the wall, terrified. She is trapped there, with no way out.

"I can't remember. I don't want to think about it."

"You're just afraid because we saw a scary movie. Go back to sleep," she orders, then goes back to her room.

After Jena falls asleep the nightmare haunts her again.

She is upstairs and opens each door in the hall. The rooms are dark. She searches, but can't find a way to escape. She stands rigid in the hall, unable to move.

She wakes up screaming, "Help me! Help me!"

Laura wakens when she hears Jena holler. This time, the older girl ignores the outburst and falls back to sleep.

Jena tries to stay away from her father whenever possible, but she can not avoid him at the dinner table. Other than this, their paths seldom cross. She watches the sadness in her mother's face. *This woman must be a saint to live with that man,* the young girl broods. *I wonder if she ever saw the dirty magazine on top of the china closet. Maybe if I write something nice for her she'll feel better.* Alone in her room, Jena jots down words meant to console.

> FOR MOTHER
> I love you more than words can say
> for all the things you do each day,
> you wash and iron and mend clothes, too,
> and tasty meals are cooked by you.
>
> I hope my music does impart
> some happiness within your heart
> for Mother Dear, I tell you true
> my heart is filled with love for you.

Jena takes the paper down to her mother. "I wrote something." She smiles. "Do you want to read it?"

"What is it?" Sarah asks.

"It's a poem. I wrote it for you."

Jena hands her the paper. Sarah holds a dish towel in one hand and the girl's gift in the other. The frail, slender woman glances at the poem.

"I don't like poetry, Jena," she remarks. She hands the paper back without reading it. Sarah continues to wipe the dishes. She does not notice the proud gleam disappear from her daughter's face. Jena goes up to her room and tears the paper to bits. She is hurt and angered by Sarah's rejection of her work. The girl believes the only person who cares about her is Sister George.

At her next piano lesson she tells her mentor, "I don't feel like I belong in my family. My parents treat me like something they would rather not have around them. I don't know why they ever had me. I think they would be happy if I just disappeared."

The intensity of her young pupil's words shocks the nun.

"You are always welcome here, Jena. Your love for music is a special gift. It can bring much joy to your life. Treasure it. The comfort music brings you is a blessing from God."

Sister offers consolation with sincerity the young girl can not remember having heard before. Jena continues to follow Sister's guidance. Most of her leisure time is spent at the piano. There are occasional bike rides with Laura and Megan. Some Saturday afternoons after practice, she goes to a movie with Laura. There she finds an escape from her surroundings.

The life she leads is an isolated one. She tries to keep out of her parents' way. She continues to pray for a place where she can be loved and feel safe.

With summer comes the week for the firemen's annual carnival. On a Sunday in August, a crew assembles the maze of tents and rides. A monstrous ferris wheel can be seen a half-mile from town. A huge carousel and a variety of rides are erected. Side-shows form the perimeter of the fairgrounds.

On a hot, humid evening Sarah and the girls walk to the amusement park. Jena stares at large pictures painted on musty, soiled canvas tents. They depict people who perform inside.

"Mother, look at the picture of the lady with a beard. And there's a fat woman on the platform. How can she walk when she's so big?" Jena exclaims. "Look, she weighs over 300 pounds."

"It must be very difficult for her. Some abnormal people work at carnivals because they can't find jobs anywhere else. This is why people pay to see them. They make a living letting others stare at them. It's a pity such people exist. But God must have a reason for it, even if we don't understand it."

"Look at the tiny people in this picture. Can we go in to see them? Can we go inside, Mother?" Jena begs.

"You are not to laugh at them," Sarah tells her.

Jena feels sorry for them. She could never laugh at them.

Sarah goes with the girls to the next tent and watches a snake-man sitting in a cage. Reptiles slide over him. The crowd listens to the snakes hiss. Jena looks in awe as the muscular man picks up a long, thick snake in his hands. It twists around his body.

"Why doesn't he get bit?" Jena asks.

"He probably has been one or more times. He must have serum available to counteract the venom if a snake bites him."

This is the first year the girls go to side-shows. They want to see every one of them.

"Here's a picture of a tattooed man, Mother. Let's go look at him," Laura urges.

All three of them are disgusted by the sight of this abnormality. Sarah grabs the girls and rushes from the tent.

"Why would anyone do that to his body?" Jena frowns.

"I can't imagine why anybody would want to have his skin punctured by needles. It must be a sin to defile one's body with ugly pictures painted all over it. This is all we're going to see," Sarah says. "No more tents for us tonight."

"I don't want to see any more, either," Jena agrees.

Sarah did not come for the side shows. She brought the girls here to enjoy the rides. The whirl-o-plane is their first stop. Up in the air they spin around and around. The girls are dizzy when they step to the ground. Next, they sway in a seat on the giant ferris wheel as it comes to a halt with them at the top. Their faces are pale when the ride finally ends.

"That's worse than when we rode down in the elevator in Bridgeport," Jena shudders. "I'm glad my feet are on the ground again."

Sarah joins them on a final ride. She sits on a wooden bench on the giant carousel. Bright gilded horses lift the girls up and down. They spin in circles as a nickelodeon blasts out strains of "The Sidewalks of New York." The girls laugh and hold onto the reins until the ponies come to a stop.

Jena wanders behind Laura and Sarah. Near the rear of the fairgrounds she stares at a group of strange-looking couples. Golden loops dangle from ears and around wrists and ankles of the women. Bright beads of orange, red and yellow encircle their necks. Their bare feet are covered with dust. Golden bracelets jingle-jangle on wrists and ankles as dancers twist and turn to lively music from guitars, tambourines and castanets.

Sarah turns back to find Jena. She grabs her by the arm. "You are not to linger in this unholy spot," she scolds.

"I want to watch them," she begs. "They're having fun. Look how happy they are when they dance."

"They're gypsies, Jena. They're thieves who have no homes. They wander all around the country to live on whatever they can get," her mother warns. "We mustn't go near a gypsy camp."

Jena glances backward as Sarah leads her away. They pass a tent with a moon and stars painted on it.

People stand in line outside.

"Why don't they go inside?" Jena asks.

"They wait to have their fortunes told."

"How does anyone know what will happen in the future?" Jena asks. She has a perplexed look on her face.

"Only God knows what is to happen," Sarah instructs her. "These people use tarot cards to try and convince others they can see what will occur in their lives. It's evil. It's a serious sin to have your fortune told. You give to another the power that belongs only to God."

"But these people are so happy," Jena objects. "They can't be so bad. God made them just like He made us."

"Just because someone is happy doesn't mean he is good. A person may suffer on earth but find peace in heaven. And some happy people can be servants of the devil and be doomed."

Her mother's criticism does not dampen the warmth Jena feels for these strange wanderers in bright colorful clothes and shiny gold jewelry.

At nine o'clock all rides come to a halt. Folks wait for the main event of the evening. The Bordeau females stand among the crowd with heads tilted toward the sky. A small, thin, blond woman and a dark, black-haired man climb a high rope-ladder. They wear skimpy, skin-tight silver outfits as they step onto a small wooden platform. A long tightrope stretches to another platform on the opposite side.

The woman lifts a long metal pole. She balances it in both hands and takes a cautious step onto the wire. Her nimble foot takes a short step. She sways back and forth and balances the pole to steady herself. Mid-way on the wire she teeters on bent knees. The pole wavers from side to side like a seesaw. She pauses, then breezes across the final section to land safely on the opposite side. The crowd cheers and claps.

The muscular man seats himself on a shiny red

bicycle. He balances another long pole across the handle bars. He rolls onto the wire and across the vast expanse. The cyclist glides the vehicle across the wire as the pole dips from side to side. The large wheels rock backward and forward as he struggles to steady himself at the halfway spot. Amid anguished "ohs!" and "ahs!" he propels the treadles onward. The wheels make a sudden burst forward and the brave aerialist joins his partner on the platform. The couple embrace. Their costumes glisten as the spotlight shines on them. The pair slips down the heavy rope to the ground as cheers and applause ring out in the night air.

Sarah leads Laura and Jena toward the exit gate. Once again the rides come alive. Barkers shout as they beckon folks to the shows. Music blares as they pass the bright lights of the carousel. They go through the gate for a late walk home.

In Jena's sly, fanciful imagination the nomads represent a happy, carefree way of life. She awakens Sunday morning as visions of gypsy dancers enter her thoughts.

After Mass, a pensive girl returns home and retreats to the back yard. In a light-blue cotton dress she sits on a white wooden lawn chair under the tall cherry tree. With pencil and paper in hand, words are swift to cover empty pages. When Sarah calls her to dinner, Jena takes her project upstairs to her room and places it on her dresser.

After the meal, Jena moves to the step of her brother's shed. She rests her head against the door. There is a slight breeze this bright sunny day. Robins twitter in the trees. Jena's thoughts drift back to the sights and sounds of a muggy summer evening. She envisions a metal pot hanging over a bright campfire. Barefoot couples spin around and around in the dusty ground in the darkness of that mystical Saturday night. She fantasizes about the love, adventure and freedom of these strange people. It is as though another spirit controls her hand as the pencil flies across the page. Her imagination runs wild as she scrawls a poem.

A GYPSY GIRL

One night I saw the gypsies
 who roam from sea to sea
and view the scenic wonders
 I long so much to see -
from tinder on a crackling fire
 shimmering sparks did fly
beneath a field of brilliant stars
 that twinkled in the sky.
These vagabonds roam far and wide
 with courage to be free
and visit unknown places
 alive with mystery.
The gypsies are the freest
 of all the folks alive,
a band of sprightly wanderers
 who struggle to survive.
I saw them join together
 around a glowing fire
to dance and sing and savor
 all that they desire.
Gypsy girls danced wild and free,
 stars sparkled high above
and slowly dying embers
 cast a spell of love.

I yearn to be a gypsy,
 to laugh and dance and love
and lay upon warm summer grass
 beneath the stars above -
I'd wander over hillsides
 through all the forest land
with my Bohemian fellow
 as we walk hand in hand -
we'd mingle with the hoot owls
 that fly through dark of night
to wile away the quiet hours
 until the dawn's bright light.
Gypsy girls don't have to stay
 beneath a roof at night
there are no chains to bind them,
 they let their hearts take flight.
If I were free to do these things
 a different girl I'd be
I'd wander over sandy shores
 and watch the roaring sea,
I'd sing and dance and laugh and love -
 how happy I would be
to end a life of endless fear
 and know at last I'm free.

    Jena puts the poem beneath her pillow. She vows to find a way to escape from this prison that consumes her with fear. Tonight she enjoys sweet reverie. She dreams of merry wanderers who sang and danced and laughed so care-free at the carnival on a hot, mysterious summer night.

CHAPTER 17
A CONSPIRACY

As fall begins, Jena embarks on a new adventure. This brisk, breezy September morning she walks to high school, a half-mile further than grade school. Classrooms are in an old, two-story brick building. Last year, Laura had Rita's sponsor, Sister Monica, for home room. She is tall, with fair complexion and eyes that twinkle when she smiles. Jena is happy to begin ninth grade with her. Laura has young, petite Sister Frances. Morning classes are religion, English and social studies. After lunch, Laura shifts to a small room for typing and shorthand. Jena moves across the hall for Latin, science and algebra.

Laura enjoys being with new classmates she met last year. Jena avoids the more affluent tuition students who come from other towns. She is pleased to wear the blue gabardine jumper and long-sleeve, white cotton blouse. The dress code gives her a sense of belonging. It eases the feeling of being different from other female classmates. More than anything else, she wants to be accepted by her peers. She abhors the ugly secret she lives with. *I'm the only girl in school who's different. The other girls don't live a lie.* The thought disgusts her.

The new studies are no challenge for her. Music continues to be the root of her existence. The hours of practice show results. Sister George advances her to more difficult compositions. Chopin becomes the girl's favorite composer. She works extra hours with Sister to perfect his

VALSE IN C# MINOR and NOCTURNE IN E FLAT.

One Wednesday after her lesson, she remains at the convent when Sister offers special help. The recital planned for last year was canceled. Not enough pupils were prepared to be presented to an audience. Jena feels no remorse. She dreads thinking about ever having to sit in front of a large group of strangers and have them watch as she plays.

Dinner is on the table when she arrives home.

"Where have you been all this time?" her father demands.

"At the convent." Her body quivers. Her voice shakes.

"The convent, hell," he fumes. "You have a piano here. You must have been with someone you don't want us to know about," he rants. His eyes remain focused on his food.

"Al, Sister had her stay after the lesson today. She has some new pieces she needs help with." This is one of the rare times Sarah defends her daughter. "Call Sister George if you don't believe Jena or me."

"I don't have to make a call to any nun. We bought that damn piano so this girl would stay home. From now on she's to practice here." He looks at his daughter as he gives the order.

Jena rushes through the remainder of her meal and retreats to her room. *One of these days I'm getting away from here.* This is a solemn vow she makes to herself.

The months drag by for the distraught young lady. As the war rages on and with conditions at home intolerable, Thanksgiving and Christmas holidays hold only a trace of joy.

When spring arrives, Jena reads in the newspaper of a jamboree to take place in Longhill. She remembers her mother's tales about the jamboree her parents went to some years ago with Uncle Ray and Aunt Peg, and how much they enjoyed the music and seeing live performers. The only thing that ruined the night for her parents was coming home to learn of the fire across the street from their house while the children were alone.

Jena devises a plot for her to attend the jamboree and escape from the turmoil at home. She talks with Laura about it on a bright spring day. As they walk to school this morning, Jena presents her plan.

"Laura, there was an announcement in yesterday's newspaper about a jamboree in Longhill next month. I know how much you like that kind of music. Wouldn't it be good if we could figure a way to go to it?"

"There's no way we could ever go," Laura laughs. "Mother and Dad would never consider taking you and me there."

"I have a plan all worked out. I know how we can go," Jena insists.

"This is one of the wildest ideas you've ever had. You know Mother and Dad will never let us go on such a long trip. There's no way on earth we can go."

"Mother and Dad don't have to know anything about it before we leave," Jena tells her. "We can go one Friday night when they are in bed. The two of us can creep downstairs and put a note on the kitchen table. *We went to the jamboree. We'll be home Saturday for dinner.* They won't hear us go out the front door. Then we can get on a bus and be on our way."

"Jena, it's another one of your crazy dreams," Laura grins. "Two of us out alone at night is a scary idea. It wouldn't be safe. Another thing. Dad would knock our heads off when we got home. He would lock us in the house forever."

"Come on, Laura. What can he do but yell at us and warn us never to do it again?" she argues. "You know he's never upset by anything you do. You're his favorite daughter. And you know it. He never yells at you. If you go, he'll never punish you." Jena looks her sister straight in the eye. "You have to go with me. I'm determined to do it and I can't go alone."

"Sure, anything I ask Dad for he gives me," Laura agrees. "But he'll never give me any more money if I do this crazy thing."

"That will never happen. He'll be angry at you only a little while. But he'll stay angry and punish me as long as I'm in this house."

"Well, maybe. But I don't have any money. Even if I did, the two of us can't travel alone on a bus late at night. It wouldn't be safe."

"That's no problem. Megan goes wild for those country singers. We'll ask her to go with us. She'll jump at the chance to see them in person. The three of us will be safe together."

The thought of something adventurous fascinates Laura. "The more you talk about it, the more I like the idea. Okay, wise guy. How do we get money for bus fares, admission fees, breakfast and lunch on Saturday?" Laura questions. "And we need money to come back."

Maybe you'll come back, Jena thinks. *But I'll never come back here. I've finally found a way to escape and not be a prisoner in my own house any longer.*

"No problem." Jena throws up her arms. "I saved money from change Mother lets me keep for candy. You know I won't go in that store alone since weird Mr. Sam bought it. I have over five dollars in a small metal bank inside my dresser drawer. I know how we can collect a lot more in the next five weeks."

"I can't believe you would dream up such a scheme," Laura gasps. She has a look of wonder on her face as she stares at her youngest sister. "How can I get enough money for me?" She suddenly is excited by the scheme Jena has contrived.

"Dad always gives you money when you ask for it.

"For the next six Saturdays you'll ask to go to the movies. Mother won't let you go alone, so Dad will give you enough money for both of us. You know he always does," Jena reminds her.

Laura is dubious. "So where do we get money for the trip?"

"Use your imagination." Jena throws out her hands with a look of disbelief. "We go on long walks and not to the movies. We can visit the old house on the hill and walk through the woods. We'll get Megan to come with us. She wears a wrist watch. She can keep track of the time."

Jena explains every detail so Laura has no excuse to change her mind. "Then we save all the money and have more than enough for the jamboree," she beams in relief.

Laura talks with Megan at lunch time. "This is a very big secret," she instructs her friend. "Jena has a plan for us to go to a jamboree a few weeks from now."

"Great! I've always wanted to go to one. What has your devious sister thought up now?" Megan laughs.

Laura tells her how they plan to save money and leave in six weeks. "After our parents are in bed, we'll meet at my house. Then the three of us will take a bus to Longhill."

"We'll get home too late Saturday night," Megan objects.

"No problem." Laura throws up her hands as she imitates her sister. "We'll eat lunch and go to the noon-time matinee. We'll be home in time for dinner."

"We better not tell anybody else about this," Megan whispers. "It will never happen if our parents get even a hint that we plan to do anything this wild."

The next weeks go as planned. But there is one exception. Laura and Megan have no idea what else Jena has planned. It is the third Friday in May. The three girls get together at lunch to check their money and make arrangements for Megan to be at the Bordeau house eleven-thirty tonight.

"Be sure you're on time," Jena insists. "We have to get the bus in front of Abe's store at midnight."

After dinner, Jena goes to her room. She takes a small suitcase from her closet and fills it with several changes of clothing, a flashlight and her small bank with extra money in it. Then she hides it beneath her bed. *I must think of some way to explain the suitcase tonight.* She pauses to think. *I know what to do. I'll tell Laura I have a change of clothes to put on before I go to the jamboree. The ones I wear will be wrinkled from sitting on the bus and in the terminal in Longhill all night. That should satisfy her curiosity.*

Jena goes downstairs and sits at the piano. *This may be the last time I play my music,* she regrets, as she practices. *But it will be worth the sacrifice if this trip frees me from this den of iniquity.* She continues in deep thought. *The neighbors and people at the bank believe Dad's such a good person. They compliment mother on what a nice family she has.* The black notes dance across the sheet music as Jena plays one piece after another. *I wonder what they'd all think if they knew the dirty little secrets about my father and how I live in fear of him. This place is a den of lies. Tonight I'll free myself.*

The girls are in bed by ten o'clock. By eleven o'clock their parents enter the downstairs bedroom. Jena and Laura dress and wait for Megan to arrive. It is after eleven o'clock. They watch for their friend from the front window in Jena's room.

The excited schemer sits on the bed by the window. Jena recalls her mother's words as they sat and talked at the kitchen table the first New Years Day Phil was away from the family. *"I wish Phil's school were closer to home so we could see him on weekends,"* Jena said. She remembers her mother's reply. *"That's what it is to grow up. He must learn to live on his own, with no family to guide him."* Jena sighed. *"I can't imagine how it will be, out there alone, without you in my life Mother."* That cold winter was so different from this warm spring night. Not only is the weather a strong contrast, but also her new desire to flee her once-peaceful home. Jena misses her brother tonight. *It would be safe for me at home if Phil had never gone away,* she writhes with regret.

A half-hour passes and still there is no sign of Megan.

"Why doesn't she get here?" Jena sulks.

"We have to wait a little longer. It takes time for her to walk from her house. She'll be here soon," Laura answers.

A full moon lights up the sidewalk. It is almost midnight. Both girls lose hope that Megan will be here tonight.

"Laura," Jena whispers. "It's twelve o'clock. I hear the bus pass the store. We'll never get to the jamboree now," she cries.

"Something must have happened at her house. She wants to go even more than we do," Laura says. "Let's go to sleep now. We'll find out tomorrow why she didn't get here."

Jena stays at her window until one o'clock. Tears stream down her face. She thinks of the suitcase under the bed and the money she saved. "I'll never get away from this damn place." But no one is awake to hear her bitter words.

Saturday, Jena wakes to a bright sunny day. Her low spirits are no match for the sun that shines through her bedroom window. She stares at the suitcase. "Damn that Megan," she weeps.

Jena is still angry when she and her sister meet Megan this afternoon. The long walks up the hill are over. Preparations for their secret journey were all in vain.

For the first time in six weeks they go to a movie.

"Where were you last night? We waited until midnight for you," Jena grabs her arm and raves.

Megan opens her mouth and is about to answer. Before she can utter a word, Jena rants on. "When I heard the bus pass down the street, I knew we would never get to the jamboree. What happened to you?"

"My mother must have suspected something was wrong. She never let me out of her sight all evening."

"It sounds like an excuse to me. You were just too afraid to go. Why don't you admit it?"

"Honest, Jena. My mother stayed in the living room past eleven. Maybe she found the money I hid under my pillow. She must have been worried why I had so much money and how I planned to use it. I fell asleep before she went to bed. Maybe we can go next week."

"Tonight is the final performance. It will be some place else next week," Jena complains.

"Well, I'm *sorry.*" Megan taunts Jena. "There are other things we can do besides go to a jamboree. Let's just forget about it and get to the movie."

They go to see "Shadow Of A Doubt." It is one of Alfred Hitchcock's most suspenseful masterpieces.

A young girl lives in a small town, just like Sage. She begins to believe her beloved uncle is a murderer. He is handsome, smart, and people think he is a good person. But the girl suspects his true, sinister nature.

Jena thinks about the story as she walks beside her sister on the way home. *That uncle's just like my father. He's evil,* she sulks.

"Don't mope so much about the jamboree," Laura scolds. "We can go to something else another time."

The jamboree is the last thing that concerns Jena now. The terror she feels comes from thoughts of what she must face when her father is in the house. She fears she'll never escape now. She turns to her only source of comfort. When she gets home, Jena goes to the piano and abandons herself to her music.

Two weeks have passed and summer vacations begin after school today. This morning the pastor will pass out report cards in the auditorium. He will name the boy and girl from each grade who achieved the highest grade average for the year.

Today when Jena enters their home room Megan rushes up to her. "I know who's getting the awards for highest average," she gloats. "Paul Storme will get the boy's award. Guess who will get the girl's?" Her face lights up. "I looked through the papers on Sister's desk before she got here this morning."

"It must be Maria," Jena says. "She always gives answers to Sister's questions in class."

"Well, you guessed wrong. Beneath Paul's name she has written, 'Girl's highest average, Jena Bordeau.'" She flaunts at being privy to this private information.

"You're joking. I hate to stand up and recite in front of the class. No one answers more questions than Maria. She'll get the award today," Jena insists.

"Well, you'll see," Megan grins. "Don't say I didn't tell you."

This news starts Jena thinking about the announcement Sister Monica made before the last algebra exam she gave to the class. She recalls the nun telling the class, *"If a boy has difficulty preparing for the test, go to Paul for help. The girls who need help, go to Jena."*

This came as a complete surprise to the girl. It made her happy that none of the other eight girls in the class asked for her help. Naturally, that led her to believe every girl knew as much about the subject as she.

When religion class ends, the ninth, tenth and eleventh grades walk to the auditorium. Father Daniels opens the ceremony with a prayer. He now presents each of Sister Monica's students with a report card. The time arrives for the special awards.

Father calls, "Paul Storme." The boy hurries to the stage. "I present you with this statue of the Sacred Heart. You have achieved the highest average of the boys in your class this year. Congratulations."

Next he calls, "Jena Bordeau." She can feel her heart beat fast as she walks to the stage.

"You have earned the highest average of the girls in your class this year. This statue of the Virgin Mary is a reward for the good work. Congratulations."

"Thank you, Father," she responds. She has an ambivalent sense of pride and guilt as she looks at the statue of Mary. Jena holds the small statue tight in her hands throughout the remainder of the program. Outside, she tells Megan, "You told me the truth. You really did look on Sister's desk. You should be thankful she didn't catch you up there."

"She wouldn't do anything to me the last day of school. She's too nice for that. I'll hate it if we have anyone else for home room next year."

Jena does not show her mother the statuette. She goes to her room and sets it on her dresser. It is Laura who tells her mother about the award. She's surprised Sarah makes no comment about Jena's statue.

"I thought Mother would be excited about the honor you got. She just listened to me tell her about it. She didn't even ask to see it," Laura reports to her sister.

"Maybe she's still upset that I wouldn't be in the May crowning. Every once in a while she talks about it when she scolds me for something I do wrong." Jena has a smirk on her face as she turns away.

This summer Jena and Laura spend some afternoons with Megan as they ride bikes past the main street of town into the countryside. Jena always diverts them to the opposite direction when they ride toward the area where Uncle Ray and Aunt Peg live. She still remembers Aunt Peg talking about her and how much her behavior has changed. It bothers Jena to think about Aunt Peg.

These hot summer days seem endless. Newspapers report battles won and lost by the countries at war. As she watches fireworks explode in the sky from her back yard this Fourth of July, she thinks about Phil. She wonders where he must be at this moment. She doubts that anyone is safe anywhere on earth. The blast of fireworks bursting through the night, shooting brilliant colors toward the heavens, becomes chaotic. To Jena, it appears the whole world has gone mad.

CHAPTER 18
A LATE NIGHT VISITOR

The Great War rages in Europe and the Pacific Islands. Likewise, turmoil persists in the Bordeau household. Sarah continues to be concerned that the strange change in her youngest living daughter's personality continues.

Sarah ponders the actions of Jena, Al and Father Karl. *Why did Jena ignore Father Karl's instructions to tell me what bothers her? What made Al suggest she was with a boy and not at the convent the other day? The rift between Jena and her father began when he returned from his first bank conference. Why would a ten year old withdraw from girls her own age and regress to infantile behavior? When Father Karl advised that Al and I resume marital relations, why was there such urgency? Al went to bed with that tramp, Holly. But how could he discuss our most sacred area of marriage with her?*

When Al approaches his wife in bed, she is rigid. She can hear Holly's loud, coarse voice ring in her ears as she tells Mary, "*His wife is a prude who doesn't like to sleep with him.*" The thought is so painful, Sarah can not respond to his advances.

"You can't reject me forever," Al blurts out.

"I'll not risk another pregnancy or dead baby," she weeps.

"If you won't fill my needs someone else will."

Al feels Sarah's tears roll onto his arm. He turns and moves from his wife's side. An ocean could fill the distance between them now.

Saturday night, Al goes to the cafe. In the dim light he sees there are no empty tables. He sits by the front door with men at the bar. Lisa serves drinks to Al and two other men who are sitting beside him. He motions her to his side.

"Tell Holly I want to talk with her before I leave tonight," he whispers.

The barmaid nods her head in agreement.

The war is the main topic everywhere.

"Al, what do you hear from Phil?" Pete asks.

"We get a letter about every six weeks. But there's very little for us to read, it's censored so much. Black marks cover at lot of what he writes."

"It's best we don't know where our boys are or what they're doing. It keeps the enemy from getting important information and avoids unnecessary panic for us," Herb declares. "The paper reports the battles are furious. It will do us no good to know if one of our boys is in the front lines. The best we can do now is pray our boys are in a safe area."

"I agree. Let's drink a toast to the safety of our boys." Al raises his glass. "This round's on me," he offers.

Lisa bends toward Al's ear. "Holly will see you later, in the hall by the men's room," she whispers.

It is almost midnight when the three men get up to leave. When Al pays his tab his friends see the two new fifty dollar bills in his wallet.

"My good luck charms," he boasts once again.

Al walks toward the men's room. In the hall he talks to Holly. "Can I see you when you're off work?"

"I'll finish in a few minutes. Scott can handle the bar and Lisa will take care of the tables. You can wait upstairs."

She looks around to make sure the hallway is empty before she hands him her key. He takes it and slips out the back door. Ten minutes later, Holly joins him in her apartment.

"Welcome back, stranger. It's good to see you." Holly smiles. "I was hoping you would be back to visit me."

"There's something we must settle if I'm to visit you again. There must be no mention of my visits to anyone. I know Abe fired you because he found out about my first time with you. I can't afford any more of your loose talk. It's most important that our meetings be kept secret. Do you understand?"

His expression is serious. His voice is firm.

"I know your wife overheard Mary and me talk when she was in the store one day. Only Lisa and I know who comes here. No one will find out about this from us. Your wife won't know about anything. I promise."

"Hell, my wife isn't the problem. She doesn't seem to give a damn who I bed-down with," he smirks. "I'm concerned for my work. No one at the bank can learn about it. I can't afford to jeopardize my job. If you can keep quiet, we can get together a few times during the month."

"You have nothing to worry about from me. I've learned my lesson."

She sighs as she holds his hand. They walk to the bedroom. As she lies beside him in bed, she purrs, "It's so nice to have a strong, handsome man here with me again."

Al arrives home an hour later. Sarah is awake when he enters their bedroom. Neither he nor his wife utter a word. He is asleep within minutes. His wife lies awake for hours as harsh words spoken between them earlier this week spin inside her head. *He's been with that wench again tonight,* she weeps.

Late Sunday morning, the two waitresses meet at the cafe. They clean glasses and dishes in preparation for the next day. As they work at the sink, Lisa asks her friend, "How was your late night visitor?"

"He was a one-night stand until last night. He's handsome, nice, and good to be with." Her face glows.

"Did he wait in the hall for you to finish work?"

"I gave him my key. I met him in my room ten minutes later."

"You trusted a stranger with the key to your apartment!" Lisa exclaims. "What's the matter with you, Holly?"

"Believe me, there's nothing to worry about with Al. If the bank trusts him with its money, I trust him with my key. Now, tell me what happened with you last night. Did you get anybody to take you home?" Holly inquires, anxious to change the subject.

An old married man wanted me to drive away with him. He said we would have to hurry before anyone would find out he was with me. He has an old beat up car. I wouldn't have much fun hiding out with him so I walked home alone."

"I like Al, even though he has a wife and four kids. I worked in Abe's store before I got this job. One day Al's wife overheard Mary and me talking in the store. I told Mary about the one time Al and I went to bed together. This is the first time he's been back since then."

"What happened?" Lisa asks. "Did his wife throw him out? Or did he get a guilty conscience?"

"Not him," she grins. "His wife wouldn't come to shop in the store after that. And she was one of Abe's best customers."

"What happened next?" Lisa stands entranced.

"Abe found out what happened. He told me he won't allow his clerks to have affairs with any of his customers' husbands, that it's bad for his business. Then he fired me."

"I'll be sure not to mention who you go with," Lisa says. "I wouldn't want to get you into any more trouble, or maybe cause you to lose another job."

At the jukebox, Holly puts on Glenn Miller's, "A

String Of Pearls." The lively beat of the music vibrates through the room.

"Some people say blondes have more fun," Lisa goes on. "Do you think if I lost ten pounds and changed from a brunette to a blonde, I might get a nice guy?"

"There's nothing wrong with your hair. It might help if you lost that extra weight, though."

"Your flaming hair is like a red light. When a man looks at it he stops dead in his tracks. But his motor runs on and on," Lisa chuckles.

The waitresses leave the cafe as Sarah and the girls return from church. As she walks up the sidewalk, Sarah hears Holly and Lisa exchange good-byes. The smile disappears from Sarah's face. She sees Holly's short, low-cut green dress and turns her head in the opposite direction.

Sarah is unusually quiet as she works at the stove this afternoon. Jena writes a letter to her brother as her mother prepares dinner. Al leaves the master bedroom. As he passes the dining room table he watches Jena glide her pen over the white sheet of paper. He walks to the kitchen. He raises his voice as he talks to his wife.

"If any one writes Phil about things that happen in this house she'll be sorry. He has enough to worry about now. He doesn't need to know about any problems we may have here."

Jena puts down her pen and walks to the kitchen. Al leers at her, turns away, and walks down the basement stairs.

"Mother, I only write nice things to my brother. I want him to know we miss him. I always tell him we all pray he'll be safe and the war ends soon so he can come back home."

"Phil doesn't write much any more. He mustn't be able to send letters from wherever he is. Your father wants you to cheer your brother up when you write to him."

"I would never write anything to make him worry or be sad. I just want to ask him if he got my last letters."

Jena takes her letter to the mailbox. Back home, she sits on the sofa and reads the Sunday newspaper. Her father's desk radio blares through the house as he listens to the baseball game. She goes upstairs to Laura's room and talks with her sister.

"Dad warned me to watch what I write to Phil. This house is like a prison. Dad won't let Sister George help me at the convent. Mother won't let me join the Girl Scouts. I wish I could be like you. Every day you go somewhere with Megan or some other friends."

"Well, you have your music. All I get to do is lay up here and listen to you practice. At least you have that."

"Sure, I love my music. But I had to beg for it. I had to wait a year before Mother agreed I could take lessons. Then she made me keep it a secret from Dad for a long time," Jena grumbles. "When she told him I practiced at the convent, he got her to buy the piano, just to keep me in the house."

"You should be happy about it. Now you can practice as long as you want."

"Remember that day I came home late from the convent? Dinner was already on the table. Dad hollered at Mother. He didn't believe I was even at the convent. He told her they bought the *damn* piano so I would stay at home."

Jena starts to walk toward her room. "Come in here. I want you to see something." She motions to Laura. When they are inside the door she takes her suitcase from the closet. "I thought I could escape from here when we planned to leave for the jamboree. I had this all packed with clothes, a flashlight and extra money. I didn't plan to come back home with you and Megan."

"Look what you got at school." Laura picks up the

statue of Mary. "You're too smart to do such a dumb thing. How will you go to college if you run away from home?"

"Dad will find a way to keep me here. He'll never let me go away to school like Phil," she sulks. "You must never tell anybody about my plans with the suitcase. If Dad ever finds out, he'll lock me in the house. I'll never be able to get away."

As Laura reaches to put the statue of the Virgin Mary back on the dresser, it falls from her hand and breaks into pieces on the floor.

"I'm sorry, Jena," she wails. "I didn't mean to break it."

"It doesn't matter. I guess no one wants to be with me. Not even God's Mother. She mustn't want to be with me either."

"That's a terrible thing to say, just because I dropped a statue of her."

"It's true, Laura. You have a lot of friends. I don't have anyone. I'm kept a prisoner in this place. It's a good thing Dad's not here when you and I go to the country on our bikes. He'd put a stop to it right away if you or mother told him I went that far away. I believe God must have allowed me to have my music. It's the only thing that makes me happy."

"What's the matter with you and Dad? Why don't you get along any more?" Laura raises her voice. It sounds as though she thinks Jena created the hostile situation. "He and I talk together. We get along good. It's Mother I can't talk to."

"You're the one she walks beside whenever we go shopping downtown. You talk with her then. I trail behind like a stray puppy dog."

Today is the last time this summer the girls ride their bikes to the country. School begins next week.

Sunday, after lunch, Sarah and the girls take the bus to visit Sister Rita at the convent. She has a big, bright smile on her face as she greets them in her spotless, white habit. They walk together around the enormous grounds. There is a soft breeze as they proceed along the long walk to the cemetery. Sister Rita points out the grave where Al's sister lies buried. *Sister Elizabeth Bordeau 1895 - 1926* is chiseled in the small, gray, granite headstone.

"Mother, did Dad see his sister's grave?" Laura asks.

"He was here after her funeral Mass when they buried her. I don't know if he's been here since then."

"I come up here often, even though I never knew her," Sister Rita states. "I feel a closeness to her, because she's my aunt and we both belong to the same religious community."

The sun is still bright when the quartet completes the tour of the grounds. Sarah, Laura and Jena board the bus for home. After supper the girls sit on the porch glider in the warm evening breeze.

The sky is filled with twinkling stars when Sarah calls to them from inside the house. "Girls it's time for bed. Make sure your uniforms are ready for tomorrow."

Laura and Jena go to their rooms to set out clothes for the next day. In the morning, another school year begins.

CHAPTER 19
A GOLD STAR

Sister Monica is at her desk when the tenth graders arrive. Megan takes a desk across the aisle from Jena, near the back of the room.

"Looks like God answered our prayers. We have Sister Monica's home room again," Megan rejoices.

For second period, Jena has tall, stout Sister Louise as her biology instructor. The nun's raspy voice belies the kind manner she displays. Biology fascinates Jena.

"I'm anxious to dissect the starfish and the frog," she tells Laura at lunch. "But I smelled the formaldehyde where samples are kept. The strong solution makes my eyes sting. With watery eyes, I wonder how any of us can examine the specimen."

"I'm glad to have typing and shorthand. I would never cut up those things." Laura takes a deep breath, then exhales.

"I saw some pictures of them. You might change your mind if you see how amazing they look inside."

"You can dissect them," Laura groans. "It's not for me."

School work and music continue to occupy most of Jena's time. With an influx of new accounts from employees at the metal works, her father extends his hours at the bank. Barry worked at the metal company before he went to the army. Now, his former place of employment contributes a vital service to the nation by constructing landing boats for the navy.

Al and John Grason meet at their annual out-of-town bank conference. He and his former boss sit in the lounge of the Royal Hotel. "Al, your work at the bank is notable. Your office is number one in the district. Sarah must be proud of you."

"I'm sure she is. With the increased work load, Sunday is the only time I'm at home all day. But she never complains. She feels the pay increase more than compensates for the hours I spend away from her and the girls."

"There's only Mona and me home. Our two sons are overseas. God only knows where they are or what will happen to them." John flicks his silver lighter, draws on a cigarette and slowly exhales a thin stream of smoke.

"We don't have any idea where Phil is either. His letters all are censored. There's not much left for us to read. That worries us when we do hear from him. He's a medic and could be in the middle of some battle zone."

"We'll never know what they are going through until the war's over." John takes a long puff, then snuffs out his cigarette in the glass ash tray. "How's Sarah dealing with all this? Has she recovered from the loss of the child? Her pregnancy, the death of the baby and Phil being overseas must be a great strain on her."

"She's back to her old self now. She keeps the house spotless and manages to shop and cook as well as ever."

The men sit in beige upholstered chairs near the circular stone fireplace in the center of the room. Bright orange flames dance above blazing logs.

"You have a fine wife, Al. Take good care of her. You should treasure such a loyal, faithful woman."

"You're right, John. She certainly is a righteous woman."

Al considers the deceptive life he and Sarah share. *The problem is, she's too good. Her stringent morals may get her to heaven, but they may send some of us to hell.*

Back home in Sage, Sarah notices a big change in Jena's demeanor the week Al is out of town. Her daughter is happy when she arrives home from school. Before piano practice she goes outside. Laura, Jena and Megan decide to go bike riding. Sarah watches from the window. *"Lord, let this be the beginning of a positive change in the girl,"* Sarah prays. Later she listens as nimble fingers fly across the keyboard as Jena practices. It has been a long time since Sarah has seen the girl with a smile on her face.

Al returns home Friday evening. At the sound of his voice in the hallway, Jena goes upstairs to her room. Sarah observes the girl revert to her strange behavior. The sad woman realizes she must continue to wait for an answer to her latest prayer.

In the kitchen, Al pours himself a cup of hot coffee.

"How was the meeting?" Sarah asks.

"Everything went well. John complimented me that Sage Bank is first in the region. He asked about you and sends his best wishes."

"How are John and his wife? It must be difficult for them with both sons in the military service."

"He doesn't complain. But he was nervous when he talked about his boys. He doesn't know where they are. He and Mona suffer like everyone else whose family is involved in the war."

Al changes from his brown business suit to a blue-striped jersey and gray slacks. He goes to the corner bar. Sarah sits in the living room, alone with her thoughts.

Jena lies awake in bed, fearful of what the future holds for her. She feels guilt when sexual feelings, awakened by her father's seduction, occasionally arouse and confuse her. With the body of a mature woman and emotions of an immature child, she lives in fear of being violated again. After tossing restlessly for hours, sleep finally liberates her from feelings of disgrace.

The house is dark when Al returns at ten-thirty. A

faint odor of beer is on his breath. He slips into bed and falls asleep. Sarah lies beside him and prays for peaceful slumber.

Al makes another trek to the barroom Saturday night. This time, he visits with Holly and arrives home after midnight.

Sunday begins another week with Al going to church alone and Sarah walking to ten o'clock Mass with the girls.

At Jena's Wednesday lesson, Sister George gives the girl a duet to learn. Another tenth grade pupil will be her partner. Cheri is exuberant. She laughs a lot and attracts attention from boys at school. But this is no problem for Jena.

Saturday morning, at the Bordeau house, the two girls practice Haydn's ANDANTE together. Jena plays treble, her partner, bass. Cheri's lighthearted laughter floats through the room each time one of them makes a mistake. They are at the piano when Al comes home at noon. When he sees the pretty, blue-eyed blonde, he takes a seat in the living room.

"It's time for us to stop now," Jena announces.

Al looks toward Cheri. "Is this a new piece for you?"

"Yes. Sister gave it to us this week." She looks at the handsome, slender man and giggles. "Jena and I plan to practice here again next Saturday."

"You can come back any time," Al tells her.

Each girl practices her assigned part alone during the week. Saturday morning, Cheri joins Jena at the Bordeau house.

Their music gets better as they spend more time together at the piano. Al is home at noon. He sits in the living room and watches the girls play their duet. Jena begins to make mistake after mistake.

"I think we practiced long enough," she tells Cheri. "I'm tired. We can work again next week."

"Where do you live?" Al asks the girl.

"I live in that big blue house on the hill. The one you can see from Main Street."

Once more her laughter resonates throughout the room. At school, boys hover around her. Now Al wants to sit and talk with her.

On the porch, Cheri tells Jena, "Your dad's nice."

He thinks you're pretty nice, too, Jena perceives.

At her lesson Wednesday, Jena tells Sister George, "I don't think Cheri can practice at my house any more. I don't want my father to complain when she comes each week."

"Then you can practice at her house or come here."

"My father will never allow me to go to her house. If I come to the convent, I have to be home before he gets home at noon."

"Perhaps it's best we forget about the duet. I can give you another new piece. I am having a recital next year. There is enough time for us to decide which piece you want to play."

This Saturday, Jena is alone when Al returns home. "Where's your girlfriend?" he asks.

"Sister canceled the duet. All her students are to begin practice on music for our piano recital next spring."

"Will she come to visit some time?"

"I don't know. We're not together much at school."

Al exits the room as Jena continues to practice.

After lunch, Jena and Laura go to the movie and watch, "Thirty Seconds Over Tokyo." Jena cringes when one of the United States' bombers crashes into the sea. She closes her eyes as an American army doctor amputates the pilot's leg in a primitive hospital in China.

"I hope Phil doesn't get hurt in the war," she tells Laura. "Do you think he's where bombs fall?"

"He may be. He's a medic. He may be in a battle or close to the fighting sometime."

"I pray God won't let him get hurt," Jena pines.

Each day newspapers give reports of battles taking place. The Bordeau family is like every other family in the nation. They hope their loved one is not involved in the latest conflict.

It has been over two months since Phil's last letter. The first week in May, Jena sends a note with his birthday card.

Dear Phil,
How do you like the dog on the front of your card? It looks like Rusty, so I had to get this one for you. I'm sending your card early so it will reach you in time for your birthday.

I often think about the sassafras and berries you brought home from the hill. I miss tossing barbells with you in your shed. I don't go in there any more.

I hate you being away from home fighting a war. I'll remember you specially on your birthday. Every day I ask God to keep you safe and to end the war soon.
Love,
Your "blood sister,"
Shorty

Phil gets the card before he sets out on a special mission. His unit spends a stormy night at sea, frightened of what morning will bring. At break of dawn, an Allied armada of 3,400 ships approaches a fifty-mile stretch of rocky coastline in Northern France. Its mission is to gain possession of Normandy.

On this gusty Tuesday a gray mist lingers. Thousands of soldiers disembark from the initial assembly of landing craft. It is the first wave of the invasion. They are deluged by a flood of missiles from German machine-gun nests secure atop a 100-foot bluff. Bullets rain down, flooding the beach with casualties. Water weeps red from blood of men who drown on their way to shore. Hundreds are slaughtered in their attempt to cross forty yards of open beach. Bodies are blown apart by millions of German mines buried beneath the sand. The lucky troops are those who manage to reach shelter near a hillside.

Phil's unit runs toward shore. The massacre continues. Heavy boots sink in the sand. His feet drag past bodies that cover the beach.

A soldier lies screaming, "Medic! Medic!"

Phil yells, "I'm here. I'm here."

He dodges bullet shells and exploding land mines as he rushes to the boy. But the lad dies at Phil's feet.

"Medic! Medic!" another voice cries out.

"I'm here, soldier," Phil bellows.

Bullets whiz past him. He leaps to the ground. As he crawls toward the injured man, a bullet strikes Phil's back. Now he, too, lies motionless.

It is afternoon when the last of 2,500 landing craft reach the shoreline. Allied planes have silenced most of the enemy artillery in time for this second wave of the invasion.

Barry disembarks from the LCI. He is too terrified to notice the vessel was constructed at Sage Metal Works. He is sickened by the sight of bodies afloat in the water. He staggers on a beach covered by a blanket of fallen comrades. Tears stream down Barry's face. He runs toward the hill, unaware his boyhood buddy lies face down in the blood-soaked sand.

All over the free world newspapers announce in bold headlines, ALLIES INVADE NORMANDY. They hail the victory and report 9,000 Allied casualties. An additional 2,500 are counted among dead heroes who sacrificed their lives in the bloody slaughter.

A short time later, Al and Sarah receive official word from the War Department. The telegram informs them their son has been killed, June 6, on Normandy Beach.

There is a gold star in the front window when Jena

comes home from the store. She runs to Sarah in the basement.

"Why did you put that gold star there?" Jena shrieks. Her voice is sharp with disapproval.

"Because your brother's been killed," Sarah sobs.

"No! No! It can't be true! Phil can't be dead!" Jena yells. Her face turns white. The hysterical girl rushes up to the living room and stares at the star. She hates that star in her window. She picks up books from the coffee table and throws them against the wall. She shakes her fists and screams, "God, why would You let Phil die? Why?"

Sarah rushes upstairs. Tears stream down her cheeks. "The war killed your brother. God had nothing to do with it," she cries.

The words hold no comfort for the devastated girl. Jena runs up to her room and slams the door shut.

Downstairs, Sarah hears Jena pound on the wall. She listens to her daughter's screams. "Why did you let this happen, God? Why? Why? I prayed that You would keep him safe and he would come back home."

The grieving mother weeps as she listens to her daughter, all alone, sob uncontrollably. "Phil. Phil," she calls out.

There is no consolation for Jena. In the stillness of night violent nightmares continue to haunt her.

She walks along railroad tracks. Her shoe is caught beneath a rail. A speeding train races toward her. She cries out, "Help me! Help me!"

In the next room, Laura pulls the covers over her head when she hears Jena shout in her sleep.

After learning of Phil's death, Otto and Nita Kale visit the Bordeaus on a sunny, Sunday afternoon.

"We're sorry to hear about Phil." Nita is crying.

"Barry hasn't written for months. He doesn't know about Phil."

"We didn't get any letters from Phil for months. Then we heard from the War Department that he's dead. Let us know when you hear from Barry."

Battles continue to rage in France. Near the end of summer the Germans surrender in Paris. For three days Barry joins thousands of Allied soldiers in wild, ecstatic, liberated Paris. On the final day of revelry, he marches with his fellow Americans through the Arc de Triompe. They parade in review before a grateful and proud General Dwight D. Eisenhower.

Barry's unit takes two weeks of rest and relaxation. He enjoys the clean, beautiful countryside. He welcomes the quiet peace of green fields and clear blue skies. The brief hiatus provides temporary solace for the weary soldier. Soon he must return to scenes of pillage and death where buildings in once-beautiful cities are now worthless piles of wood, mortar and stone. Many villages and towns are completely destroyed. He sits on soft, green grass and writes a letter home.

Dear Mom and Dad,
This will let you know I'm well and not injured. I'm in the beautiful countryside on leave. I saw General Eisenhower when Paris was liberated. What do you hear from Phil? We lost contact with one another a good while back. If I see him I'll let you know. Be sure to write any news you hear. Tell the Bordeau family I said hello. I send you my love.
Your son,
Barry

Barry continues his tour of duty. In this latest letter from home, Nita writes him news about his friend.

My Dearest Son,

Your father and I are so relieved to hear you are safe and able to enjoy the beautiful countryside.

I'm sorry to tell you this. Your good friend Phil was killed June 6, in France. His parents got a letter from the War Department a short time after they read about D-Day in the newspaper....

Barry can not bear the news. He crumples the letter in his fist, then throws it on the ground. *My friend was on the beach when I was there. Among thousands of bodies I passed, I never saw Phil. I couldn't save him. We never said good-bye,* he mourns.

The exhausted soldier is severely depressed when he heads back to the front lines. He is angry at the enemy, the war and himself. He casts his eyes to the heavens and shouts, *"God, why do You allow this to happen? Why did my buddy have to die?"*

Here at home, Jena fights her own private war with recurring nightmares.

She is on a bridge. Below is the river where Phil would swim. She walks halfway across. A huge hole, the width of the bridge, appears. Jena spirals down, down, down through the giant orifice. As she is about to hit water, she jumps up in bed.

Her screams waken Laura. The older girl has grown used to hearing her sister cry out at night. She no longer rushes to Jena's room when she hollers. She knows the girl will slip back to sleep once she stops crying. Laura pulls a cover over her head. Moments later, she drifts back to dreamland.

CHAPTER 20
RISE VICTORIOUS

Newspaper and radio reports on the war are constant reminders to Jena of her brother's death. Al's hostility and Sarah's aloofness push the girl deeper into solitude. As she begins her fall music lessons, Sister George announces plans for the spring recital.

"The program will start with the youngest pupils and end with the most advanced student. There will be twenty performers. You will be number nineteen. Mark Sanger will perform last," she tells Jena.

"What composition am I going to play?"

"I would like you to study VALSE TRISTE. If you feel comfortable with it, you will perform this piece. Mark will play RUSTLING OF SPRING."

Jena leafs through the pages. "Will I be able to perfect this during the next eight months? I hope to be ready. It looks very difficult."

"It's quite advanced from what you have done the past five years. But I'm sure you can master it in time for the recital."

Sister's confidence encourages her zealous student. With each spurt of enthusiasm from the nun, Jena becomes more encouraged to strive for greater achievement. She does homework after school then spends hours at the piano. She begins with familiar compositions. Soon the walls echo with repetitious notes of music by Sibelius.

Every day, Jena either begins or ends practice with

the lively, ARAGONAISE. Sarah never makes any mention of her daughter's music anymore. She once said it is her favorite piece. Jena finds reprieve from her fears in the fiery, rhythmic music from the opera, "Le Cid." She feels joyful as she recalls visions of spirited gypsies as they frolic in the night.

As evening approaches she is consumed by fear of falling asleep. Demons invade her reverie. The latest nightmare continues to cause nights of sporadic slumber.

As she walks across the bridge at the edge of town, a huge hole appears in the cement. She plunges down, down toward the water. She is about to plummet into her brother's beloved Deer River.

A plea for help disrupts a calm, cool night. Jena wakens. Her body continues to tremble as she tosses in bed, frightened to venture back to that dark, mysterious avenue that leads to endless torment.

Al is not bothered by bad dreams. Sleep brings him contentment. Persistent denial accords him little feeling of responsibility for his crime. *The major blame belongs to Sarah. It is her aversion to my natural masculine desires that caused this disaster,* Al fantasizes. *Sarah shirks not only her duties toward me, but to our daughters. She wants to keep Jena ignorant of the female functions of her young body. Not only has she caused this rift in the family, but I am reminded of that diabolical act every time I look at Jena. Enough of this grief.* He sighs and rolls on his side. He sinks into a deep sleep, alone in the double bed.

Al continues his affair with the barmaid from the neighborhood cafe. He keeps a key to her apartment in a secret pocket in his wallet. Most Saturday nights, after Holly finishes work, she joins him for their clandestine meeting. When he returns home from his late-night visits, Sarah is repulsed by the smell of liquor on his breath. Their pretentious relationship has become a way of life for the couple. Only necessary conversations occur between them.

Valentine's Day arrives on a cold winter morning. Sarah brings in a red envelope from the mailbox, addressed to *Mr. Al Bordeau*. There is no doubt in Sarah's mind what the envelope contains. On this day for romance the betrayed, angry woman is sure what kind of card is enclosed. She places several envelopes on her husband's desk.

After work, Al does his usual chore of sorting the mail. He opens the large envelope and finds a glossy valentine. On the front is a big red heart. Inside is a bunch of bright red, heart-shaped balloons, afloat among fluffy blue clouds. *Come fly with me where hearts are free,* is inscribed beneath the art work. Although there is no signature, Al knows Holly is the Cupid who sent it.

He displays a rare smile at the dinner table. He eats his meal in silence. Sarah notices Al has not changed from his navy tweed suit to his casual clothes before coming to the table. She and the girls are at the dinner table when he gets up, puts on his coat, and leaves the house.

Al hears Holly's coarse laughter above the noisy crowd when he enters the bar. He squints his eyes as he glances around the smoke-filled room. At the bar he is enticed to stay, as he stares at Holly's red dress. The low-cut neckline displays profuse cleavage. Her brightly painted lips and thin penciled brows are encircled by flaming tresses.

"You look nice tonight. How did you like your mail today?" she whispers. The glint in her eyes reveals her pleasure with his presence and his wide smile.

"Red balloons to match your fiery hair. I can't visit tonight. Saturday I'll float by to see you."

"It will be a night you won't forget," she grins.

"I'll be there. You can be sure of it."

Holly walks to a corner table to serve another patron.

Al has a glass of beer then exits by the front door.

At home, Sarah finds it difficult to hide her sorrow from the girls. She sits with a somber face, dressed in a floral cotton dress, silent as she sips hot coffee.

She has never seen the low-cut black blouse, short skirt and fancy white apron the waitresses wears at work. Tonight, she would resent Holly's special Valentine Day dress even more.

"Why did Dad go out on a Wednesday?" Laura asks.

"He must have to meet someone." She evades a direct answer. *Forgive me, Lord, for the deception. I know where Al is, but You know I must shield my daughters from knowledge of their father's affair. Help me solve this problem,* she prays.

With the girls in the living room, Sarah searches for the red envelope in Al's desk. She finds it in a top drawer. Tears run down her face as she reads the valentine. *"God will punish that harlot for what she does,"* Sarah mutters to herself. She puts the card back in the desk and returns to the kitchen.

She places the last dish in the cupboard as Al walks in the room. She does not detect an odor of beer on his breath, but that silly grin remains on his face. *Thank God he came back right away. He must remember tomorrow's a work day.* She breathes a sigh of relief.

Outside, a high-pitched siren wails. Every person on the street runs for cover. Al hangs heavy blankets over all the downstairs windows. Civil Defense workers walk from house to house. They check that no glimmer of light shows outside.

Sarah shakes visibly as a single candle flickers from the center of the dining room table. She paces around the room and listens for the sound of planes. Her hands tremble as a rosary slips through her fingers. Flashes of red, yellow and blue sparkle from the small, clear, crystal beads.

"God save us! Lord save us!" She prays the words over and over. Seated at the table, Al and the girls hear static crack through music that drifts from the radio in the living room.

"When will these blackouts stop?" Laura asks her father.

"Not until the war is ended," Al replies.

"It's been more than three years since the war began. No enemy planes have bombed our country since Pearl Harbor. Why do we have to watch for them now?"

"If the enemy ever comes over here the Sage Ship Yard will be a prime target for them to hit. We can never let our guard down until the war is over."

"Our ration coupons will continue until then, too, I guess," Laura laments.

"An allotment for food and gasoline each month is not much of a sacrifice," Sarah interrupts. "Our boys give their lives so we can live in a peaceful country. We'll never see Phil again," she weeps. "I don't want you to mention that what we must do without is too much to give up. Just remember what it's like for our servicemen. Stop complaining. Just pray this war is finished soon."

"Laura can't stand the cotton stockings we wear. She's upset we can't buy nice nylons," Jena remarks. "Today she told me she wants to use leg make-up like some other girls do."

"There's no nylon for stockings. Laura is too young to use leg make-up," Sarah comments. "Our airmen need every source of nylon for parachutes. Wearing cotton hose is no sacrifice. It's merely an inconvenience."

"Thank God," the woman sighs when sirens sound the all-clear. The lights are turned on and blankets are removed from the windows. Sarah lays aside her rosary and sits in the living room in an effort to regain her composure.

While the home-front remains safe, the war continues to take a heavy toll in other countries. Millions of military and innocent civilians lose their lives throughout the world. President Roosevelt is ill when he meets with Prime Minister Churchill and Marshal Stalin in Yalta. The Allied leaders form plans for the unconditional surrender of Germany.

The President returns to Warm Springs, Georgia as the war in Europe nears an end. As the Commander-in-Chief sits for his portrait one spring day, he lapses into a coma and dies.

It is shortly after dinner when the Bordeau family hears the news over the radio.

"This war kills every one. It killed Phil. Now President Roosevelt is dead," Jena wails.

"I won't mourn for the President," Al bellows. "He knew before the Japanese bombed Pearl Harbor what was about to happen. He did nothing to prevent the war. It's because of him, Phil is dead."

"Our President wouldn't allow a war to happen," Jena objects. "He would do something to stop it."

"You don't know what you're talking about. War is all about money and politics," Al argues.

Later this evening, Jena asks her mother, "Why would Dad say the President would let our country get into this war?"

"There are some questions that have no answers. Men and women think differently about these things."

While the nation mourns, leaders throughout the free world offer condolences for the beloved leader. A brief memorial service is held at the President's Episcopal Church at Hyde Park, New York. There is no eulogy during the fifteen minute service. A single plane circles above the small gathering as he is lowered into his final resting place.

The gloom of war dissipates slightly as the giant tree outside Laura's window emits the fragrant aroma of cherry blossoms. She is happy to have Rita's old room. The scent permeates the air and brings with it hope for peace.

Now that spring is here, Jena spends extra hours each day at the piano. The final two weeks before the recital, strains of **VALSE TRISTE** fill the house.

The long-awaited day comes too soon for Jena. She changes from her Sunday dress to her recital gown. All the girls wear long dresses. The boys will wear suits and ties. Sarah shortened Rita's peach, organdy prom gown to fit Jena. The nervous girl's brunette hair forms soft curls around her flushed cheeks. She walks slowly to the curb and cautiously slides into the taxi. "I feel awkward in a gown and high heels, Mother."

"You will feel better when you're with the other girls," Sarah tells her. "All of you will feel uneasy this first time in a long dress."

Jena paces backstage as one after the other, eighteen pupils complete their performance. Sister faces the girl.

"You will play well, Jena. You have practiced long, hard hours and made no mistakes at practice yesterday. I know your performance will be perfect." Sister grasps both of Jena's hands. "Just concentrate on your music. Now take a deep breath and relax."

Jena walks across the stage. She hesitates with each step, afraid of falling. The shiny wooden floor is smooth. She takes short steps to keep her balance and arrives at center stage. She glances at the audience and eases herself onto the bench at the baby grand.

There is silence. She takes a deep breath and opens her music. The slow, soft whisper of a waltz fills the auditorium. It builds with motion and expression, then grows more forceful with less movement.

The hall is filled, but Jena is not aware of the audience. She concentrates on each note as she plays music by Sibelius. Sister George is elated as she watches from backstage.

Once again the music increases in motion. It ends soft and slow. The final measure completed, Jena picks up her music and bows to enthusiastic applause. She walks backstage to the open arms of her mentor. Mark Sanger ends the program with a flawless performance of RUSTLING OF SPRING. Sister George is delighted with the success of the recital.

Jena returns home with a great sense of accomplishment. It was worth hours of arduous practice. She feels victorious. The phone rings as she changes from her peach gown to a blue Sunday dress. Laura answers the phone and calls upstairs.

"Jena, some lady wants to talk with you."

The excited girl rushes downstairs.

"This is Miss Lorenzo, your neighbor. I was at the recital today," she informs the girl. "I want you to know how much I enjoyed your performance. You were very poised as you walked across the stage. I did not know such a talented musician lives in the neighborhood."

"Thank you, Miss Lorenzo. It's very nice of you to call and say that."

"You should be aware that your talent is appreciated. I look forward to your next performance."

"I'll try my best. Thanks for calling," Jena exclaims.

"Laura," Jena yells, "You'll never guess who just called."

"Well, who was it?"

"It was Miss Lorenzo, the lady from across the street. She's the one who sings opera." Jena is breathless.

"What did she want?" Laura asks.

"She was at the recital. She said I was poised and

that I am a talented musician." Jena beams. "But I really wasn't graceful. I was just afraid I'd fall on the floor in high heels."

"You should be good. You spend all your time at the piano."

"It's good Mother let me take music lessons all these years. I never have a problem of what to do in my spare time. You're not home much anymore when I practice. You go dancing or bowling with your friends almost every evening."

"Well, you were great at the recital this afternoon."

The following day headlines proclaim V-E DAY. Less than four weeks after the President's death, there is victory in Europe. Adolph Hitler is dead, and now two million Nazi surrender to the Allies. A document of unconditional surrender is signed by General Jodl. The historic event takes place in General Eisenhower's headquarters, a little red schoolhouse in Rheims, France.

"Neither the President nor Phil can enjoy the victory," Jena tells her mother. "Our leader lies in a lonely grave in New York. And Phil is buried far away in our grandparents' country," she cries.

Thousands celebrate throughout the nation. Traffic stops as people line the streets. They sing and dance and kiss every one in sight. It is chaotic ecstasy.

There are other parts of the world that can not share this revelry. The entire battle is not over. Troops in the Pacific continue to die. Plans are made for the invasion of Japan.

Many senior boys will enter the service after they graduate. Girls make preparations for the prom. At school, Jena overhears girls discuss what gown they will wear the coming week.

"Did you ask Dad for money to buy a gown?" she asks Laura.

"There isn't any reason for me to want one. You

know I'm not going to the prom."

"You go to dances and other places with your friends. You could go if you wanted. One of the fellows could take you. Why don't you go with one of them?"

"None of them are allowed at our dances. The nuns would throw a fit if I go with a boy from the public school. Sister wants us girls to go with guys from our class," Laura gasps.

"Rita and Bob went to their prom together. It's odd. Rita had all the fun in her high school years. Then she dumped Bob and went to the convent." Jena rolls her eyes in amazement.

"My friends don't go to our school. I have a lot of fun when I spend time with them. You should get out and enjoy yourself sometime, too."

"Even if I wanted to, there's no time for that. I have another recital next spring. I need to practice a lot more now. I want to play even better than I did this year."

"Well, suit yourself. I'm going to enjoy myself."

Laura has a quiet graduation. There is no big dinner or party at home. After the ceremony this afternoon, she makes plans to go to a big celebration at Megan's house.

"Why is she having a party?" Jena asks.

"She's going to the prom with some senior boy. He expects to leave for the army soon. Megan's combining a graduation dance with a farewell party."

Jena watches her sister put on a blue silk dress and navy pumps. Laura brushes her curly blond hair, puts on rose-colored lipstick, and leaves for a fun-filled evening. Jena goes downstairs and seats herself at the piano.

It seems the Great War may be close to an end this summer afternoon. Tokyo is in shambles and the Japanese people have been warned to evacuate Hiroshima and Nagasaki. Japan ignores the Potsdam Declaration. It refuses the demands for an unconditional surrender of all Japanese armed forces.

On a hot August day one B-29 bomber drops a single bomb, the power of 20,000 tons of TNT, over the city of Hiroshima.

Japan still refuses to surrender.

Two days later an atomic bomb is dropped on Nagasaki. It is the greatest devastation in the history of humankind. It is 44 months after the sneak attack on Pearl Harbor that Japan surrenders. Headlines shout the news, V-J DAY JAPAN SURRENDERS.

While the free world celebrates, a lonely soldier walks, dazed, along the streets of New York City. In his hand he clutches a newspaper that announces the war is over.

An Army lieutenant turns from the crowd and goes to the disheveled loner who wanders toward the wharf.

"Hey buddy," he shouts, "come join the celebration."

Apparently the soldier does not hear a word. He continues to stroll toward the water. The lieutenant grabs the man's arm.

"What's your name, soldier?" he bellows.

Stunned, the young man looks at the older man's uniform.

"My name is Barry Kale, Sir." His response is abrupt. He raises his right hand and salutes the officer.

"Why are you walking alone, corporal?"

"I'm looking for my buddy, Sir," Barry shouts.

"Where is your buddy?"

"I left him on the beach, Sir," Barry wails.

"What beach would that be?"

"Normandy Beach, Sir. I must get Phil off the beach, Sir." The soldier tries to pull away from the lieutenant's grasp.

The officer clutches Barry's arm and leads him from the wharf. He guides the perplexed soldier to the street. "I'll help you find your buddy," he murmurs.

"Taxi, taxi," the lieutenant shouts.

"Cabbie, drive us to the nearest hospital," he orders.

World War II is over. The festivities continue in streets and homes. But for many there is no victory, only scars to carry for a lifetime. The casualties of war include not only the dead and physically disabled. Barry is among those who sustain mental wounds. A desperate soldier holds a newspaper in his hand as he searches for a buddy who remains alive only in his memory.

High on a bluff in Normandy, France, Phil lies in a grave marked with a simple white cross. He rests with thousands of other American heroes who died so their loved ones could live in peace. His pal sits in a hospital, segregated from the outside world. In his mind, the disoriented young man continues to search for a friend that he will never find. For Barry, his greatest battle has just begun.

CHAPTER 21
COMMENCEMENT

The final school year begins. Last year, Sister Monica talked with Jena concerning the girl going to college. The nun calls the student to her desk before class begins today.

"Jena, if you plan to attend college you must prepare for it immediately. You must complete the forms and arrange for finances."

"I'll never get enough money, Sister. I don't think my father will pay for any tuition. He once told me how expensive it was for my brother. Phil worked summers and during school terms to help with expenses. He was in his third year but never got to graduate." Her expression is sad, but it also reveals disappointment with her impending future.

"With your grades, you should be able to get a scholarship. I can help arrange it for you. But it must be handled immediately."

Sister hands the girl several papers from her desk. "It is necessary for your parents to help you complete these forms. You must impress upon them the urgency to handle this right away."

Jena decides it is time to set aside her anger. She goes to talk with her father. As she stands at the doorway of her parents' room, she thinks about Sister insisting she handle the matter right now. Her father is at his desk, preoccupied with paper work. He looks up at her when she enters the room.

"What's the matter now?" he asks gruffly.

"Sister Monica told me to talk with you tonight. She said you should help me fill out these papers if I intend to go to college next fall."

She voice quivers. She speaks fast so he can not question her about any trouble he thinks she got into. She hands him the forms. It is obvious, from the look of amazement on his face, this is a big surprise from whatever he expected to hear.

"What makes you think it's possible for you to go to college? That requires a great amount of money. Where do you think it will come from?" He keeps his eyes on the papers in front of him.

"Sister told me my grades are good and she will help get a scholarship for me. That will take care of the money." She is not sure where her strength comes from. She answers in a firm, steady tone to let him know she does not expect any financial assistance from him.

He turns toward her. He has a stern look on his face.

"College is not only about money. It takes a lot of planning. Do you have any idea what you want to study?"

His tone becomes derogatory. Jena feels her body quiver.

"I know what I want to do. I want to study to be a doctor." Her answer is abrupt. It is too abrupt. She answers too fast, and her reply sounds argumentative. She immediately regrets her intense response.

Al's aggression turns to anger.

"What makes you believe you're college material? Your grades may be good in high school, but college takes long hours of hard work."

"Sister thinks I will be able to do the work. She wants to help me apply and get the necessary finances. If she has faith in my ability, I must be qualified."

"You know how difficult medical practice is for Doc Mueller. He works long hours and has no time for anything else."

"But I don't want to be like him. I want to work with children." She pours out her secret desire in hopes that her father will at least sign papers so she can apply.

"You want to be a pediatrician?"

Jena believes her father is about to agree to her request. "No, not that kind of doctor. I want to be a child psychologist." She answers too fast and reveals another secret.

"You mean you want to mess around with kids' minds? Those head doctors are all crazy themselves," he sneers.

The word *psychologist* ignites a fury in the man. It quashes all her hopes he will accept her request. His strong objection to her choice of study and his contemptuous reply make it all too clear what his answer will be. "No daughter of mine will go to college. The only reason girls go away to school is to be with boys."

His sinister accusation fills her with fear. But she remains persistent in the pursuit of her dream.

"That's not why I want to go. Sister wants to help me. Why won't you fill out the papers?" she pleads.

"You heard me. This discussion about college is over."

Al picks up his pen and continues his work.

Jena's eyes fill with tears as she retreats to her room. *If Laura wanted to go to college, Dad would have allowed her. I should have used my brains and not told him what I really want to study. This is the last thing I'll ever discuss with him. He'll never get another chance to ruin any plan of mine. Never again,* she vows.

The despondent girl arrives in class Monday morning. Once again Sister Monica call Jena to her desk.

"Where are the forms I gave you to fill out?"

"I don't have them." Jena gives no reason. She just stands dejected as she faces the nun.

"I told you we must takes care of your applications now. Did your parents help with the papers?"

"My mother told me to talk with my father. He and I discussed money and a scholarship. I thought he was going to help me. Then he asked me what I wanted to study."

Jena hesitates to tell the nun how her father got angry or the rest of their conversation about girls going to college to meet boys.

"He must have been happy to hear you want to pursue the medical profession," she smiles.

"Oh, no. He wasn't. When he learned I want to be a child psychologist, he got angry. He said they were all crazy themselves." Jena turns her head and looks at the side blackboard. "He said the reason girls go away to school is to be with boys, and no daughter of his would go away to college. Then he refused to talk about it again."

"I'm taking two of your classmates to the hospital this Saturday. They want to become nurses. I want you to come with us. You may decide this is a medical field you would like."

"I'll go to the hospital if you want me to. But I don't want to be a nurse. I believe there are children I can help if I can get the proper training."

"Make a visit to the hospital with us," Sister insists. "You may decide to be a nurse like Sister Rita."

Saturday morning, Sister Monica and three senior girls go by bus to Bridgeport. At the hospital, when Jena sees blood in an operating room, her stomach feels queasy. She is more convinced than ever this is not her field of study.

"Sister, I don't want any part of the nursing profession. The gory side of medicine can be handled by girls with stronger stomachs than mine."

Now, more than ever, Jena becomes obsessed with the desire to get away from her father and the hostile environment at home. She continues to isolate herself from family and schoolmates. Megan is the only classmate with whom she occasionally associates. She finds solace in the beauty and imagery of music. For hours each day she strives to perfect Rachmaninoff's PRELUDE IN C SHARP MINOR for her recital next spring.

It is a brisk autumn day when Jena arrives home from school and sees Nita Kale seated on the sofa beside Sarah. Barry's mother holds a tissue to her eyes. Jena listens to the woman talk to Sarah.

"I know how hard it is for you to accept Phil's death. Otto and I got a letter from the army, also. It informed us that Barry's in a veteran's hospital. He doesn't remember his name or know where he's at," she sobs. "He keeps repeating he has to find Phil. They were both on Normandy Beach, on D-Day. But Barry never saw your son or knew of his death until I wrote him the tragic news."

"Nita, I'm so sorry," Sarah cries. "Isn't there something the doctors can do to help him regain his memory?"

"When Barry was found wandering on a wharf in New York, he had a worn deck of cards in his pocket. It seems Phil had them with him when he died. One of Phil's buddies gave them to my son. Barry doesn't recognize the cards," Nita says.

"Jena gave them to her brother the night he left for the army. Phil told her he and Barry used them together their first months in camp."

Jena rushes into the room. "Mrs. Kale, please show me the cards. Phil wrote me he always carried them in his pocket."

"I don't have them, Jena. The doctor at the hospital wants to keep them." She weeps. "He thinks someday

Barry may remember when he and Phil played with them together. They may help restore his memory."

Nita continues to sob. Sarah gets her a glass of water.

"I'm sorry that Barry is ill." Jena puts her hand on the woman's shoulder. "Can Mother and I go with you the next time you visit Barry?"

"That may not happen for a long time." Nita takes another tissue from her purse and wipes tears from her eyes. "The doctors need more time to work with him. They wrote us that our son won't know Otto or me and seeing him may only cause us more pain."

"Why do these things happen? God should not allow wars to happen. Good people shouldn't die. Why doesn't He stop people from fighting?" Jena wails.

"Men cause wars, not God. He gives every person a free will. Evil men make wars. You must never blame God for tragedies brought about by wicked men," Sarah cautions her daughter.

Jena kneels by her bed this evening. Tears stream down her cheeks as she prays. *"God, take care of Barry. Help him get well and remember the good times he had with Phil. And God, please let Barry remember about the cards he and Phil played together. Amen."*

In the still of night, once again her slumber is invaded by a familiar nightmare.

Jena sees the river where Phil would swim. She is halfway across the bridge. A huge hole in the cement prevents her from walking any farther. She falls through the opening. Down, down she goes. She is about to hit the water.

The sound of her scream wakens the frightened girl. Jena lies rigid in the dark, silent room. Tears soak her pillow. She lies motionless as she struggles to cast the nightmare from her mind. She listens to the clock tick out the minutes and remembers times she and Phil spent together on the hill. The fun they shared in her brother's shed remains a vivid memory. She recalls the shiny deck of cards she gave him when he departed for the army one cold, snowy winter night.

"God, why did Phil have to die? Why must Barry stay in a hospital where he can't even remember any of the good times he shared with my brother?" In the still of the night, Jena lies awake and begs God to send her sleep with peaceful dreams.

With the arrival of spring Jena approaches the final months of school. Sister Bridget directs an operetta to be presented by the twelfth grade for Senior Class Day. Jena is in the chorus of "The Vagabond King." She delights in the play's lively music and characters. Her imagination fancies fiery gypsies who sing and dance around a bright fire. As her classmates click castanets and jingle metal tambourines to the rapid music, she envisions those happy wanderers at the carnival. The golden bracelets twist and jangle as dancers' bare feet fly across the sand. Their loud laughter and boisterous songs drown out the crackle of flames that soar in the night air. Sights and sounds echo round and round in her mind.

In school Jena rehearses for the operetta. At home she practices for the recital. Weekdays Laura works in the credit office at Paragon Department Store. Most evenings she goes bowling, dancing or to movies with friends.

At school the girls talk about what gowns they will wear to the senior prom.

"Did you get a new gown for the prom?" Jena asks Megan.

"No. I won't be going. I'm going steady with Lenny, the fellow who took me to his prom. He stayed in the army and will be away a few more years. I'm glad I got to go when I was a junior. I'd hate to have never been to a high school prom. Why don't you want to go, Jena?"

"Even if I wanted to, there's no time. My recital's in a month and I have to practice a lot now. I want to play even better this year than I did the first time."

"You don't have to worry about that. With all the hours you spend at the piano, you'll do great."

The determined girl practices the difficult Prelude over and over again. From the loud, deliberate opening, through a soft passage, to an agitated rush that follows, firm fingers glide through the difficult composition. She continues past the loud repetition of the prime tempo to the very soft conclusion.

The day of the recital comes all too fast for Jena. On this bright Sunday afternoon Laura is in her sister's room as Jena steps into a pink batiste gown and white leather pumps.

"It's a good thing Rita got this for one of her school dances," Jena remarks. She fumbles with the back zipper.

"Let me help you with that," Laura offers. "You're so shaky you'll get the thing stuck."

"I'm nervous because so many people will be there. I want this to be a good recital." With a pensive look she adds, "It will be my last one and I want it to be perfect."

At the auditorium, Sister George gives final instructions to each of her pupils. She holds Jena's hands and declares, "I'm sure you'll deliver a flawless performance. Mark will be the final performer. You and he will highlight the program."

Cheri completes FUR ELISE, and walks off stage. Jena crosses the stage, sits at the piano and opens her music. She takes a deep breath and begins to play the Rachmaninoff Prelude.

The opening chords are loud and clear. At the eighth measure the music is very soft. She concentrates on each note as she plays and reaches the tenth measure of the composition.

In the stillness of the auditorium, a familiar voice rises to the stage. Jena turns toward the audience and sees Al seated beside Sarah in a front row. She lifts her hands from the keyboard when she hears her father speak to her mother.

Backstage, Sister George whispers a prayer. *"Dear Lord, let Jena continue. Don't let her start the piece over again."*

The stunned girl is not able to read any notes. Her mind goes blank. She picks up her music, bows to the audience and whispers, "I'm sorry." Jena returns backstage into the open arms of her mentor. The piano she loves now becomes an instrument of doom. She sobs hysterically.

"I'm sorry, Sister," she cries. "I heard my father and saw him out front. My mind went blank. I couldn't see any of the notes. I'm sorry I ruined your recital," she mutters between sobs.

"Don't cry, Jena. It will be all right." Sister stands with the young girl and holds her arms around her heartbroken pupil. "I heard someone talk, also. I'm sorry you are so upset," she says softly.

Mark Sanger walks across the stage with empty hands. He memorizes the music for his performances. He waits for complete silence before he begins to play. In the quiet hall he commences the cadenza of the WARSAW CONCERTO. He continues powerful chords and concludes to a thunderous applause. He bows and walks backstage. He goes outside without a word to Sister or any of the students.

"Did I spoil Mark's performance?" Jena cries to Sister.

"He was upset that you didn't complete your composition. It is nothing for you to feel bad about. Mark was very good and the audience enjoyed the recital. That should help heal your broken heart." Sister wipes Jena's tears. "Go home and don't worry about what happened today," she insists.

There is no phone call for Jena when she arrives home today. She places her music in the piano bench and goes to her room.

At the dinner table this evening no mention is made of the recital by Al, Sarah or Laura. They all want to put the incident out of mind as soon as possible.

Jena finds it impossible to forget about the tragic event. Monday morning, Cheri corners her classmate at school.

"After the recital your Dad told me he liked how I played. What happened to you?" She gives one of her giddy laughs. "Why did you walk off the stage before you finished your piece?"

"Nothing happened to me," Jena snaps. "I was nervous and couldn't remember my music."

"You had it on the piano in front of you," Cheri giggles.

"It was too hard for me to read the notes. Just be quiet about it. I don't want to talk about it any more." Without another word, Jena turns and walks away.

At the operetta rehearsal this afternoon, Jena remains by herself. Even the merry music from "The Vagabond King" does not lift up the girl's downcast spirit.

The day before the play, Jena goes to Sister Bridget. "Since I'm in the chorus and not a main character in the play, will you allow me to work backstage tomorrow?"

"You practiced so long with us." Sister has a curious look on her face. "Why don't you want to sing tomorrow?"

"I get nervous in front of an audience. I ruined Sister George's piano recital last week. I don't want to be on stage again." Jena vehemently states her decision.

"If you don't want to sing in front of the school, I'll let you work backstage. I hope by tomorrow you'll change your mind and decide to join the chorus."

Jena is restless all night. Her decision remains the same. But she worries Sister will change her mind and force Jena to appear on stage tomorrow.

In the morning she carries out a well-thought-out plan. When Sarah summons her daughter for school, the young girl does not answer.

"Jena, get up," her mother calls once more. "You'll be late for school."

"I don't have to go today. Sister told me I won't have to sing in the operetta." Jena is not concerned that what she shouts down to her mother is a half-truth.

Sarah goes upstairs to her daughter's room. "I can't believe Sister would let you miss your class play. Now get out of bed and get dressed."

"Sister knows I ruined this year's recital. Yesterday, I told her I don't want to sing in front of the entire school and maybe do something to mess up her operetta. She said I won't have to sing. Honest. This is the truth."

"I'll accept your word on it. But just why do you do such strange things? Why can't you just try to be like the other girls?" Sarah looks disgusted at Jena.

"I can never be like them. I'm different now." Suddenly, she stops, afraid she has already said too much.

"Some day you may regret the things you avoid now," Sarah warns. In her head spin dire words her daughter has thrust at her in a moment of anger, "*I'm different now.*" The impact of that irate statement frightens Sarah. *What is Jena hiding?*

At school, Sister Bridget calls Megan to her desk. "Do you know what happened to Jena today?"

"I got a phone call from her before I left home. You told her she doesn't have to be in the chorus. She said there is no reason for her to come to school today."

"That is not the exact truth. I told her she could work backstage if she didn't want to sing. I'll speak with her tomorrow. Go now and put on your costume."

The operetta is a success. Everybody enjoys it.

Megan phones Jena when she gets home. "You got a free day. Sister is angry about it. She is going to talk with you tomorrow. I never thought you would miss any kind of musical production. You even missed Senior Class Day."

"I don't ever want to stand in front of an audience again. Sister George is disappointed I stopped playing before I finished my music at the recital. And Sister Bridget really did tell me I didn't have to sing in the chorus. So I just stayed home."

"I'll be glad when we're done with school next week. I didn't look for work yet," Megan says. "Your sister went to work the week after she graduated. Did you find a job?"

"I'm going to apply at Paragon this Saturday. Laura's been there a year. Maybe she can pull some strings to help get me hired. I'll take whatever job is available."

"Our family goes on vacation every August," Megan boasts. "I'll look for a job when we get home. I'm not anxious to start working. September will be soon enough for me to begin."

When Jena enters the classroom Thursday morning, Sister Bridget draws her aside. "Where were you yesterday?"

"You said I didn't have to sing in the operetta. There was nothing for me to do backstage so I stayed home."

"I said you could remain off stage. I didn't give you permission to miss a day of school," the nun scolds.

"Really, there was nothing for me to do," she repeats.

"It was your Senior Class Day. And you missed it. I'm very disappointed in you." Sister has a stern look on her face.

"I'm sorry, Sister." As she turns to walk away, Jena adds, "Anyway, I'm sure you're the only person who missed me."

The nun stares at Jena, unable to offer a suitable reply.

When her daughter returns home, Sarah wants to know, "What did Sister say about you missing school yesterday?"

"She said she's disappointed in me."

"What excuse did you give?"

"I told her no one needed me there." She turns from her mother in a gesture of indifference. "That's what I told her."

Jena retreats to her room. She changes from her uniform to a paisley print, thin cotton dress then goes to the piano. As music floats through the rooms, both mother and daughter find solace from a weary situation.

Saturday morning, Jena walks to the Paragon store. She goes to the personnel department and fills out an application form.

"My sister works in the credit office," she volunteers.

"Yes, I know. Laura is a good worker," Vera, the personnel manager answers. She takes a sheet of paper and hands it to Jena. "Every applicant must take a physical exam before working here. Take this form to your doctor. Bring it back after he completes it."

When she returns home Jena tells her mother, "I have to get a physical exam like Laura did. After Doctor Mueller fills out the report I can start work."

After lunch, Sarah and Jena sit side by side as they travel by bus to Bridgeport.

"Are you sure you want a suit for your graduation present?" her mother repeats.

"I hardly ever wear anything but Rita's and Laura's hand-me-downs. I want something new of my own, something that isn't altered to fit me." Jena's expression is the look of doom.

"Your sister got a birth stone ring last year. She will have it forever as a nice memento of her graduation."

"I saw it, Mother. I don't want a ring like Laura's or a wrist watch like you gave Rita. I just want a new suit."

"I'll never understand you, Jena," Sarah laments.

They exit the bus in front of the department store where Jena saw Santa many years ago. The elevator ride disturbs the girl's stomach now just at it did then. On the fifth floor a clerk shows a navy suit to the young girl.

"Please, no navy," she tells the elderly woman. "For four years I wore dark uniforms at school. I want something bright."

Jena tries on a melon gabardine suit she likes.

"This is a nice color for you," the salesclerk tells Jena. Sarah agrees, pays the lady, and hands the parcel to her daughter. The young girl now owns her first suit.

Jena carries the box to the first floor. The aroma of cafeteria food brings recollections of her former visit.

"I want peach pie with ice cream," she tells the waitress.

Sarah has her favorite, apple pie a la mode.

After lunch, the pair boards a bus for home.

Laura follows Jena upstairs. The older girl shakes her head when her sister opens the box.

"Why did you ask for such an unusual graduation gift?"

"I want something to wear that's all my own. I don't want jewelry to keep in a drawer for a keepsake of my graduation. It's just another day," she shrugs her shoulders.

"I remember when Rita had a great party at home the night she graduated," Laura recalls. "It lasted past midnight."

"We sat on the stairs and watched the couples dance. Mother served a nice lunch for them," Jena recalls.

"I thought you and I would have a party, too. Things sure have changed here. Last year the only difference between graduation day and any other day was the cap and gown I wore at the ceremony. Then Megan had a big party at her house."

"Only one thing is special about my graduation," Jena says. "I will have a job that lets me escape this place every day I'm at work."

Sunday afternoon, Sarah, Laura and Jena go to the school auditorium. Megan and Jena sit next to one another on stage in their white cap and gown.

"Why doesn't Father Daniels cut the long speech and just hand us our diplomas?" Jena whispers.

"He has to preach about what a great life we're about to begin," Megan smirks. "I don't know what's so wonderful about living and working in a small town like Sage."

The pastor hands out diplomas and shakes the hand of each graduate. After the ceremony, the graduates remove their caps and gowns backstage. Jena listens as her classmates discuss what parties they will attend. She returns home and spends a long evening in the solitude of her room. *Soon I won't be sitting in this house alone. I'll break away from this place and meet new people when I begin my job.*

Jena lays across her bed and daydreams as she plans her exciting new life.

CHAPTER 22
THE WORK PLACE

Monday morning Laura starts her vacation. It is the day of Jena's appointment with Doctor Mueller.

"Come with me Laura. I never went to the doctor by myself. After I'm done there we can take my paper to the store. Then I can find out where I'll work."

"I'll go with you this time. But after this, you'll have to make the visits alone."

This is one of the few times the younger sister goes to the waiting room. As the girls browse through old, outdated magazines, Miss Winters opens the office door and calls out, "Jena Bordeau, the doctor will see you now."

Jena looks at her sister. "Come in with me Laura."

"I'll wait out here. You'll be out in a few minutes."

Jena sits in a chair beside Doctor Mueller's desk while he reads her file.

The nurse leads her into the next room. The doctor examines the girl's ears, nose, throat, back and chest. He takes her pulse and blood pressure. Back in his office, Jena sits by his desk and watches him fill in spaces on the medical form.

"It's been a few years since you were here. I see you have been taking good care of yourself. Your exam shows you are doing very well." The doctor's voice is coarse but not unpleasant.

Jena feels at ease with him today. She is not afraid.

"Mother makes us eat good. I got my exercise walking back and forth to school. Now I can walk to work every day."

"Even though you are in excellent health, the state health department requires a blood test before you can begin work. It will take a few seconds for Miss Winters to draw some blood. Then you will be done here."

Miss Winters leaves the room. The doctor lowers his head as he signs the medical report. Jena notices how thin his hair is since she last saw him. It has turned white as the jacket he has on.

The nurse returns and ties a rubber tube around the girl's arm. Jena becomes tense. She stares at the nurse. Her face turns pale. Jena is frightened when she sees the needle in Miss Winters hand. "What's that for?" she shrieks.

"It's how we draw blood to be tested." Her voice is soft and calm. Her blue eyes sparkle.

The terrified girl turns her head as the nurse brings the needle to her arm. Jena hears her say, "Make a tight fist."

Miss Winters bends to steady Jena's arm. The phone rings. The nurse walks across the room to answer it. Jena snaps the band from her arm and grabs the paper from the desk.

"I don't want you to stick that needle in me," she cries. "I don't want you to do it." Jena runs out the side door.

Doctor Mueller is stunned. He goes to the door and summons Laura from the waiting room to his office.

"When Miss Winters was about to take a sample of your sister's blood, Jena got hysterical. She ran out the side door. She was outside before I could stop her. Go after her and bring her back here. Tell her to bring that paper with her." He speaks in a stern, gruff voice. "Jena must have her blood tested if she wants that job."

"All right, Doctor," Laura promises. "I'll tell her."

"What's wrong with that girl?" Miss Winters asks the

doctor.

"She had a lot of pain from broken bones. She must be afraid of being hurt again."

Laura catches up to her sister two blocks from the office. "Doctor Mueller wants you to go back and see him. Why did you run out of the office? I don't understand why you are so afraid. Getting a blood test didn't bother me."

"I don't want any needle stuck in me," she groans.

"It's just a little pinch on your arm. You know you can't work at Paragon if you don't get that blood test. The doctor wants you to take the medical form back to him right now."

"Doctor Mueller signed the paper. I'll just hand it to the lady in personnel and not mention anything about that stupid test. If she insists on it, maybe I'll go back to the doctor."

She looks her sister in the eyes and smirks. She raises her eyelids. "Or I might look for another job."

"You'll be sorry if you don't get hired," Laura says. When the girls arrive home neither mentions to their mother what happened at the doctor's office.

After lunch, Laura and Jena go to the personnel office at Paragon. Jena hands the health report to the secretary. The tall, blond woman glances at the paper. She looks at the front side, turns it over and sees the doctor's signature. She does not notice there is no check mark in the space by the words, *blood test*. At the file cabinet, she places the paper in a manila folder, then closes the drawer.

"Jena, be in the cafeteria seven o'clock Monday morning. You will always enter and leave work by the employees' entrance in back of the store. Laura can go with you now and show you how to get there." She looks at the older sister. "Enjoy your week Laura. I'll see you again next Monday."

As the girls walk home, Jena gasps in relief. "The

secretary didn't even read the doctor's report. She just glanced at it to see if it was signed by Doctor Mueller. She must think all tests are completed when forms are handed back to her. You worried for nothing," Jena laughs.

"She might notice it later. What will you tell her then?"

"Oh, she may never have any reason to look at my file again." Jena waves her hand and dismisses the thought.

A tall, plump girl with auburn hair and rosy cheeks greets Jena her first day at work. She is young and her brown eyes sparkle as she speaks.

"I'm Jan," she smiles.

The new trainee stands immobile in the large cafeteria. Her hands are folded tight in front of her.

"There's nothing to be afraid of," Jan remarks. "This week I'll show you what we're to do each day. Have you ever cooked on a grill?"

"No. My mother cooks all the family meals."

They walk across the room to the cooking area. Jena's eyes open wide as she stares at the large grill and coffee-makers.

"Is it hard to cook on the grill?"

"It wasn't for me. You just watch what I do. I'm sure it will be easy for you, too." Jan fills two glass carafes with water. "It's important you set these on dry hot plates."

Jena fills two more carafes. Her instructor shows her how to brew fresh coffee.

"You must remember never to place cold glass on a hot surface. We have to keep four pots going all morning. The men who come early may want cold cereal, or Canadian bacon and eggs for breakfast. Later, most customers want donuts, toast or rolls with their coffee."

"What if a customer asks me to cook this morning?" Jena's face is intense as she watches Jan place a row of mugs on the counter.

"I'll cook the next few days. Many of the same customers come in every morning. They're nice and will know you're new. After a week, you'll be ready to use the grill."

Eggs, bacon and small boxes of cold cereal are placed near the grill as they prepare for the morning rush.

"The customers help themselves to rolls and donuts. Just keep their coffee mugs filled. Some men will tease you because you're new. But don't let their jokes annoy you."

Jan instructs Jena as they stack plates on the front counter. She looks at the large clock on the wall.

"It's time to bring down the fund. Go to the cashier on the fifth floor. Tell her you work in the cafeteria. She'll give you money for the register."

The trainee returns downstairs. She removes bills and coins from a brown pouch and puts them in the register drawer. Jena remains behind the counter. She looks at her first customers as Jan unlocks the glass doors on the front of the building.

Some customers confirm Jan's prediction of friendly humor. Jena shudders as she listens to their witty chitchat.

"So you're Jan's new helper. Did she tell you to keep the coffee hot and be sure not to burn the bacon?" one of the men laughs.

Jena's hand shakes as she pours him coffee. She focuses her eyes away from the customer when she rings up the sale and places change in his hand.

"Thank you," is all she can manage to say.

"Good luck in your new job," he remarks. She watches as he exits the front door with a group of men.

"All the business men in town must come here," she mentions to Jan. "How can you put up with some of their wisecracks?"

"You have to ignore their remarks. Soon they'll let

you alone. The more it bothers you, the worse it will get. Just laugh back at them. You'll learn they're nice and mean no harm."

Some morning patrons return at lunch time. But most of the mid-day lunch crowd Jena waits on for the first time. They are anxious to be served and return to work. She catches tidbits of casual chatter as she serves orders of soup and sandwiches. The commotion disappears when workers head back to their jobs.

The two waitresses breathe a sigh of relief as they stand in the quiet of an empty room. Jena is happy when dishes are put away and the cafeteria is clean and in order for the next shift. At four o'clock she goes to the hallway with her trainer and stamps her card at the time clock.

"You did good today, Jena," Jan smiles. "Was it as bad as you thought it would be?"

"There's a lot for me to learn. And I'm not sure if I'll be able to get used to the jokes from some customers."

"Once you get to know them it'll be better. Believe me. They'll joke until you show them it doesn't bother you. It will happen sooner than you expect."

"All that bothers me now is how tired I am. Thanks for all your help. I'll see you tomorrow."

Jena waves as Jan turns toward a green car in the parking lot. She waits outside the door for her sister.

"How do you like the job?" Laura asks.

"It's hard work. A girl named Jan teaches me. She worked here a few years. She must be older than we are. I like her."

The girls walk at a slow pace. The hot sun beats on the pavement. Jena wipes perspiration from her forehead.

"I'm glad there are fans in the cafeteria. By next week I should know how to use the grill." She sounds confident. "What kind of work is there to do in the office?"

"I handle customers' bills and help people open new accounts. There will be more for me to learn as time goes on. By the way," Laura grabs her sister's arm and laughs, "would you like to open a charge account now that you have a job?"

"They're training you real good. Already you sound like a true company person. You'd better wait until I get a pay check in my hands," Jena grins. "I should earn about $55.00 a month. After taxes, Social Security and rent I'll give Mother, there'll be about $44.00 left for me each month."

Jena pauses to assess her future finances. "Perhaps you're right. I'll need a charge account to buy some new clothes. It was good to wear uniforms, but I'm happy we are done with them."

"I'm glad they hired me for an office job," Laura cheers. "I'll make about $80.00 a month. After deductions are taken out, there won't be much left for me to spend. The men wear suits and the women nice dresses when they're at work. My first pays will go to buy some good clothes." She raises her brows and tilts her head. "I'll give mother rent money when she asks for it."

"I want to start saving money. I plan to save ten dollars every month. Maybe someday I'll have enough to travel to Europe. Or maybe Hawaii." Jena gazes thoughtfully into space.

"You'll have to work and save all your life. Or else rob a bank!" Laura laughs. "Why would you want to go to those places, anyway?" She mocks Jena for considering the idea.

"When we saw "Heidi," I decided it would be nice to visit Switzerland and see the Alps. Then, after we saw "The Man In The Iron Mask," I thought it would be nice to go to France and see the country our grandparents came from. I imagine Hawaii must be like paradise. That may be the closest I will get to heaven." She answers quietly, as if to wish out loud might prevent it from ever coming true.

"We'll be lucky if we ever get to take trips to

Bridgeport," Laura complains. "You can dream your far-fetched dreams Jena. I'll plan for things that could really happen for me."

At the dinner table neither Al nor Sarah questions the girls about their jobs. Communication has diminished almost to a state of nonexistence within the family.

"Pass the butter. Pass the salt. Are there any more potatoes?" Such remarks constitute meal time conversations.

Sarah proceeds with household tasks in her usual manner. She makes random comments on chores to be done or groceries to be bought. But she never mentions the girls' jobs.

Al continues his regular routine. He leaves for work after breakfast and returns home at dinner time. Some summer evenings he talks with Laura when they sit on the front porch swing. Jena notices her father talks more to her sister than to his wife. There is never any conversation between him and Jena.

There were lots of pretty women in the magazine I found on top of the china closet, she recollects. *He must enjoy that kind of woman.*

What she doesn't know is that her father makes frequent visits to the redhead who tends bar and waits tables in the corner cafe. Al finds a lot to talk about when he is with Holly. He is a different man when he is away from his job or his family.

The first two weeks at Paragon, Jena is engrossed with her work. The jovial, red-cheeked coworker is a blessing. Jena learns to use the grill and be polite to customers. When she looks into Jan's steady brown eyes she feels she has found a person she can trust and perhaps have as a friend.

The second Friday at work, Laura and Jena cash their first pay check at the cashier window. The company holds back a week's pay from all employees. Today the girls collect a one-week pay. Outside, they open the sealed envelopes.

"I have eleven dollars!" Jena exclaims. Her eyes light up as though she found a pot of gold.

"Good Lord, Jena," Laura says. "It's only eleven dollars."

"But it's mine. It's all mine." She clutches the money as she spins around on the sidewalk.

When she arrives home, Jena shows the money to her mother. "How much do you want for rent?"

"Whatever you give me." Sarah's face is somber and devoid of any emotion.

"I put $2.50 away. I want to start to save some money each pay. Will two dollars be enough for you?" Jena asks. "If you want more, tell me."

"This is all right." Sarah puts the money in her apron pocket. She is heedless of her daughter's joy.

Upstairs in Laura's room, Jena shows her sister $6.50 she puts into a thin leather wallet. "After dinner let's go to the store and celebrate. Grace will be at work tonight. This time I can have someone wait on me," Jena chuckles.

The girls sit at a corner table in the cafeteria. "Bring us a hot fudge sundae with lots of whipped cream on top," Jena tells Grace. "You aren't very busy this evening. Has the boss been in to check on you yet?"

"No. But don't worry about the big sundaes," Grace answers. "C.L. and his wife are out of town. We'll be busy after the football game but he won't be here to check on us."

"This is my sister." Jena introduces the two. "She works in the credit office. She's been here a year."

"Hi Grace. Would you like to open a charge account? We get a dollar for each new customer we sign up this month."

"I can't get a credit card. I'm still in high school.

Anyhow, part-timers don't make enough money to open an account. You should know that after working here for a year."

"My sister tried to sign me up today when I opened my first pay envelope," Jena grins. "I told her she learned real fast to be a company person."

Agnes, the other part-timer, is behind the counter. Two young fellows are sitting on bar stools. The pretty high school girl is laughing at something one of them tells her.

"Do they work here?" Laura asks Grace.

"No. They're a couple of clowns. They come here the evenings Agnes works. She always laughs at their silly jokes. I don't know much about them."

On the way home Jena tells her sister, "I saw the boys look at you a lot when we were at the table."

"They seem like a lot of fun. Maybe we'll see them the next time we go for a treat."

"If we see them again I'm sure you'll get to know them. I could tell the tall one would like to meet you by how he kept looking at you."

As they walk home, Jena feels a glimmer of hope. *Some day I might meet some good people and be happy.* Tonight she strolls in the warm summer air spinning dreams of a future that might bring happiness.

CHAPTER 23
NEW ACQUAINTANCES

The girls collect their second pay today. On this hot, humid evening they walk to the store to treat themselves once more. Again, the same fellows stand at the counter. Agnes continues to laugh at their jokes.

Grace takes large hot fudge sundaes to the girls. "Those guys have their eyes on you," she tells Laura.

As Jena and Laura enjoy their treat, the fellows saunter over to their table.

"Hi, I'm Lon," the tall, lanky one speaks up. "This here dude's my friend Mel. We saw you in the store last week. Do you live around here?" He squirms and grins as he talks.

"We live about eight blocks away, on Elm Street. Where do you two live?" Laura asks.

"This joker lives on the next block. I live two blocks away," Mel speaks up. "Do you come here every Friday? I never saw you in the store before last week."

"We work here. I work in the credit office. My sister started work in the cafeteria three weeks ago," Laura tells him. "Where do you two work?"

"I'm looking for a job. Lon takes care of his sick mother. His father works days. Lon's housekeeper, cook and nurse when his father's away. He gets out weekends and evenings."

"It's time for us to get home," Jena reminds her sister.

"Can we walk home with you?" Lon asks Laura.

"It's a long walk to our house then back to your place. Don't you have anything better to do than walk across town with two girls you don't even know?" Laura is amused.

"Not us. There's not much to do in this town. The walk will do us good and keep us out of trouble."

Mel laughs at his friend's humor.

"If you don't mind the heat, it's okay with me. What do you think, Jena?"

Jena looks at the short, quiet one and decides he looks harmless. "It's okay with me, too."

Lon shuffles along beside Laura. His blue eyes watch her every move. Mel walks with Jena. He talks about sports and the way Lon cares for his mother.

Laura laughs at the jokes Lon tells. "What do you do when you're not at work?" he asks.

"I dance, bowl and sometimes go to a movie. I go to the ice rink in winter." She carries on a light, merry conversation with the happy-go-lucky guy.

"What do you do, Jena?" Mel asks.

"I play the piano most of my spare time." *I wish I could be as friendly and talk as much as Laura,* she thinks. "What do you like to do?" Jena asks Mel.

"I like sports. I go swimming in the summer and to football games in the fall."

"Where do you go the days Lon cares for his mother?"

"A lot of the time I am there with him. His mother is bed-ridden. She's a nice, friendly lady. But I like fall best. That's when Lon and I go hunting on week-ends. We shoot deer and rabbits," he answers proudly.

"How could you shoot those pretty animals?" she gasps.

"We eat them. It saves money on food."

Jena walks behind her sister. She admires her beauty and cheerful personality. *Laura attracts men like honey attracts bees*, she muses.

She is jolted from her private thoughts by Mel's voice. "Do you have a boyfriend?" he is asking.

"No. I don't date anyone. Do you date Agnes?"

"Yes. We went to some movies together. She graduates from high school next year. I met her at the store a couple months ago."

Jena is silent for a short while. Finally she speaks out. "She's pretty and friendly. She must like you and Lon. She always laughs when you talk with her."

"We've been out together a few times. I can't make up my mind about her." He stares at his feet as he shuffles beside her.

She feels an attraction for this shy, awkward guy. This is the first time she's walked with a fellow. She enjoys his company but fears a friendship with him. Ambivalent feelings appear as they walk side by side down the streets of town.

A short distance in front of them, Laura and Lon are engrossed in an animated conversation. Mel and Jena watch the comic antics of his pal. Lon twists and turns as he tells jokes. Laura laughs in delight at the humorous banter of the young man by her side.

"How did you and Lon get to know each other?" Jena asks.

"We live close to one another. We've known each other all our lives. We're closer than most brothers."

"Do you have any brothers or sisters?"

"No. I live with my mother and a cat named Thai."

"You have a cat named Thai? Where did you ever get a name like that for a cat?" she laughs.

"He's just a common alley cat. But my mother treats him like pedigreed royalty. He gets treated like a member of the family, like a spoiled kid."

"Do you like cats?"

"Sure. And they like me."

When they arrive at the Bordeau house the girls say good-night by the front steps.

Tonight Jena's joy is two-fold. She gets her second pay and she finds a friend.

This extraordinary weekend passes pleasantly for her. She sits at the piano Saturday and plays soft music by Chopin and Liszt. She feels her world take a turn for the better.

Jena goes to bed with anticipation of a brighter future. In three weeks she has learned much from Jan. The customers are friendly and she now enjoys her work in the cafeteria.

Monday morning Jena wakens to the fresh invigorating air of a sunny summer day. As she rides the bus to work her spirits soar with expectations of pleasant things about to happen in her life.

"Do you think we'll see those fellows again?" she asks Laura on the way home from work.

"Who can guess what will happen with those two clowns? I'll say this, they're different from any boys I've ever met."

"They're comical, but nice. I hope we see them again."

"This is the first time you've ever been interested in any boy, Jena. For your sake, I hope you see Mel again."

Friday afternoon, the boys come in the store. "What do you want to order?" Jena asks.

"We'll both have chocolate sodas," Lon answers.

As Jena rings up the sale, Laura comes in on her break. Lon watches her as she approaches the table. "Can we walk you girls home after work?" he asks Laura.

"Jena's done at four. She waits an hour for me. You can keep her company. We have to hurry home, though. Dad wants us to be on time for dinner. We'll be here later and you can walk us home then."

The fellows stay until Laura meets her sister at the

employees' door. "We'll see you later," Lon reminds them.

The evening walk home is another fun time.

The next week, the boys drop by the store to meet Laura on her daily afternoon breaks. Friday evening Lon mentions there is a dinner-dance on a party boat the next night.

"Lon and I have never been on a boat ride. Have you girls been on a paddle-wheel steamboat?" Mel asks.

"We've never been on any boat," Jena tells him. "I've been to Bridgeport three times. Twice with my mother and last year with Sister Monica. She took some senior girls to see the hospital and nursing school."

"The boat doesn't stop in the city. It docks here in Sage, cruises up the river and passes Bridgeport. Then it turns around and comes back to let the people off here. There's dinner on the ship, too. Would you girls like to go with us?" Lon asks.

"It sounds like fun. But Mother will have to give her permission before Jena can go."

As they walk together, Jena asks Mel, "Why do you want to take me on a boat ride if you plan to go steady with Agnes? What will she say if I go with you?"

"I don't have to worry about Agnes. I've made my decision about her." He strolls along. His eyes are focused on the ground.

"What did you decide?" She is anxious to hear his answer. It may explain why he asked her to go with him tomorrow.

"I asked you to go on the boat ride, not her. I won't be taking Agnes out again".

Mel wants to date Jena. It's too good for her to believe.

"Why did you decide to take me?"

"Lon and I have fun with you and your sister. Agnes is fun, but she doesn't talk about anything that interests me."

It's true, we can talk together. He needs someone to listen to him talk about his family and things he likes to do. Mel and Lon must use comedy to hide their shyness, she imagines.

At the house, Laura talks to her mother. "Lon and Mel want me and Jena to go on a boat ride tomorrow. It's the first time the boat will stop in Sage. Can we go with them?"

"How well do you know these boys?" Sarah studies how the boys behave as she stands inside the screen door.

"We've seen them at work the past four weeks and they walk home with us a lot," Laura admits.

Sarah steps onto the porch and talks with the boys for several minutes.

"If you boys promise to have the girls home before midnight, they can go with you," she tells them.

"We'll have them home on time, Mrs. Bordeau," Lon says.

"We'll be here at six o'clock tomorrow," he tells Laura.

Saturday is a perfect evening for a dinner-dance aboard ship. The sun is warm and there is a soft breeze.

A large crowd has gathered on the dock when Mel and Lon arrive with the girls. At seven o'clock the boat starts its smooth journey. The couples sit at a table adorned with a red rosebud in a crystal vase. It is centered on a white linen table cloth. The band plays soft music as, table by table, the passengers fill plates with food from a lavish buffet.

After dinner, the four join other folks on the dance floor. After two awkward attempts to keep in step with the music, Lon suggests, "Laura, let's go on deck and view the sights."

Mel is just as clumsy. He and Jena follow close behind. The foursome stands above the paddle wheel. It sprays a fine mist in the air as the wheel spins forward.

Skyscrapers are aglow with lights as they cruise past Bridgeport. Music from the giant calliope fills the air. The steamboat makes a wide half-circle and heads down stream. From the top deck they watch the boat being tied at the dock.

The group walks home under a star-lit sky.

"Thanks, Mel, for a wonderful evening," Jena tells him.

"It was a great night," Laura agrees.

The fellows fumble with their hands as they stand at the door. They shift from side to side and comment about the good time they had.

"We'll see you again at the store," the fellows call out as they walk toward the sidewalk.

It is eleven-thirty when the girls go to their room. Jena slips out of her pink floral dress, puts it on a hanger and takes it to the closet. She places her white low heeled pumps on the floor beside her dresser. She puts on a cotton nightgown and goes into Laura's room.

Her sister is still wearing her new blue dress. She's laying across the bed. Her navy pumps are scattered in the middle of the floor.

"Why don't you get dressed for bed?" Jena asks her.

"I'm too tired. I'll get up in a few minutes. My feet hurt from walking in these new shoes."

"What did you think about those guys tonight? I was surprised to see them in a suit and tie. They looked sharp. I'll bet this is the only time we see them all dressed up."

"Those fellows are full of surprises. They acted pretty nice, too. Lon didn't make as many wisecracks as he usually does." Laura sits up. "I'm going to change for bed now. You better go to sleep. We have to get up from Mass tomorrow. If you want, we can talk about this tomorrow."

"Good-night, Laura. Thanks for asking Mother to let me go with you."

"Good-night, Jena. I'll see you tomorrow."

The girls are asleep when Al comes home. Sarah knows by the odor of his breath, tonight is not the time to tell him the girls went on a boat ride with boys.

Sarah joins Al with a cup of coffee before early Mass. The best time for her to talk with him is when the girls are not present.

"Laura and Jena went for a ride on the boat that docked here last night."

"You didn't mention anything to me about you going on a boat ride with them."

"I didn't go. They went with two boys they met at the store. For several weeks the boys walked the girls home. I met them. They are nice fellows."

"You allowed Jena to go on a boat ride with a boy?" he raves. "The first time that girl goes out you let her go with a stranger? What's wrong with you? Why didn't you ask me first?"

"You weren't home to ask. I could see nothing wrong with her going. Laura was with her all evening and they were home before eleven-thirty."

"You don't know what goes on outside in the real world. You stay secluded here. No one is safe in that jungle out there." His face turns red. "I'm sure Laura was safe. She can take care of herself. But Jena could have been anywhere on the boat. She could get in a lot of trouble. That's what was wrong about you letting her go out last night," he bellows.

"She needs to get out with people her own age. She knows how to behave herself," Sarah protests.

"She'll go wild with too much freedom. She'll get in some kind of trouble before long," he persists. "You mark my words."

Al is at church when the girls have breakfast. Sarah does not mention the argument she had with their father. She looks at Jena and wonders what secret Al and her daughter share. The seeds of mistrust and suspicion, sown long ago, nag at her once again. She will always look at Jena with apprehension. She worries about the veracity of Al's premonition.

Sunday is great for Jena. She greets the new day with excitement. She is oblivious to her mother's suspicions or her father's hostility. Her mind is filled only with thoughts of more happiness to come.

Mel and Lon continue to meet the girls at the end of their work days. On their walk home this hot afternoon they plan for the Fourth of July holiday.

"Laura and I can pack a lunch. We can spend the day at Franklin Park," Jena volunteers.

"There will be games and a band," Lon adds. "We can watch the fireworks after dark."

It is noon when the four of them arrive at the park. They have hot dogs and potato salad, fresh fruit and cookies. Tennis and races occupy their daylight hours. After a dismal attempt to dance, they all sit and listen to the band until dark. While the band plays the last song they walk from the building. They sit on the warm grass and watch bright colors light up the dark sky. Fireworks burst through the night like thunder. The sky becomes a giant kaleidoscope of brilliant red, blue, yellow, and white sparks. The quartet joins the crowd as they stroll down the hill.

On the Bordeau porch the fellows say good-night. For Jena, a wonderful holiday comes to an end.

CHAPTER 24
DAWN OF ROMANCE

Lon is strongly attracted to Laura. He admires her soft blond curls, bright blue eyes and slim body. She is seven inches shorter than her five-foot-ten companion. But Laura does not share his ardent feelings. After the boat ride she told Jena, "I like Lon. He is good natured and a nice friend. But I could never form a serious relationship with any man now. At nineteen, life holds too much excitement. I treasure my freedom and want to enjoy it for awhile."

Mel is the first person Jena permits herself to trust. She is attracted to his impish grin, thick crop of brown hair, and deep brown eyes that sparkle when he laughs. She is five inches shorter than the five-foot-six lad. With the same hair and eye color, and similar stature, Jena suspects they could be taken for brother and sister.

I remember mother once saying that when a couple gets along well together and are happy, they even begin to look like brother and sister. Maybe it's a good omen that Mel and I resemble one another, Jena happily reflects. She feels as safe with Mel as she once did with Phil. Although she has strong feelings toward Mel, she fears any physical contact with him.

As they walk together this evening he tells her about his childhood. "I was six months old when my father left my mother and me without telling her he was leaving.

Since he always fancied himself a big-time gambler, mother figures he went away to make his fortune."

"Where is he now? Is he successful and rich?"

Jena can tell this is a painful subject by the look of dejection Mel displays and the sadness in his voice.

"This is like talking about a stranger or a distant relative, not my father. Mother doesn't know where he is. She never hears from him. A long time ago an acquaintance of his told her my father was involved with a casino in Las Vegas."

Mel turns his eyes away from her. He wipes tears from his face. "It's been eighteen years since he went away. I don't remember ever seeing my father."

"Do you ever wonder what he's like now?"

"Yes. Someday I hope to find him. I'm sure he must want to know his son." Mel glances at his shoes and shuffles them against the cement sidewalk.

As Jena listens to his story, she feels the pain and sorrow Mel reveals. But she can not share her pain with him. She is terrified to tell him about what happened between her and her father. She fears if he learns she has been damaged, he will never want to date her again. The only way her secret will be safe is if they remain good friends. He must never learn of her strong feelings for him.

"I'll pray that some day you and your father are reunited," Jena says. Mel just stares into space. He remains silent.

The following evening Mel takes Jena to a movie. They see "A Tree Grows In Brooklyn."

Francie Nolan is an impoverished young girl. Her father charms her with wonderful dreams. Mrs. Nolan considers her alcoholic husband a failure. It is the mother who holds the family together. The young girl does not understand the conflict between her parents. Francie loves her father and the scrawny pine tree he brings home for Christmas. She is devastated when her beloved father dies. But only after his death does she learn to appreciate and love her mother.

Mel and Jena discuss the movie as they walk home.

"I never had my father share a Christmas with me. It's almost like he's dead."

"But you know he's alive. Someday you may find him and spend Christmas together. You must have faith," she tells him.

"If I ever do find him, we'll get to know and love one another." His voice is tense, emphatic. "I'm sure of it."

"Maybe some fathers don't deserve love," Jena suggests.

"That can't be true. Even Francie loved her father. And he was a hopeless alcoholic."

Dream your dreams, Mel, Jena thinks. *Some day they all may be shattered.*

As they part at the front door he reminds her, "I'll be here with Lon at seven tomorrow. One of my friends will drive us over to the farm for the hay ride."

Saturday evening Art and Doris arrive at the Bordeau house with Mel and Lon. Laura and Jena join them in Art's old, black sedan. At the barn the short, chubby, gray-haired wagon master shouts a loud, "Giddup" to a pair of work horses.

"Giddup, you two," he goads the animals.

Songs and laughter burst through the brisk fall air as the wagon jostles the group through the open countryside. Chilled by the crisp, cool breeze, the couples cuddle close together. Mel's strong arms encircle Jena's petite body. The group stays warm, huddled on a thick bed of straw. They sing under a star-filled sky as the wagon returns to the barn.

The old farmer helps the men build a bright bonfire. The aroma of warm apple cider and hotdogs stirs up healthy appetites. Roasted potatoes, corn-on-the-cob and sizzling hotdogs are quickly devoured. Apple cider washes them down. One, two, three plump marshmallows are jabbed onto sharp, pointy twigs. The group holds sticks over a dwindling flame. White lumps become hot, soft, brown morsels.

Art and Doris drive the happy couples home. Jena is glad Laura is there with her. There are no hugs or kisses at the door. Only pleasant good-nights.

Friday evening Jena was concerned that someday Mel's dreams would be shattered. It is Sunday, two days later. But it is Jena who is about to find her world torn apart.

It has been years since Mel attended Mass. As Sarah, Laura and Jena leave church today, Mel is waiting outside to see Jena.

He greets her with a surprise invitation. "I want you to come with me and meet my mother today."

"I can go after dinner." There is a puzzled look on her face. "Why do you want me to go?"

"She wants to meet you. She has something to tell you."

"Is this news about your father?" Jena asks.

"No. You'll have to come to the house. She'll talk to you there. Don't worry about it. You two will like each other. I'll pick you up after dinner," he says, then walks away.

"What's this all about?" Sarah asks her daughter.

"I don't know. I can't imagine what she wants to say to me. I'm just as surprised as you are."

Jena cannot hide her anxiety at the dinner table. She dabbles with her food, eating only a few tiny morsels .

"What's the matter with you?" Al growls. "You've not

eaten any of your food. Are you sick or what?"

"No. I'm not sick," she mutters.

"Mel wants to take her to meet his mother. She's nervous about meeting her," Sarah speaks out.

"What the hell's going on between you two? Has something happened that his mother knows and we don't?" he grumbles.

"There's nothing wrong," Sarah interrupts. "They went out all summer together with Laura and Lon. His mother probably wants to meet the girl her son goes with." *I hope that's all there is to this,* she worries.

"It sounds like a lot more than that to me. There better not be anything going on between you two," he warns.

Al's harsh insinuations only upset Jena more.

"I'm not hungry." She winces and pushes her chair away from the table. "I'll wait in the living room until Mel gets here." She sits at the piano and calms herself with music.

Mel arrives and rescues her from the stormy atmosphere.

Mrs. Schmidt opens the front door. The tall, frail woman holds a large striped cat in her arms. Mel introduces his mother to Jena.

"This must be Thai," Jena says, as she pets the animal.

"Yes it is. He's just like a big baby. He gets all the attention in this house." She confirms Mel's statement.

As they sit in the living room, Jena is shocked to see the cat leap over the sofa and chairs. He shocks Jena when he jumps on her lap.

"Thai, come over here," Mrs. Schmidt commands.

The cat ignores her order.

"Come here Thai," Mel says. The cat purrs and runs to him.

It is Jena who decides to opens the discussion. "Mrs.

Schmidt, Mel told me you have something to tell me. He didn't say why you asked him to bring me here."

"He did an impulsive thing a couple weeks ago. He wants me to meet you before he goes away," she weeps.

"What do you mean, he's going away? Where's he going?" Her eyes open wide and her face grows pale.

"Friday morning he told me he joined the army," she cries.

"When did you join the army, Mel? Why didn't you tell me yourself?" Mel sits on a floral upholstered chair across the room from Jena. He sees her shocked expression. "We talked about the important things in your life. Why didn't you tell me this?"

"I didn't know how to tell you. My mother wanted to meet you. The only way for you to know one another was to bring you here and have her tell you the news."

"When are you leaving?" Jena asks.

"Eight o'clock tomorrow morning."

"I'll be at work. We won't even say good-bye." she cries.

"I hate good-byes. We can go down to the store and have a sundae now. I don't want a big farewell downtown tomorrow."

Each woman has her own private sorrow. Mrs. Schmidt will lose her only child. He has been her life all these years without her husband. Jena will miss her first, close friend.

The thin, nervous woman rubs her hands together as she paces between the sofa and the living room chairs. She had her husband leave her years ago, now she must live alone, without her son. Her heart has just been broken for the second time. It is impossible for her to ease the heartache of a stranger.

"Mel will write us. Come to see me soon," she tells Jena.

"Basic training will end in December. I should be

home for the Christmas holidays. Mom, you and Jena can get to know one another better while I'm gone."

This bright remark does not cheer her. The woman gazes at her son. Her pale face is strained. Tears roll from her swollen eyes down her face. Her hands tremble as she holds Thai.

"I'll be back as soon as I take Jena home."

"You be sure to come back to see me, Jena," she sobs.

"I will, Mrs. Schmidt. I promise I will."

As they walk from his house he tells Jena, "I told Lon to bring Laura to the store."

There is no laughter in the cafeteria as the quartet eats hot fudge sundaes. Jena and Mel hold hands as he walks her home. This evening she does not fear being close to him.

"Lon is really going to miss you. The two of you are like one another's brother. When did you tell him the news?"

"When I signed the papers two weeks ago."

"It makes me sad that you never mentioned Friday at the movie or last night at the hay ride anything about you leaving."

Lon is depressed knowing his best friend is going away. To add to his pain, he is infatuated with Laura, and he can not conquer her free spirit. As they walk home this cool fall night, she gives him more crushing news.

"I met a nice man at the store the other day. He's taking me to a movie Saturday."

"What's the dude like?" Lon sulks.

"Steve is tall, blond and twenty-four years old."

"He must be some nice gent if you like him. He mustn't be a crude dude like Mel and me," he frowns.

"There's nothing wrong with either of you. I'm too young to go steady. It's time that I get to meet other fellows."

He can tell by how she talks about this guy she must like him a lot. "You never went to a movie alone with me. Not like Mel and Jena did last week," he complains.

"You never told me you wanted to. It was fun being with you, Mel and my sister. We laughed and had plenty of good times these four months. That's what's important. It's important for people to have fun when they're together."

Her words crush his spirit like their shoes trample the crisp, red and gold leaves that are scattered along the sidewalk.

At the door, Lon tells Laura good-night for the last time.

"Good-bye Mel. I'll see you at Christmas," Jena sighs.

It will be three months before she talks with him again. She spends a restless night thinking of Mel leaving tomorrow.

Two weeks pass before Mel sends a post card with his new address. Jena sends a short letter to him this evening.

By the end of a month Mrs. Schmidt gets a short letter from her son. The next day there is a letter in the mail for Jena. During one of the girl's visits to Mrs. Schmidt, the woman offers her letter for Jena to read. Both of their letters are much the same. *The food is lousy. He lost ten pounds. It rains every day. His muscles ache from so much exercise. And he looks forward to letters from home.*

Jena mails a letter to him every week. By the time Mel finishes basic training, each woman has received three letters from him. Lon got four letters from his buddy. Each time one arrives, Lon takes it to Mrs. Schmidt for her to read. No one has received a letter from Mel the past three weeks.

It is a cold, snowy evening. Laura answers the front door at the Bordeau house. It is two days before

Christmas.

"Jena, there's someone here to see you," she calls out.

The younger sister walks from the dining room to the kitchen, afraid to enter the hall. "Lord, let it be Mel," she prays.

There in the hallway stands a slim, handsome soldier. He looks so good in his neat, trim uniform. Jena is elated. She feels as if her heart has burst inside her.

"Mel," she shouts. "I didn't expect you today."

"I wasn't sure when I'd get here. I thought it would be nice to surprise you. I just came by to let you know I'm home." He grins. "I dropped my duffel bag at home. I have to spend the evening with my mother. She's waiting for me."

"When will I see you again?"

"Do you want to go to Midnight Mass with me tomorrow?"

"Yes. I'd love to. What time will you be here?"

"I'll pick you up at ten-thirty. The church is small and our choir sings carols the half-hour before Mass begins. We'll have to be there early to get a seat."

At the dinner table Sarah tells Al, "Mel and Jena are going to Midnight Mass together. He stopped here to see her today."

He looks at Jena. "That's one smart man home on furlough. Don't let him get you in trouble while he's home."

Her happiness has made her oblivious to his innuendo. Joy fills Jena's heart this bright Christmas Eve. Light, fluffy snowflakes settle on Mel's khaki uniform. Winter, her favorite season, she's with Mel, her best friend. This is a wonderful time for the young lady.

"No other soldier looks as handsome as you do," she says.

He retains his impish grin. He lowers his eyes and

bows his head. His blushed cheeks reveal the confident soldier to be the same fellow who went away a few months ago, too bashful to appreciate a compliment.

"What did your mother say when she saw you in uniform the first time?" They hold hands. She looks into his eyes.

"Nothing. She just cried." Pause. "She wants me to spend all my furlough with her. I told her there are friends I want to visit while I'm home."

"I hope she doesn't mind you taking me to Mass tonight."

"She doesn't know I'm going to church. It would shock her. I haven't been to Mass for at least five years. She thinks I'm out with Lon."

Jena is overcome with joy as they enter the church. There are many lovely ornate statues trimmed with gold. She sits beside Mel and listens to the choir sing carols. The service is beautiful.

As they walk home snow continues to fall. Mel gives her a brief kiss at the door.

Earlier this evening Laura, Jena and Sarah decorated inside the house. In the wee hours of the morning, Jena walks into a living room aglow with bright colored bulbs and twinkling lights. Gold garland hangs from branches of a tall pine tree.

Sarah takes mugs of hot chocolate into the living room for her and the girls. They sit and admire the holiday splendor. Al lies asleep in bed. The women unwrap their presents from under the tree. Two gifts remain unopened. One for Al, another for Mel.

Sarah hands her husband his gift at breakfast.

Mel visits his girl in the afternoon with a gift in his hand. "Merry Christmas, Jena. I hope you like this."

She opens the red ribbon and shiny gold paper to find a three-pound box of milk chocolates.

She reaches under the tree and hands him a small

box.

"Merry Christmas, Mel." Her face is aglow. The silver identification bracelet has his name engraved on it.

"Thanks, Jena. It's a great gift."

"Remember me when you wear it," she smiles.

Mel and Jena take a walk in the snow before he leaves to spend time with his mother.

Lon and Mel stop to see her at the store Friday. "Would you like to come hunting with us tomorrow?" Mel asks.

"Sure. I like to walk in the woods."

Mel does not ask Jena if he and Lon can walk her home after work. Laura will be there, too. He knows Lon doesn't want to talk to her about the new beau she has.

Saturday morning Jena dresses in heavy slacks, her old sport coat, heavy boots, a wool cap and mittens. The fellows have on heavy parkas and boots. She leaves after breakfast.

Lon leads the way across the bridge. They climb a rocky hillside and come to a secluded glen. Mel sets five empty pop cans on a thick log.

"I'll show you how to fire a rifle," he boasts. He aims and fires. Bullets whiz by. All the cans topple to the ground. He hands the gun to Jena. She holds it with the stock against her shoulder.

"This gun's too big and heavy for me," she complains. "My hand can't reach far enough down the barrel."

She gives the gun back to Mel.

"Let's hunt some rabbits," Lon says.

Crisp leaves crackle beneath a blanket of snow. It is past lunch time. They have not seen a single rabbit.

The three adventurers retreat down the hill and retrace their steps over the bridge. Lon parts company with his friends at his front door.

"I'll see you later at my house," Mel tells him. "My Mom's looking forward to your visit."

Sunday Mel and Jena spend their last time together at a movie. She has no interest in the love story of a half-breed Indian woman in love with both sons of a cattle baron. But she is happy to sit close to Mel with his arm around her shoulder.

She feels her heart beat fast as, hand-in-hand, they walk home. On the porch, they say good-bye. "Thanks for the movie, Midnight Mass, the candy and the good times we've had. Write and tell me how you're doing. You don't write often enough," she reminds him.

"I had a nice time, too. You'll hear from me, and I'll see you when I get home again." He kisses her good-bye and goes off into the cold, snowy night.

Jena continues to write her weekly letter to Mel. Her first answer, dated January 31, informs her of his transfer overseas. Mrs. Schmidt continues to share her mail with Jena. In an April letter she learns her son will go on leave with some buddies to Naples. He has not mentioned this to Jena.

During a visit to Mrs. Schmidt, Jena tells her, "Something terrible must have happened to Mel when he was on leave. I haven't heard from him for six weeks."

"Oh, Jena," she answers, "nothing happened to him. Just be patient. He'll write soon. Soldiers sow their wild oats when they're away from home."

"Is that what Mel's doing when he goes on leave?"

The woman knows by the look on Jena's face the girl is upset by the idea. "Don't worry about it. He likes you a lot. He told me he went to Mass with you Christmas Eve. He thinks a lot of you to go back to church after so many years. He's just like all other red-blooded boys who want to be men. Don't worry about what he is doing. You'll get a letter soon."

As Jena walks home alone, the thought of Mel with other women disgusts her. The naive girl does not want a man who is with other women. She is disillusioned by what Mrs. Schmidt told her. She knows now why his mother didn't show her his last letters. Mel must have told her about the women he spent time with in Italy.

I'll never write to him again, she vows. *Dad tried to warn me. He was right. Soldiers learn a lot in the army. Men are lustful and dishonest.*

The dreams she had for a wonderful life with Mel are shattered. She feels a friend she trusted has betrayed and abandoned her. The ache in her heart is unbearable. Her once-beautiful friendship with Mel comes to an end.

CHAPTER 25
SECRETS REVEALED

The Bordeau family continues its regular routine. Sarah attends to house chores. Al remains manager at the bank and continues his clandestine affair with Holly. The girls walk home together after work.

Jena often sees a despondent Lon at the store. He knows she and Mel no longer write to one another, but she refuses to say what brought about the end of their friendship. He never asks about Laura or the fellow she dates.

Jena has worked at Paragon a year. She knows the regular customers. On weekday mornings a group of policemen comes in for coffee and doughnuts. For the past two weeks a new officer has been with them. Jena believes Sergeant Price is up to his usual pranks when he teases her about the patrolman next to him at the table.

At the register he whispers to her, "Brock doesn't have a girl. He comes in to see you every day. You two would make a good pair. Give the guy a break. Go to a movie with him." The sergeant is acting as a self-appointed liaison between Jena and his new patrolman.

"I've never heard of a policeman whose boss must get a date for him. You can stop the jokes now," she answers.

For several days Jena is subjected to the same inquiry. She remains dubious until the day Brock speaks to her.

"Show Boat" is on stage at the theater. Would you like to go to Bridgeport to see it Saturday evening?"

"That's a musical. Are you a musician?" she asks.

"No. But I like different types of music."

"Did your boss put you up to this? For the past weeks he's been talking about us going out together."

"I didn't know what you would like to do. Somehow he found out you are interested in music and told me. When I read about the stage show in the newspaper I thought it is something you would like to see. Will you go with me?"

"Sure I will. I've never seen a live musical."

Saturday, Brock arrives in a shiny green Chevy sedan. Jena fears being alone in the car with him. She hardly knows the man. At her first light opera she is enraptured by the professionals who perform. The scenery is spectacular in the open air theater. Her biggest surprise is that Brock enjoys good music.

She realizes the fears she had about him are groundless. The ride to town, the stage show and the stop at a restaurant for ham barbecues are nice experiences. Brock is polite and considerate. She can't understand why a policeman would be insecure about asking a girl for a date.

Brock and Jena go to dances, movies and musicals Fridays and Saturdays in June. One evening he takes her to the local bowling alley. All the heavy balls she throws land in the gutter.

The fondness between the two is apparent by the way they look at one another during his coffee breaks in the cafeteria. Today, Sergeant Price, the *matchmaker*, reminds Brock about the policemen's annual family picnic.

"Both you and Jena can meet your buddies' families. Will you be there next Sunday?"

"I'll be there Sarge. Will you go with me, Jena?"

"All the people will be strangers to me."

"I've only been with the force two months," Brock tells her. "I'd like to get to know the families of the men I work with. But I won't have a good time without a partner."

"You'll like them, Jena," the sergeant tells her. "The only way to find this out is if you come and meet them."

"I'll try to talk her into going," Brock tells his boss.

At noon, Sunday, Jena is on the porch swing as Brock drives up to the house. His partner Tom is in the back seat with his wife Sue. Both couples wear slacks, jerseys and tennis shoes. Jena begins to relax as she rides with the friendly couple.

At the park, Sue introduces Jena to the women and children. Brock strolls his girl around the picnic area to meet the men who work in the office at the station house. Beneath the warm sun, the couples swat the birdie in a game of badminton. At the annual softball game, it's men against women. The women boldly ignore the rules, to no avail. The men win by a score of sixteen to four.

At the barn, the kitchen crew sets up a table with the buffet. There are various ethnic foods; containers of cabbage rolls, pierogies, German potato salad, lasagna, moussaka and enchiladas, representing the various nationalities present. Among deserts are crisp apple streusel and savory baklava.

In the evening, adults and children dance to lively polkas, swing tunes and soft melodies played by a quintet.

Even without fireworks to light up the sky, this is a nice summer celebration for Jena.

On the porch, Brock reminds her, "The sergeant told us the people are like a close family group."

"Yes, he did. And I'll never doubt his word again. You got to meet the wives and children, too. Tom and Sue are so pleasant. I had a great time today."

The prolonged time together gives Brock and Jena

time to know each other better. Theirs is a friendship with no serious entanglements. She feels secure with him.

Saturdays in July and August they attend more operettas in Bridgeport. Jena enjoys the lively productions of "The Desert Song," "No, No, Nanette," "H.M.S. Pinafore," and "The Student Prince." Music draws the couple closer together.

This evening, Al is not home. Jena invites Brock inside the house to listen to her at the piano. She plays selections of Chopin, Beethoven, and her mother's favorite, ARAGONAISE.

"That sounds good," he tells her.

"When I studied music, there were times I would rather practice than eat."

"Why don't you continue to study music?"

"The nuns give students private lessons through twelfth grade. Dad wouldn't let me go away to school. I just play for my own pleasure now."

Jena enjoys being with Brock. The young policeman develops a love for his friend. One night as they ride home, without giving Jena any hint of what he is about to say, he blurts out, "Why don't we get married?"

In instant shock, it takes several seconds before she answers. "Brock, I can't get married."

"Why not, Jena? Don't you like me?"

"Of course I like you. But we don't know each other well enough for marriage."

"It will soon be six months since we've been going together. We both like the same things and we get along good. Why shouldn't we get married?"

"It's just too soon for us to start a life together."

"Will you think about it? Tell me you'll at least think about it," he pleads.

"I'll think about it for the future," she promises.

They continue going to movies and dances. The holidays will soon be here, and Jena has not met any of

Brock's family.

"Mother and Dad would like to meet you. Will you join my family for Thanksgiving dinner?" he asks.

"I should spend that day with my parents. My oldest sister lives at the convent and my brother was killed in the war. Only my other sister and me stay at home now." She makes it sound crucial, like Sarah and Al can't do without them. "Maybe you can take me to visit them at Christmas time."

"I'll tell my parents you'll be there Christmas day, for our annual family dinner."

"My sister will be home with Mother and Dad Christmas day."

Laura has been dating a manager at Paragon the past year. When Steve proposes marriage, her heart cries out, "*yes.*" But strong religious convictions cause serious doubts. Unable to make a decision, she summons advice from her father, believing his wisdom will help put an end to her confusion.

Although secretly disobedient to church laws, Al demands his children faithfully adhere to them.

"You can never marry a man who rejects his Catholic faith. This morning you went to Mass alone. Steve ignores the vows made at his Baptism and Confirmation."

"But we love one another. I'm sure one day he'll return to the church for me."

"It may be you who loses the faith, not him who returns to it. How long would you continue going to Mass alone?"

"I'm sure he will change if we get married," she sobs.

"No priest will sanctify a union between you and a fallen-away Catholic. No one from our family would be permitted to attend a wedding at another church. Think how you will feel on your wedding day if all of Steve's family is at the ceremony and no relatives of yours are there."

Torn between love for Steve and the wrath their marriage would provoke from the priest and her family, Laura refuses the diamond ring the man offers her after the dance Sunday.

Jena goes to her sister's room when Laura comes home.

"Why are you crying? Are you sick?" Jena asks.

"No. Steve and I broke up. This was our last date together."

"You two get along so well. What happened?"

"Tonight he gave me an engagement ring for my birthday. He doesn't practice the Catholic faith any more. And I won't marry out of my religion. Now it's all over for us," she cries.

Monday morning Laura goes to personnel and notifies the secretary of her resignation. On her lunch hour she applies for a job with a local attorney. For two weeks Laura manages to avoid Steve at the store.

Al has not voiced any objection to Jena's dates because her boy friend is a policeman. His buddies walk patrol and keep surveillance of the bank at night. Al can't afford to risk problems between the local police and the bank.

When Christmas day arrives, Brock takes Jena to his house. Both his father and mother are average height and have shiny silver-gray hair. The man has a bright smile. Ben and Ellen Sorrel have four grown children. Like his father, Ben has repaired shoes all his adult life. He is well-known in Sage.

"It's nice to finally meet Brock's girl." The father shakes her hand with a firm grip. His blue eyes sparkle.

His mother is friendly, but serious. Her brown eyes look as though she has experienced much stress or sorrow. Brock's brother Hank, has blond hair, blue eyes and a fair complexion. Jena wonders why such a handsome man is still single at thirty-nine. His thirty-seven-year-old sister Alma, is short and plump. She has brown hair and eyes, like her husband Lex. He, too, is short and stout. The couple has two children. Lex Junior is ten. He has red hair and brown eyes. Shelly, his eight-year-old sister, has hair and eyes the color of her parents. Alma and Lex look so much alike, they could be mistaken for brother and sister. Jena again recalls the prophetic words of her mother: *"When a happily married couple lives together a long time, they even begin to look like sister and brother." These two must be very happy together*, Jena presumes.

Hilda, his twenty-seven-year-old sister, is a redhead with hazel eyes. Her thirty-five-year-old husband, Russ, is a tall, blue-eyed blonde. The couple is childless. Jena notices the only thing these two seem to have in common is their height.

"When will we hear an announcement from you two?" Hilda asks them at the dinner table.

"It's too soon for anything like that to happen with Brock and me. I won't be twenty-one for two more years. My parents want us girls to reach legal age before we make major decisions in our lives."

"Jena has worked at Paragon eighteen months. We met seven months ago. I'll let you know when there's any news for you to hear," Brock informs his curious sister.

While Ellen and Hilda work in the kitchen, Jena, Alma and the children play a game of domino on the dining room table. The men sit before the living room fireplace and listen to the football game broadcast on the radio. It is a pleasant visit for the young woman, not tense like the atmosphere at home.

The following day the Kales visit the Bordeaus.

"Your holidays must be very sad with Barry away," Sarah sympathizes with the couple.

"Barry has been transferred to a veterans' hospital in Bridgeport. We went to see him yesterday," Nita tells her.

"When can I go to see him?" Jena asks.

"My dear, it will be quite some time. He's been under treatment over two years. The doctors still haven't made much progress with him." She wipes tears from her eyes as she sits beside Sarah on the sofa.

"What does the place look like?" Al inquires.

"We walked past six huge buildings for the patients with physical injuries. Then we walked to a white brick complex that houses psychiatric patients. The walls are light blue and white ceramic tile. The surroundings are so pleasant. I was sure it would cheer up Barry." Nita brushes tears from her face.

"Did your son recognize you and Otto?"

"Sarah, it's so sad," Nita cries. "He's so withdrawn from reality. It breaks my heart to see him sit and stare into space. He looks at us when we talk to him. But he doesn't say a word."

"What do the doctors say about him?" Sarah asks softly.

"The psychiatrists hope to make a breakthrough soon. They feel that if he remains in this condition much longer, it is quite possible Barry may be hospitalized for the remainder of his life."

If the psychiatrists would just let the young man alone, he could get through this on his own. He just needs time. He doesn't need those damn shrinks prying into his childhood to dig up whatever secrets may be buried there. His early years have nothing to do with his war trauma. Al fumes in silence.

Otto's grim expression reveals his agony. "The doctors told us not to give up hope. I don't know when we will be able to visit him again. The future looks bleak. I feel God would have been more merciful if Barry had been killed in the war. His illness is too great a burden for us," he confesses.

"Don't say that, Otto," Nita cries. "We must believe

our son will get well and come home to us someday."

The mention of death upsets Jena. She still thinks about Phil being gone forever. This oppressive visit with the Kales causes Jena a resurgence of guilt. They are so sad, but her happiness with Brock and his family yesterday lingers today.

Winter passes as Brock and Jena continue their courtship. On this bright spring morning the three policemen make their regular appearance in the cafeteria with Sergeant Price. Jena follows them as they walk to the table. The three patrolmen appear to be about five-foot-six. The sergeant is slightly taller, with thin gray hair and blue eyes. He is heavier than the well-built officers. The youngest one has auburn hair and green eyes. Brock and Tom both have brown eyes and brown wavy hair. Both are twenty four.

Jena serves them their usual coffee and doughnuts.

"When will you two have some good news for us?" Sergeant Price asks.

"That all depends on my girl, Sarge." Brock looks at Jena.

"What do you have to say young lady?"

"I'm only nineteen. I have a lot of time yet."

"Don't make this young man wait too long. Before I knew what happened, I found myself turn old and gray." Sarge runs his hand over his head.

"When there is anything new to tell, Brock will let you know. Until then, you and his family will just have to wait."

The couple swims at the lake on hot weekends. On their ride home from a boat ride on the lake this warm Saturday in June, Brock puts the momentous question to his girl once more.

"It's a year since our first date," he reminds her. "Have you thought any more about us getting married?"

"Yes, I have." She remembers the many nights she

lay awake agonizing over the situation. *How can I tell him I'm not good enough to be his wife? It will surely end our relationship.*

"Well, what is your decision? When can we tie the knot?" He takes his eyes from the road ahead and glances at her.

"Brock, I doubt we'll ever get married."

He pulls over to the berm of the road and stares at her.

"Why not Jena? Tell me what's the matter." His hands grip the steering wheel. His pale face has an intense expression.

"I'm not the kind of person you think I am." She lowers her eyes and turns away from him.

"What do you mean?" he stammers. "Is it because you don't love me?"

"Love has nothing to do with it," she whispers. "I'm just not the girl you would want for a wife. That's all I can say."

"But I know you're good. We haven't done anything wrong. We like the same things and have fun together. Why don't you want to marry me?" He sits behind the wheel, stunned.

"It's not you, Brock. I can't marry any man." She cries. "If you knew what's wrong with me you would change your mind."

"I would know by now if there was something the matter with you. I think you're just afraid of getting married."

There's a lot wrong, she regrets. *And he has a right to know why I can't marry him. He won't love me anymore after he learns what happened. God, help me,* she silently prays.

"You think I'm good and innocent. I'm not the pure girl you want for a wife. That's what's wrong," she weeps.

The car sits to the side of the road. All is quiet. The

shocked expression on Brock's face lasts but a few seconds. Tears roll down Jena's face. It is Brock who breaks the silence.

"Tell me what happened." His voice is strained. He speaks in a slow, serious manner.

"I was hurt when I was young. That's why I can't marry you. I can't marry anyone." She keeps her face turned from him.

"How old were you when it happened?"

"I was ten."

"It can't be your fault. You were just a child."

"It doesn't matter whose fault it was. The fact is, I'm damaged. I'm not good enough to be anyone's wife," she cries.

"What did your parents do? Did the man go to jail, at least?"

"No. I never told my mother about it."

"My God, Jena. Why didn't you?" Brock raises his voice.

"Because I couldn't. She would hate me for it."

"Good Lord, girl. No mother would condemn a daughter for being sexually assaulted," he exclaims.

"Oh yes, she would," Jena yells. "Because it was my father who hurt me. I was afraid to tell her. Looking back now, I think she must have known what he did. But she never did anything about it. She did nothing at all," Jena sobs.

Before he starts to drive again, Brock takes Jena in his arms. Tears stream down her cheeks.

"I want to marry you Jena. Nothing has changed for me."

They ride the remainder of the way home in silence. It is dark outside when Brock stops the car in front of her house. He looks at Jena huddled beside him. He listens to her whimper.

"I don't want to go in that house. Can we just drive

somewhere and talk for awhile?" Finally, she looks at him.

"Whatever you want, Jena. It's okay with me."

Brock drives to the edge of town. He sits close to her beneath the glow of a full moon.

"I love you, Jena. This does not stop me from wanting to marry you. But I think we should talk to someone about what your father did."

"No!" she shouts. "You must never tell anyone. My dad would go to jail, and my mother would hate me," she cries hysterically. "You must promise not to tell anyone."

"But Jena, the man did a terrible thing to you. It is a serious crime. He must be punished for it."

"No," she insists. "I don't want anyone to know about it. A woman should enter marriage pure."

"That's a nice dream. If it always happened that way, very few couples would be married. What matters is that we love one another." He holds her close and whispers, "What happened to you long ago doesn't change how I feel about you now."

"A man or woman should not have been with anyone before they marry each other," Jena repeats.

"I love you, Jena. But it won't be my first time either." He bears his soul to the woman he wants for his bride.

Now it's Jena's turn to be shocked. "If you loved someone before me, why didn't you marry that girl?" Her body trembles.

"I never loved anyone but you." His voice is subdued.

"Then what happened?" She is insistent.

The silence of the cool night is interrupted by the hum of crickets. Their noise grows louder as Jena and Brock sit under the stars sharing one another's secrets.

"When I was overseas during the war, I went on leave with some soldiers. *Hey Brock, let's find us a woman,'* one fellow tells me. *'What kind of a woman do you like?'"*

Brock pauses, not sure how to tell this to Jena.

"What did you tell him?" She urges him to continue.

"He turned to the other guys when I didn't know what to say. *'Hey fellows, the kid never had a woman.'* They all laughed at me because, at age twenty, I had never been with a woman."

"Then what did you do?" She feels nauseous. But she wants to hear his story.

"They led me to a small hotel on a side street. It was a shabby building. But my buddy told me, *'It's not how it looks on the outside. What matters is what goes on in the inside.'* *'What should I do when I get inside?'* I asked him. *'Don't worry about that. The woman knows what to do. She'll take care of everything,'* he told me. Then he laughed again. An old woman opened the door and led me through a hallway. At one of the doors a blond woman took me into a squalid room. A dim light bulb hung from the center of the ceiling. Rumpled sheets were on a large bed."

Jena sits and stares at him, astonished. This is the first time she has ever heard of such things.

"What did she say to you?" She is breathless.

Brock continues nervously. *"'Don't be shy, soldier,'* she told me. *'This must be your first time. You pay me now, before we start.'* Minutes later, we lay on the bed. The act is over in a matter of seconds. I vowed it would never happen like this again."

"I've never been with another woman since," he confesses.

Jena is relieved when Brock's shocking confession is ended.

"Let's never, ever mention our past sins again," Jena says.

At two o'clock Brock asks her the most important question of their lives. "Now will you marry me Jena? You really have nothing to feel ashamed about with me."

"I'll marry you Brock. But not yet. You work twelve hours a day. The sergeant said he will hire another man so you won't have to work so much overtime. I want to wait until you have an eight-hour job before we get married."

"If I work those long hours we can have enough money in a few years to put a down-payment on a house."

"I want us to spend time with one another after we are married. My parents never go out or do anything together. I want us to enjoy being married. Later, after we have children, I want us to spend time with them. That's what marriage should be all about. That's how it must be for our family."

"I'm sure the boss can take care of the hours I work. We can plan the wedding, and when the time is here I'll be on eight hours," he assures her.

Jena drifts off to sleep with her head on his shoulder. At five-thirty, the sunrise wakens them. "Let's go to six o'clock Mass before I take you home," Brock suggests.

"Good. I'll get home when Dad is at seven-thirty Mass."

When Brock stops the car in front of the house, Sarah is outside. When she hears the car drive up she stops sweeping the porch. The woman shakes her head from side to side. The fire in her eyes reveals she is more than upset. Sarah is angry. As agreed upon, Brock drives away as Jena walks from the car to the front porch.

"Where have you been all night?" Sarah glares at her daughter.

"We sat in the car and talked. We didn't do anything wrong. We went to Mass before we came home."

"You should thank God your father isn't here now. Get to your room before he comes home," she orders.

Jena goes into Laura's room instead. "Can we talk?" she asks her sleepy sister.

"What do you want to talk about now?" Laura yawns.

"You and Steve dated a long time. I was surprised when you two broke up. I need to know something. I think you will be the best person to help me."

"I'm not sure I can help you with anything. You tell me something. What is so important that you have to wake me so early in the morning?" Her sister yawns again and stretches her arms.

"Brock wants us to get married. But I'm nineteen and he's twenty-four. We dated a year. But I may be too young to marry him. What do you think?"

"Listen to your heart, Jena. Don't let anyone change your mind. If you love Brock, marry him," she says emphatically.

The following Saturday, Brock takes Jena to Bridgeport. They pick out a solitaire diamond, then go to a dance in town. She gets home before midnight.

Inside the house, Jena sees Sarah in the living room. "Where's Dad?" the girl asks.

Sarah arches her brows and squints her eyes. "Your father's not home. What's the matter? Why do you ask?" Her mother stares at the excited young lady.

"Nothing's the matter. Tonight Brock gave me a diamond ring." Jena holds out her hand. "We want to surprise his family. I want you to keep it a secret until we tell them."

"Your father will be angry if I don't tell him."

"You mustn't say anything to anyone until we tell his parents." The words rush out of her mouth. "You must promise me you won't. When I tell you tomorrow, act surprised. Dad will never guess you already know," she insists.

"I don't understand this, but I'll keep your secret."

Sunday after church, Brock and Jena go to his father's shop. Ben has his back to them as they enter the door. He has a broom in his hand, sweeping scraps from the floor. Jena loves the aroma of new leather that permeates the small room. On a side shelf are various sizes of heels. She gets a whiff of the rubber as she walks by her future father-in-law. Ben looks up.

"What are you two doing here? You didn't come to help clean the shop. Did you?" He lets out a soft laugh.

"We want you to be the first to hear the news." Jena holds out her left hand to him. She looks at her diamond ring.

"Congratulations. When's the big day?" He smiles at her.

"In the winter. I want a small wedding with just our families. I don't like to be with a lot of people." Jena tells the truth.

"Brock, go tell your mother. She should me home from Mass now. She'll be happy to hear it. Good luck to the both of you."

He hugs Jena and shakes his son's hand.

After showing his mother the ring, Brock takes Jena home. Her parents are in the living room when Jena takes Brock inside.

"I thought you two were going to the lake," Sarah says.

"We went to see Brock's parents after Mass. We wanted to show them what he gave me." Jena reaches out her hand so both her father and mother can see the ring.

"When did he give you that?" Sarah pretends to be surprised.

Al's face becomes flushed as he looks at the bright diamond.

"Last night. Dad wasn't home so I couldn't show it to both of you then. We wanted Brock's and my parents to see the ring before anyone else found out about it." She mentions this with a bright smile.

"When will the wedding be? I thought your sister

would be the first one I would walk down the aisle," he scowls.

"Jena wants a winter wedding," Brock says. He doesn't look at her father for fear Al might see the anger and disgust he feels for the man.

"We're going to the lake now. I want to go upstairs and show Laura my ring." She is anxious to get out of her father's sight. Brock waits outside on the porch for Jena to come out.

"Jena, I forgot to tell you. Laura's not home. She went out with that young lawyer she works with," Sarah calls upstairs. "You'll have to surprise her tonight."

Mother, if you only knew, she thinks to herself. *This ring will be no surprise to my sister.* Jena smiles when she thinks of the conversation she had with Laura the past week.

In the evening, Brock arrives in a tan dress suit. Jena wears a peach, dotted-Swiss dress. Her soft curls are pulled back from her face. She carries a white clutch bag that matches her low-heeled pumps. Brock pins an orchid on the dress of his fiancee. She wears it when they go on a boat ride to Bridgeport. They celebrate their engagement at a dinner-dance as they sail along the river.

When Jena goes up to bed this evening, Laura meets her at the top of the stairs. She grabs her sister's hand.

"Let me see your ring," Laura grins. "That's some rock. Wow. Dad sure is angry Brock didn't talk to him before he gave this to you."

"It's too late for him to do anything to stop the wedding. We went and told Brock's parents first. Now, too many people know about it. I'm glad you helped me decide what to do," Jena tells her. She stands with her arm extended as she admires her new ring.

"I'm going to have fun while I'm young," Laura declares. "I've decided to wait until I'm near thirty before I marry." Laura has tears in her eyes as she goes into her room.

"Let me know if there's anything I can do to help with the wedding. I hope you and Brock are happy together," Laura tells her sister. Jena does not see the tears roll down Laura's face as she closes her bedroom door.

CHAPTER 26
A TIME TO LOVE

Al faces his wife as she serves him his morning coffee.

"Why would Jena keep it a secret that she and the cop were to get engaged?" he asks. "It shows she's too immature to think about marriage now."

"She's happy for the first time since she and Mel stopped writing. This past year she has been happy with Brock. It seems like her mind is made up about what she wants to do."

"It's a mistake. She's too young to know what she wants. He's too old and experienced for her."

His objections surprise his wife. "We were their same ages when we married," she reminds him.

"That girl has a lot to learn. Maybe the engagement won't last," he grumbles, and walks from the room.

Monday morning at the store, Sergeant Price is pleased to see the ring on Jena's finger.

"You can give this cupid credit for bringing the two of you together," he boasts. "When's the big day?"

"Sometime this winter," Brock tells his boss. "Jena wants me to work an eight hour shift before we set a date. Then we can post our banns and get married."

"What does that mean?" the sergeant asks.

"It's an announcement of a forthcoming marriage. Before a couple can get married, it must be published in the church paper six weeks prior to the wedding," Brock explains.

"You two plan the wedding. I'll take care of your work schedule after you get back from the honeymoon," Sergeant Price tells him.

Brock and Jena select furniture and household items for a four-room apartment. In five months the living room and bedroom will be paid for.

"In another month the stove, refrigerator and table set will belong to us," he tells Jena. The items are on hold at the store.

Sunday, after Mass, the couple visits Father Karl in the rectory. It is a balmy fall day. The short, middle-aged priest sits at his office desk. He has a pleasant smile as he greets them.

"We want our banns to be published, Father. We've been engaged four months. We plan to be married in two months," Brock informs him.

Father takes a slip of paper from the desk drawer. He writes Jena's and Brock's name, Baptism and Confirmation information on the form.

"Ours will be a small wedding. Only our families will be invited to the church. And I want to be married in a suit. Is that permissible Father?" Jena asks.

"The size of the wedding does not matter. And what you wear is insignificant. The important thing is that you will receive the Sacrament of Matrimony in the sight of God, in His house," Father tells them.

"We want a Low Mass with one priest. Tom and Sue Harret will be our attendants. Jena wrote down the titles of the music we have chosen. Here is the money for the Mass, Father." Brock reaches across the desk and hands the priest a check.

It is a late fall day when Jena and her mother go to Bridgeport to shop for a trousseau.

"I won't be married in a gown and veil." Jena springs the news to her mother as they ride the bus to town.

"Your father will want you to wear them when he

walks down the aisle with you," Sarah objects.

"The priest said it's not important what I wear. The church requires only that we have a wedding Mass," Jena replies. "I've decided to wear a beige, tailored suit."

"What will people say? This is not what your father planned for you and Laura. He will be angry about this. You must change your plans," she pleads.

"I'll not waste money on a gown and veil to wear only one time. I can wear the suit all winter."

"This is another of your stubborn ideas. And what strange idea do you have for a place to live?"

"We found an apartment. Brock and I picked out all the furniture, too," Jena informs her mother. "We made the arrangements for the Mass with Father Karl. Our banns will be in the church bulletin this Sunday. It's too late to change any of our plans now."

"Your father will be angry you plan on wearing a suit when he walks down the aisle with you." Sarah wrinkles her brows and shakes her head from side to side. Her hands are clasped together tight. "I don't know how to tell him," she sighs.

"You don't have to worry about anything, Mother. I will tell him. I'll tell him when the time is right." *That's not the only thing that will anger him. He will not get the chance to ruin my wedding day. He'll just have to live with the embarrassment of whatever plans I make for my wedding,* she reflects.

Jena refuses to be moved by Sarah's emotional display.

At the store, the women ride the elevator up to the fifth floor. The flip-flops in the girl's stomach bring back memories of the first time she visited the store. Once again, she shares a rare, pleasant event with her mother.

The salesclerk helps Jena choose a suit for her wedding. Sarah selects several tailored dresses for her daughter. Jena is amazed by Sarah's excellent choice of current styles and designs in clothing.

When they return home, Jena shows Laura her beige wedding suit, six dresses and two pairs of shoes. Included in the package are delicate lingerie and a soft peach nightgown.

"This will be our last Thanksgiving and Christmas holidays together, Laura. Six weeks from now I'll be married and away from this place. When I pack a suitcase to take on my honeymoon it will be a happy time. The first time I planned to leave here, when we were to go to the jamboree, it ended in disaster. I'll not let Dad or anyone else ruin things for me this time."

The following Friday, Jena celebrates her birthday with Brock's parents. Ellen serves cake and ice cream before she and Ben leave for their daughter Alma's house.

"We'll be with Shelly and Lexy until Alma and Lex are home from the football game. We won't be home until midnight. Enjoy your birthday, Jena," Ben tells her.

When they are alone Brock spreads a heavy afghan on the floor before the fireplace. Jena opens the blue velvet box and admires the pearl earrings Brock gave her after dinner. Orange flames dance to the crackle of blazing logs in the fireplace. The two sit and share tender moments as soft music flows from the radio. Enticing kisses lead to passionate embraces. Soon strong desires erupt. The couple experience a sexual encounter. The spontaneous union startles Jena.

"This wasn't to happen until we are married." She is overwhelmed with feelings of degradation and guilt.

"We love one another. Our wedding is in six weeks. There's no reason for you to worry," Brock assures her.

This is a bittersweet union as she savors this new found pleasure. As they lay before the fire and watch flames turn logs to embers, Jena secretly grieves as old fears return to haunt her. It is past eleven o'clock when they leave the house.

Brock stops his car a block from Jena's house.

"You should know how to drive before we are married. Slide over to the driver's seat," he tells her. He opens his door and goes around to the passenger seat. Jena's hands shake as she puts them on the steering wheel.

"There's nothing to it," he tells her.

He instructs her how to steer and turn the wheels. She makes a right turn from Main Street onto Elm Street. At the corner she accelerates the gas and veers sharply to the right. The car jumps the curb, crosses the sidewalk and lands in front of a thick hedge. Jena shakes. She clings to the steering wheel.

"Brock, come over here and drive this car." She sits staring at the tall hedge, her hands clutching the wheel. "Please, Brock, come over here and put this car back on the road."

"You can do it. Just straighten the wheels. Then put it in reverse. This is how you'll learn."

She follows his instructions in a state of shock.

"Now push easy on the gas pedal and back onto the road."

She backs the car onto the street and turns off the ignition. "You drive it up to the house. I don't want to drive anymore."

Brock takes in Jena's pale face and frightened expression. "We all make mistakes the first time we drive," he says. "There's no reason for you to be afraid. Just drive straight up the road and stop in front of your house."

Jena realizes she must move the car up the road herself. Her body continues to shake as she parks the car at the curb.

"You did okay for your first try. This is my fault. I'll have you try again in the daytime, not at night."

As they walk toward the porch, Brock suddenly bends over. A sharp moan disrupts the stillness of the night.

"Brock!", she shouts. "What's the matter?"

"I have a pain in my stomach. It must be the spices my mother used in the food."

"Your face is white. You must be sick," she cries.

"I'm just tired. I'll be all right after a good night's sleep. This is nothing for you to worry about."

Jena's first shock was in front of the fireplace tonight. A few minutes ago she almost wrecked the car. Now Brock is ill. It has been a disruptive evening for the young lady. She trembles as they stand at the door.

"But I do worry about you. What are you going to do?" Her eyes fill with tears.

"I want you to rest tonight. The truth is, I have a stomach ulcer. It acts up once in awhile. Don't worry. Believe me, I'll be all right, Jena. I'll be here to take you to Mass tomorrow."

Brock kisses her good-night, gets into his car and drives up the street. Jena quivers. Tears run down her face as she walks into the house. Al waits for her in the hallway.

"I heard you and Brock talking loud outside. What's the matter? Did you and your policeman have a fight before the wedding?" he sneers. "I said you two will never make it to the altar. It's time you take my advice."

"We didn't have a fight. It's nothing like that. Brock got sick just before he went home," she cries.

"Well what the hell do you expect? You know these soldiers come back from war all messed up. Look at Barry. He doesn't even know his own parents. The doctor told them it seems like Barry will spend the rest of his life in the hospital."

"If it weren't for Phil, Barry, and all the other soldiers who fought for our country we might still be at war now," she argues. "We're free, thanks to them. Brock has an ulcer. There's nothing the matter with his mind," she cries. "This has nothing to do with us getting married."

"Well, you better think again. It has everything to do with it. Did he tell you before tonight he was ill? How can you trust him about anything when he keeps this a secret from you? You'd better decide not to marry him before it's too late. A man you can't trust won't make a good husband."

"He may be a better man than some others I can name."

"What do you mean by that?" he demands.

"Whatever you want it to mean." Jena turns away from her father and goes up to her room in tears.

Brock stops at a nearby phone booth. He calls his childhood friend, Doctor Jason. Five minutes later, the two men meet in the doctor's office. Brock explains what happened at Jena's house a short time ago.

"Do you have any medication for your ulcer at home?" the doctor asks.

"I should have enough for a few days."

Doctor Jason hands Brock a white slip of paper. "Here's another prescription." He frowns. "If you don't slow down and get more rest your next attack could put you in the hospital again. I don't want that ulcer to start bleeding."

"Things will be less hectic for me after the wedding. Jena and I won't be going out so often. We'll be relaxing at home."

"I want to see you in another week, Brock. Call Monday and talk with my nurse."

"Thanks for seeing me so late. I'll make an appointment and see you soon."

Jena is shaken by Brock's sudden illness and Al's demand that she reconsider her wedding plans. *Is Dad right? Did Brock hide other things from me? It's too late now to change the wedding. Our banns will be in the church paper tomorrow.* She sobs as she considers her father's warning.

Tonight she is haunted by a recurrent nightmare.

She is in a long, narrow hallway with many doors. One by one she looks into each room, searching for an exit. It is black inside. She leaves each door ajar. She leans on the wall, trapped in the hallway. There is no escape.

Jena is still worried when she awakens in the morning. Brock is bright and happy when he takes her to church.

"How do you feel now?" she asks. She looks closely at him. He shows no sign he was ill last night.

"I'm fine. I told you not to worry." He does not mention his visit to Doctor Jason after he left her at the door.

After Mass, Jena shocks him as she talks about the conversation she had with her father last night.

"Dad met me inside the door. He warned me I should cancel our wedding. He thinks you are hiding more than your illness from me. I don't know what to believe now."

"I told you about the woman overseas. That's all I have to admit that concerns us now. It's been two years since I had a problem with my ulcer. This is the first attack I've had since then. There's nothing to worry about. There are a lot of people who have ulcers. If I get sick after we are married will you stay married to me?" he asks.

"Of course I will. Why wouldn't I?" she exclaims. His question shocks her.

"Then why should it matter now? I take care of it. I have a purple heart for my injury in the war. But I'm all over that wound now. It doesn't interfere with my job. And it won't cause problems after we're married."

His voice becomes harsh now.

"Your dad's just worried that I'll find out about him

and you. He'll do anything to keep you home where he thinks his secret is safe."

"I'm sorry I didn't trust you. You're right. I'll not let Dad ruin my life forever. I won't," she promises.

When Sarah returns from church she shows Al the church bulletin. Jena's banns are in it. "It's still not too late for her to get out of this mess," he tells his wife.

He is going to explode when Jena tells him she'll wear a suit when he walks her down the aisle, Sarah fears. She remembers she wore a long white dress and large white hat for her wedding. He knows she was two months pregnant at the time. She doesn't remind him of this now. He is furious enough about Jena's wedding.

Al's hostility does not deter the couple from completion of their plans. Their new furniture arrives at the apartment the week before the wedding. This same Saturday Sue has Sarah, Laura, Brock's mother and sisters, and a few women from the store to her house in the evening for Jena's bridal shower.

When Brock takes her home he hands her his wedding gift as they say good-night. Jena opens the lid of the blue velvet jewelry box and music plays, "I Love You Truly." The pearl necklace matches the earrings she got for her birthday.

"The pearls are beautiful. The necklace will be perfect to wear on our wedding day, Brock. Thank you."

The following Saturday, Jena wakens to a cold wintry day. As she waits in the living room for Sue, Al goads her. "It's time for you to get a move on. Sue will be here soon. It will take you time to get into your gown."

"I don't need much time," she announces. "It will only take a few minutes for me to put on the suit I'm wearing."

"What the hell's the matter with you?" he yells. "I'll not walk you down the aisle with you wearing a suit."

"You won't have to. I decided to walk down the aisle

without you, all alone."

She sees fear and rage in his eyes. Now he must realize the anger and contempt she held toward him for nine long years.

"Brock understands why I want to wear a suit and walk down the aisle alone. He is the only one I have to please today. We both agree that you and mother should sit together in the pew with Laura and Sister Rita."

Jena turns from him and walks defiantly up to her room. She pays no attention to the heated conversation in progress between him and his wife.

The bride-to-be is in her room. She is dressed when Sue arrives. Her bridesmaid wears a light blue suit. Sue smooths loose strands of shiny brown curls and applies rose lip color and a tinge of rouge to the nervous bride. After Sue goes downstairs to talk with Tom and Brock, Laura closes the bedroom door.

"Jena, did Brock get anything to take on your honeymoon?"

"We have everything we need in our suitcases."

"Good Lord Jena, I don't mean clothing. On the way to the hotel have Brock stop at a drugstore. You don't want to get pregnant the first time you two get together. Do you?"

It would help me to understand what Laura means if she had talked to me about this before today. There's no time now. I wish she had explained about getting pregnant before this. I wonder what he should buy at the drugstore. Jena thinks about her and Brock on her birthday. *That was our first time together.*

All thoughts of Laura and her advice vanish as Tom drives Sue and the bridal couple to church. The shiny green Chevy pulls to the curb in front of the old red-brick building. The morning air is cold and crisp as delicate snowflakes dance in the breeze and drift to the ground. As the couples walk from the car to the large wooden doors they are caught in a billow of soft lacy flakes. Jena delights that her wedding day is during her favorite time of the year.

Inside the candle-lit church, Ben and Ellen sit with Hank, Hilda, Russ, and Lex and Alma with their children. Across the aisle sits the Bordeau family. Al is beside Sarah in the pew with Laura and Sister Rita as his youngest daughter walks down the aisle alone. His stony face can not conceal the anger he feels. He is embarrassed what people will think when he does not walk his daughter down the aisle. The thought that Brock might know the reason for Jena's suit and her solitary walk to the altar torments Al. *Everyone will think Jena has to get married. That's the only reason a woman doesn't wear a white wedding gown. No one will suspect there may be an ulterior motive for her unusual actions. Only Brock may know Jena's real reason,* he contemplates in the stillness of the church. *I'll find out later if he really knows what happened between Jena and me. I can't be bothered at this time with what Sarah thinks. But it is imperative that I find out what Brock knows.*

Sarah's calm expression hides feelings of disillusionment and pain caused by her husband's betrayal the past years. She sits beside him engrossed in her own thoughts.

Thank You God, for letting Jena find happiness. Please let this day mark a new beginning for all of us. I can learn to accept Al seeing that tramp Holly. But I can no longer look at Jena every day and live with suspicions about her and my husband.

Jena enters the church from the vestibule. She sees Brock's family in the front pews. Across the aisle from them she sees her parents with Laura and Sister Rita. Uncle Ray, Aunt Peg and their four daughters sit behind them. In the next pew are Jena's God-parents, Bill and Marie Reinor. Aunt Marge, wearing an old head scarf, sits alone in the back pew. Al's brother is not at the wedding. Other church members are gathered sporadically throughout the church to attend daily Mass.

Brock, Tom and Sue take their place in the sanctuary. Soft strains of "Ave Maria" flow from the pipe organ as Jena walks down the aisle. Sarah is uneasy watching her daughter about to wed, dressed in a beige suit and pillbox hat. She stands beside Brock, who is dressed in a brown serge suit. Throughout the ceremony Al remains rigid. When the couple exchange vows he looks at the floor, not at the bride and groom.

Jena beams as Father Karl announces, "I now pronounce you man and wife."

Soft strains of D'Hardelot's "Because" drift from the balcony to the congregation below as Brock, Jena, Tom and Sue retreat to the vestibule. The bride and groom, with faces aglow, exit the church into a gust of wintry snow. They dodge tiny missiles of rice thrown at them amid billowy snowflakes.

"We'll meet you later at the restaurant," is heard through the wind as the bridal party rides away.

The two couples arrive at Aristo's Restaurant in time for dinner. Jena ignores her father's sullen mood. She repeats her promise to herself, *Nothing or no one will interfere with the joy Brock and I share on this most important day of our lives.*

Sarah and Jena are talking together in Aristo's private dining room. Al waits for Brock to be alone before approaching him in the foyer.

"You're the reason my daughter embarrassed me today. She should have worn a white gown and veil and had me by her side."

Brock's face turns red. He clenches his fists.

"She is ashamed to have you for a father. That's the real reason for our modest ceremony. Don't you dare accuse me of being the cause of my wife's decision to omit you from the service. It's because of you she is not wearing white today. The blame is all yours. You know it. Now accept it."

Brock raises his hand to strike his new father-in-law. From the corner of his eye he sees Jena enter the foyer. Brock lowers his hand and turns his back to Al. The bridegroom smiles as he and his bride enter the dining room and join their guests at the table.

Brock made arrangements to spend two weeks touring the sights and seeing shows in New York City. It is evening when the newly-weds depart for their honeymoon. They travel to Bridgeport for their wedding night.

At the Grand Hotel, the bride stands close to her husband at the reception desk. Jena keeps her hand firmly anchored to Brock's arm as the bellhop leads the guests to their room. Inside, they rifle through their suitcases and prepare for bed. Jena is nervous as she puts on her new peach nightgown. The two rest warm and secure in each other's arms. In this tender moment Jena feels secure. All her fear is gone as the happy couple joins together as one to begin their new life as man and wife.

They arrive in New York City Sunday evening. There are cold blustery winds as Brock drives onto Lexington Avenue. He parks his green Chevy and escorts Jena into Hotel Shelburne. The bellboy carries their luggage to the tenth floor.

After dinner, Brock takes Jena to see "Dead Reckoning," a movie starring Humphrey Bogart, her favorite movie star on the wide screen.

It is about twenty minutes into the movie.

Jena sees a man and young girl seated in the row

directly in front of her and Brock. Jena watches the man put his arm around the girl. He slips his hand inside her blouse. Jena leans her head toward Brock and complains.

"Look at him. That man is older than you. That girl can't be older than twelve."

The girl must have overheard the remarks. She turns her head toward Jena. Their eyes meet. There is fear on the young girl's face. In this fleeting moment Jena recognizes the shame they both share.

"You can stay and watch the movie if you want. I can't sit here and watch that man abuse that child. I'll wait in the lobby for you." She stands up to leave.

Brock gets up and follows Jena down the aisle. In the lobby the groom criticizes his new wife.

"You told me Bogart is your favorite actor. You like to see every one of his movies. Why don't you stay and watch this one?" He takes her arm and looks into her eyes. "I don't understand why you should get upset seeing that man and girl together. It doesn't involve you."

The memory of what happened to her nine years ago flashes through her mind. She grieves for her stolen innocence.

"I can't sit and watch a child being abused and not be able to do something to help her. It does involve me. You should understand how I feel. I will never regain the childhood I lost. I can't watch the same thing happen to someone else."

Jena squeezes her hands in tight fists at her sides. She looks away from her husband and walks on.

"You have to put your past behind you, Jena. You must stop letting other people's actions disturb you. We all have things we want to forget. Be thankful you had a nice house to live in when you were young. That's more than I had."

"Your house is nice. And you have good parents."

"My parents had seven kids crowded together in one

bedroom. We always lived in that small two-bedroom house. There was never enough money for Dad to provide all the necessities our family needed. When we were old enough for paper routes all the boys worked to help with finances."

"Where are the other three kids? I only met four of you." Jena is mystified by her husband's revelation.

"I was five when my sister Claire died at fifteen from pneumonia. I hardly remember her. My brother Bernie was twenty four, and Gus was twenty six when they died on D-Day."

She sees pain on his face before he lowers his eyes and turns away from her.

"My brother Phil was killed on D-Day, too. And his best childhood friend is now in a mental hospital," she sighs. "The war has ruined so many lives."

Brock is anxious to change the subject.

"Well, we'll not raise our kids in a small house like my parents did. I want a large family. As soon as we save enough money I'll get a big house for us. It will have enough bedrooms for all our kids."

"I want to wait at least a year before we start having babies. I want six children. We should have them three years apart so we can spend time together with them. Your boss should have a new schedule for you when we get home," she reminds him.

"If there's an opening, I'll be the first one to get it. That's what the boss told me," he casually remarks.

Jena's face turns white. She looks into Brock's eyes and murmurs, "But he promised you would work only eight-hour shifts after we married. He promised you. I want us to spend our evenings together. We'll never have much time alone if you keep working twelve hours every day."

Brock hears the panic in her voice.

"Let's not worry about that now. We should be

happy these two weeks together. We can talk about that when we get home."

Jena is speechless. She feels deceived. There is a gusty breeze as they rush back to the hotel. As she nestles in Brock's arms tonight fear spins through her being like the turbulent wind whirling through the streets of New York City.

Sergeant Price must have told Brock his hours will not be changed when we get back. He told me this evening he'll have to wait for an opening. I wonder how long Brock has known about this. He let us make plans for our wedding and never told me about it. A feeling of misplaced trust creeps through her mind. She feels her happiness begin to fade.

She lays awake thinking about what lies ahead after they get home from the honeymoon. With her husband sleeping peacefully by her side, Jena reviews the lonely life her mother lives.

I could not bear to be home alone all week. I want my husband to share more than breakfast, dinner and bedtime with me. I saw my mother live for years like this, Jena laments.

Doctor Mueller is about to retire and close his office. For her pre-nuptial physical, Jena went to a young, new doctor in town. *I'll go see Doctor Marc when we get home. Maybe he can tell me someone I can talk with. I have to get help for the problem with my father. Brock and I can talk with him together. Then we can get to the problem of honesty and trust in our marriage.* Her thoughts are put to rest as Jena falls asleep.

During their two weeks in New York, the couple goes to Mark Hellinger Theater, Liberty Island and into the Statue of Liberty, visits The Cloisters Museum of Art, Greenwich Village, and shopping in Macy's Department Store. Jena contemplates the future as her husband lays asleep beside her.

Jena and Brock pack their suitcases as the honeymoon comes to an end. They begin the long ride home to Sage for the start of a new life together. Jena sits beside Brock as he drives down the interstate highway. Whatever lies ahead for her and Brock, her faith in God gives her confidence that He will bless their marriage with love, children and happiness. And for now, she is grateful He has blessed her with a time to love.

THE END